Victim No More

Women's Resistance to Law, Culture and Power

edited by
Ellen Faulkner &
Gayle MacDonald

Fernwood Publishing • Halifax & Winnipeg

Editing & design: Brenda Conroy
Cover design: John van der Woude
Printed and bound in Canada by Hignell Book Printing
Printed on paper containing 100% post-consumer fibre.

Published in Canada by Fernwood Publishing
32 Oceanvista Lane
Black Point, Nova Scotia, B0J 1B0
and #8–222 Osborne Street, Winnipeg, Manitoba, R3L 1Z3
www.fernwoodpublishing.ca

Fernwood Publishing Company Limited gratefully acknowledges the financial support
of the Government of Canada through the Book Publishing Industry Development
Program (BPIDP), the Canada Council for the Arts and the Nova Scotia
Department of Tourism and Culture for our publishing program.

Library and Archives Canada Cataloguing in Publication

Victim no more: women's resistance to law, culture and power
/ Ellen Faulkner & Gayle MacDonald, eds.

Includes bibliographical references.
ISBN 978-1-55266-295-3

1. Feminism. 2. Women's rights. 3. Women—Social conditions.
I. Faulkner, Ellen II. Macdonald, Gayle, 1956-

HQ1155.V52 2009   305.42   C2008-907764-4

Contents

In memory of Dr. Judith Catherine Blackwell, 1944–2005,
sociologist, women's studies advocate, mentor, friend.

To honour the life and work of Dr. John Patrick McKendy, 1949–2008,
who died far too soon and who embodied the essence of peaceful resistant practices
in the name of social justice and in the face of violence.
Peace to you, John, rest in it.

To resistant women wherever they are found;
may these words speak to your life.

Preface

When we first started talking about this anthology, we wanted to create an alternative to what we saw as a depressingly large body of literature on the female "victim," whether of violence, of patriarchy, of law or of culture. Similar to Norma-Jean Profitts' path-breaking work (2000) on the transformation of the "victim" to a woman of empowerment, we wanted to document those stories, trace the problems of law and examine international settings to see how women fared. Ellen sent out a call for papers (CFP, to use the academic lingo) to many different women's list-serves. We received over sixty enquires and expressions of interest and thirty-two very fine abstracts. Obviously, we needed to choose which ones to publish. We originally conceived of this volume as dealing with women's responses to law — for example, what is referred to as the "re-victimization" of women who end up in court after violent attacks. We soon realized that victimization comes in many forms and that law as a framework would not "hold" all of the work we had uncovered. We moved, then, to a more encompassing framework — one of resistance. Included in this book you'll find work on war victims, political and ideological victims, victims of sexual violence. What links together all of these diverse topics is the concept of resistance, or the ways in which individual, collective, local, national and/or international forms of resistance work to enhance women's lives. It is our wish that this volume gives the reader the hope we managed to find in these pages.

Acknowledgements

We could not have completed this book without the help of many people. The students in Gayle MacDonald's 2007 third year Sociology of Women and the Law class at St. Thomas University, Fredericton, provided valuable comments on the manuscript. Feedback from anonymous external reviewers also strengthened the final manuscript. We wish to thank many people for their direct encouragement and assistance with this book. We are deeply indebted to everyone at Fernwood Publishing for their work and completion of this book, in particular, Errol Sharpe, who believed in the idea of this book and provided invaluable feedback throughout the process of conceptualizing, editing and structuring. Beverley Rach (production) and Brenda Conroy (editing) of Fernwood provided excellent pre-production advice. Debbie Mathers (typesetter) prepared the manuscript for the design process.

We would like to thank the research assistants who worked very hard to help us complete this project: at St. Thomas University, Mary-Ellen Green and Patti Wheatley, and more recently, Tania D-Alusio Tyler, for her patient editing of the final manuscript; Jessica Beaulieu and Jennifer Servos, Department of Sociology, Brock University.

Finally we could not have completed this project without the valuable assistance provided by our administrative assistants, Anita Saunders, Department of Sociology, St. Thomas University, and Linda Landry, Jill Debon and Viola Bartel, Department of Sociology, Brock University.

Lastly we thank our families and friends...

Ellen: To Gayle, for thinking of this anthology and mentoring and nurturing me along the way, many thanks. Thanks to my colleagues at Brock University for their support, in particular: Michelle Webber, Nancy Cook, Kate Bezanson and Mary-Beth Raddon (Sociology) for coffee and lunches; Ifeanyi Ezeonu, Merijean Morrissey, Ana Isla, May Bletz, Heather Gordon, Janice Hill, Tricia Vause, Ed Borowski and Judith Blackwell for movies and dinners. Thanks to June Corman, Judith Blackwell, Ann Duffy, Merijean Morrissey and Jane Helleiner (Sociology and Women's Studies) for supporting my research. Thank-you to Norma Jean Profitt and Linda Coates for sharing their thoughts on resistant practices. And finally, thanks to my family for their ongoing encouragement.

Gayle: To Ellen, for liking the idea and for working so hard to see it realized, thank-you, thank-you, thank-you. To Riley Veldhuizen, many thanks for the stickers and green tea during the week from hell. Thanks to Eris and Breagh MacDonald-Rahn for asking that penetrating question: "Another book, Mom? Again?" and for actually sticking around on the last book launch. Thanks to Josephine Savarese (Criminology) for always bringing beer and asking good questions. Thanks to Jeannette Gaudet (Romantic Languages) for helping me remember why friendship is so important. And finally, to Jo Lang: many thanks for keeping the home-fires from burning, for tai-chi, for tango, for playing and for love.

Introduction

Agency and Resistance

Debates in Feminist Theory and Praxis

Ellen Faulkner and Gayle MacDonald

Feminism's third wave is built on both the politics of second-wave feminism and the backlash that responded to it within a postmodern, neo-liberal world, where culture rather than politics is taken to be the key area of resistance (Miller 2008: 28). Feminist activism began in North America as a collective movement. The "personal is political" became its rallying cry, its mantra for a revolution for how to think/act about and to understand the differences between the sexes. Many achievements came as a result of this foment: pay equity, day cares, sexual assault centres, and transition houses for battered women and their children. No longer could legislators, policymakers or pundits ignore the plight of women. No longer would jokes about women's roles be easily delivered in Parliament.[1] Indeed, the Democratic race for leadership in the U.S. showed for the first time how a white woman or a Black man could actually become president of the United States, something some of us thought we would not live to see.

But what does all of this mean to the women's movement? Backlash in the press, such as resistance to Mary Koss's research on date rape on university campuses and to Take Back the Night marches and No-Means-No date rape campaigns (Stringer 2001; Roiphe 1993; Wolf 1993; Kamen 1993; Koss and Harvey 1991; Gilbert 1991, 1992, 1993; Koss and Oros1982; Koss 1988), spell out a feminism that, for the most part, is no longer the "in" social movement. It's considered passé (Gillespie 1994). Moreover, negative publicity has been used to bolster claims for financial cut-backs to feminist organizations. In 2006 the Conservative government "cut funding to the Status of Women Canada secretariat and to the Court Challenges program that funded citizens and groups fighting laws they believe violated the Charter of Rights and Freedoms" (Mallick 2006). Then the Tories "killed all funding for women's groups that do advocacy, lobbying, or research" (Mallick 2006). This signalled that a diversified political challenge is necessary to combat neo-liberal policies. Environmental movements (largely spearheaded by women) have become more compelling to youth as they look forward to a resource-ravaged planet and all of its incumbent difficulties. Books on disasters of all types environmental (Jacobs 2004; Rees 2004; Smith 2004; Aptekar1994) and capitalism gone amok (Klein 2007, 2001) comingle in people's consciousness with self-help books on everything from Tantric sex to Buddhist mediation.[2]

We argue, however, that there are movements still afoot (Boyd 2004), collective, individual and cultural, and many of them involve women. We argue that collective action on class, race and gender has changed emphasis, reoriented into issues of identity politics (Mathen 2004; Spivak 2008, 1988; Spivak, Chakravorty and Harasym 1990), of cultural challenge and of legal resistance (MacKinnon 2008). This resistance is largely due to a reaction to the circumstances, labelling and experience of the female "victim."

In this anthology, we trouble the concept of victim. We do so to enable the reader to see the work of women in resistance. We hope to offer the beginnings of a framework of resistance, one that explores the moments *beyond* victimization, how women do not stay crushed and broken, but move on, build and grow. We note the types of resistance as we find them, in settings of collective or individual political organizing, legal reforms and cultural norms and labels that criminalize. We find these examples in arenas of political resistance, identity formation and as tools of survival.

Activism Revisited

In the eighties feminists focused on anti-pornography, anti-prostitution, anti-censorship and pro-workers' rights, initiatives that presumed the workability of the "woman as victim" model. This model attempted to empower women by suggesting that the sexual assault victim, the sex trade worker, the woman victimized by pornographers or sweatshops and the woman sexualized in her trade union could be a survivor rather than a victim. This was a necessary political step and one we do not hesitate to support. Further, the movement has transitioned from a collective politic to individual resistance, and some individual resistance tactics have morphed back into a collective politic. We see this as a necessary political step in the next frontier of women's rights, the international stage. This transitioning was, in part, a direct response to issues imperative to the movement, identity politics arising from postcolonialist resistance, for example, and transnational feminisms both fusing and fracturing simultaneously. Rather than an aberration, or a seemingly erratic pattern, such political patterns are not only effective but highly "on the ground" responsive to issues that women face everyday across the globe. Not unlike the resistance to global capitalism, the tendency to "umbrella" women's resistance (Lewis 2005) at the international level has fractured some movements, fused others. But the women's movement lives on, largely reactive to the label of "victim" and seeking changes on both individual and structural levels.

Early feminisms, for all their achievements, stayed in a victim framework. Women were rendered passive, yet again, not by patriarchal ideology, but by reductionist explanations of the place of women: battered, assaulted and harassed. But to *name* these issues, as critical as that is for the healing of women so victimized, is but part of the political battle. Woman-as-victim is not an emancipatory cry that encourages all women to join efforts in combating patriarchy. It is, at its core, highly analogous to the right-wing, conservative agendas that would keep women politically passive, smiling stewards of male futures, still adhering to "men's way" in the boardroom and the bedroom. It is not what our mothers and sisters intended, at all.

The early movement was narrow. It had to be. A wide net, a grand focus, could not have achieved what our foremothers needed — whether that was the vote, shelter from harm, pasteurized milk, pay equity or extended maternity leave. This strategy had its victories but it also had its problems. For example, feminism as it used to be rarely included women of colour (Moraga and Anzaldúa 2003; Bhopal 2002; Allen 1992; Ware 1992; Omolade 1989; Spelman 1988; Giddings 1985; Lorde 1984; Avakain 1981; hooks 1981; Smith 1979; Hood 1978; Joseph and Lewis 1981) or fully explained differences of sexuality (Atkinson 1974; Myron and Bunch 1975; Rich 1980; Cornwell 1983). Some women were still marginalized, particularly so when it came to discussions of women and the law. Discussions of child custody in North America, for example, did not include what was happening in Europe, and discussions of violence, even on a structural level concerning sexual assault, could not explain fully the systematic rape that war has produced in the past few decades.

Alternatively, those who choose not to conceptualize women as victims argue that women's work in the sex trade industry, pornography and the underground economy is empowering for women. Turning victim language on its head, sex trade workers who fight for union rights suggest that archaic notions of consensus building and transformation are just that — archaic, so that the models of sex discrimination feminism represents often do not work for all women. True resistance, therefore, can be found through examining the *specificity* of women's conditions, the legal, social and cultural structures that disempower women, and the transformative power of negating the label of victim. Resistance then becomes a way of life, a survivor response or a political action. *Resistance is manifest either individually or collectively, at the local level or at the level of the state, as a first response or a last resort.*

What is unique in this collection is the rapport between this scholarship and resistance, relative to women's relationships to law, politics and culture (Chunn, Boyd, Lessard 2007; Boyd 2007; Boyd, Young, Brodsky and Day 2007; Boyd and Rhoades 2006). Through narrative, theory, field-work, case studies and/or legal policy, this anthology documents resistance in particular ways. Women in these chapters resist dominant practices in the social world in favour of more fluid, resistant and life-giving strategies to enable change in their own lives. By exposing language, experience and legal policy to this type of analysis, we can more fully understand the nature of the resistant experience for what it is, a subversion of normative practice.

In thinking about the ways in which women resist, we can turn to North American women's political awakenings, involvement with the battered women's movement, the sexual assault crisis centre movement and women's studies courses as examples. Participation in annual Take Back the Night marches, No-Means-No date rape campaigns and women's collectives entailed mobilizing, lobbying and fundraising, all of which contributed to social justice and social change for women. These actions for social change liberated many; yet, the promise of liberation had its contradictions. Research on racism in the women's movement, for example, has been resisted in women's studies programs (Moraga and Anzaldúa 2003; Bhopal 2002; Allen 1992; Ware 1992; Spelman 1988; Giddings 1985; Lorde 1984; Avakain 1981; hooks 1981; Smith 1979). But what of the resistance strategies employed by women cross-culturally? Are the strategies of resistance available to North American women viable alternatives to, say, women in Europe?

Theory and Praxis

The forms of resistance we observe in this anthology are wide-ranging. Activism is a highly visible form of resistance, and known to most. There are others. For example, legal responses to women's social problems are not necessarily recognized as resistance. Law reform and legal challenges are considered institutional responses, which do not fall into the same category as political protests. But as this volume attests, international actions, such as the response to war crimes in Bosnia (Goedl) and analysis of the United Nation's mobility clauses and the implications for child custody (Bromwich) can indeed be categorized as resistance, and resistance of the most critical kind.

Resistance is rarely documented as a powerful political strategy, especially when women are its primary agents. As an institution and as praxis, law rarely has room for agency, and even less so for the agency of women. Women are most often depicted in particularized ways by law, most significantly, as victims, usually as sexualized victims. As Mary Eberts has often indicated, law deals only with the sexual aspects of women's lives: pregnancy, motherhood, sexual assault. Less visible in legal cases are the more common places of women's victimization: of work, of pension and of increased tax burden (Johnson 2002). One salient reason for this is that law acts as a social mirror (Bell 1994), reflecting back to us how we socially organize the world in gendered terms. In other words, if we organize the world in ways that only emphasize women's sexuality, we render invisible those areas of women's lives in which other types of victimization occur. There is no room in this scenario, for example, for women who are victims of war, of harassment at work or of international child abduction. The means by which women from diverse backgrounds are able to resist depends on context, location, support and the ability to strategize in order to survive with dignity and determination. In this volume, we present women who all have the ability to resist, despite differences of class, race, gender identity, and ethnicity and nationality.

Law does not usually recognize resistance *as* resistance (Jeffrey and MacDonald 2006). Collective political action, individual actions or legal challenges by social groups are considered suspect. Claims to knowledge and power are often considered anormative, or simply ignored (Foucault 1976, 1977). Despite such examples, there have been considerable concerns among feminists about relying on legal structures to further women's interests (Smart 2002, 1995; Smart and Brophy 1985). These concerns stem in part from the patriarchal legacy in law, reflected in the dominance of men in virtually all aspects of law making and law enforcement, including the judiciary, the legal profession and Parliament. At the same time, some feminists favour using legal institutions as part of a broader effort to change society. There has been ongoing interest not only in studying the impact of particular laws and measures on women, but in taking a more introspective look at how women are treated within the legal profession and the courts (Hagan and Kay 1995; Brockman 2001).

First- and second-wave feminists resisted oppression and domination, and, through consciousness raising, political action and transformation, fought to have women recognized within law. Marxists and radical feminists questioned participating in the legal system because it was created and sustained by a "dominant sex class" (Smart 2002; Smart and Brophy 1985). Poststructuralists and postmodernists deconstructed damaging labels applied to women who do not fit neatly into dichotomous legalistic categories and have questioned the workability of the legal institution itself. The transformation of social, political and legal institutions might signal to women that they have won the battle, but lost the war. Liberal humanist values seem to prevail within formal social institutions, leaving out diverse voices and experiences. The "legal woman," like the "rational man," reconceptualized by feminist theory, remains white, middle class, propertied, married, heterosexual and educated. Those who do not fit within the dominant conceptual framework often become othered and excluded. This is the case for women who experience sexual assault (Coates and Ripley), abuse (Rosenberg), sexual harassment (Profitt) or even addiction (Toner), all of which appear in this volume.

To summarize, much consciousness raising in the women's movement for social change (for example, Betty Friedan's *The Feminine Mystique*, Simone de Beauvoir's *The Second Sex*, Germaine Greer's *The Female Eunuch*, Del Martin and Phyllis Lyon's *Battered Wives*, Ti Grace Atkinson's *Amazon Odyssey*, Mary Daly's *Gyn Ecology*) drew upon stories women told of how they resisted male domination. These political analyses allowed women to document experience and make connections with other women so that the personal became the political, in the process breaking down barriers between women and providing alternative methods of resistance and survival. However, fractures in the women's movement challenged these political alliances, threatening to disconnect women from each other over issues of identity, location, class and race. Feminist theory became weakened as it attempted to be too many things to too many diverse groups. Further, it became evident that feminist theory may "need" victims perhaps a little too much.

What we mean by this is that victim precipitation models that fail to investigate context, specificity and intersectionality have ended up labelling and re-imposing social control mechanisms (Elias 1993). What is problematic about this direction is not the presence of victims but the absence of chronology; the treatment of victimization as fixed, rather than fluid, as a state of being, rather than a "journey of life" process. Simply put, victims do not stay victims. They heal, regroup, move on (Profitt 2000). Those who do not move on, who stay crippled by the experience, are a minority. An example that flies directly in the face of the construction of victim is included in recent work (Jeffrey and MacDonald 2006) on sex workers. Radical theory encourages us to transform our thinking about women and men who work in the sex trade, educating us about the workers' agency to organize, unionize and enjoy the work that they do, a far cry from the victimization model consistently used by feminists (LeMonchek 1997; Jeffrey and MacDonald 2006).

Agency, for feminist theorists, has been "embodied" in the subject of dissent and enacted, at times, through political protest (Parkins 2000; Stern 2000). It may be that second- and third-wave feminisms have more in common than they believe. Resistance can include both an understanding of the institutional and personal oppressions women experience while at the same time providing options for self-determination, through individual identity, or political and/or collective social movements.

New Social Movements

Those who criticize the apolitical nature of (some) new social movements tend to see modern society as predominantly capitalist. Although they may have transcended traditional Marxist positions on the role of "old social movements" they remain wedded to a conception of capitalism as a systemic form of domination that must ultimately be challenged in political terms. (Buechler 1995: 453)

Despite the contention that there has been a "fall" from collective to individual resistance there is no consensus that this fall from grace ever took place. Historian Charles Tilly documents a long history of social movement in the West as a result of large-scale social changes and political conditions, so that "social movements still select tactics from essentially the same repertoire of contention that became established in the nineteenth century" (quoted in Staggenborg 2008: 4). According to Tilly, "social movements are one form of contentious politics," which included "special-purpose associations or coalitions and engaged in strategies such as demonstrations, petition drives, public statements, and meetings — various tactics that make up the modern social movement repertoire" (5). "Based on this contentious politics approach, Sidney Tarrow (1998: 4) provides a succinct definition of social movements as 'collective challenges, based on common purposes and social solidarities, in sustained interaction with elites, opponents, and authorities'" (Staggenborg 2008: 5). Suzanne Staggenborg argues that it is necessary to consider the historical context of the multiplicity of modern social movement themes and forms of agitation. She concludes that modern social movements are extensions of, rather than apolitical and ahistorical forms of, contentious politics.

Given the historical lineage of social movements and their common characteristics over time, the argument that an economic class base is required to drive collective action requires reassessment. Rather than reject economic issues, new social movements extend the focus on class to include claims for recognition of environmental issues, globalization, feminism, gay and lesbian issues, and Aboriginal protest (Larana, Johnston and Gusfield 1994; Mooers and Sears 1997; Kauffman 1990; Staggenborg 2008; Buechler 1995; Marcus 1982; Kaplan 1979, Ramos 2008).

However, Steven M. Buechler (1995:450) thinks that there is little consensus on anything to do with new social movement theories in relation to older Left leaning forms of political activism. New social movements may be part of a cycle of movements — drawing from the cycle of protest in the sixties and seventies influenced by the New Left and feminism. Buechler argues that unfortunate dichotomies are created when theorists try to define what is political versus what is cultural. Buechler agrees with McAdam (1994) that "all movements are cultural in some way" (Buechler 1995: 451). All movements play a representational or symbolic function. Buechler writes: "all movements take explicit or implicit political stances... [and] are complex and cannot be explained using inflexible binaries" (451).

A number of characteristics of new social movement theories validate the cultural theoretical perspective. First, such theories "represent a major form of social activism whose social base is sometimes best defined in something other than class terms, whether that be gender, ethnicity, race, sexuality, or age" (Buechler 1995: 456). Second, these theories "may be best characterized not in terms of a social base rooted in conventional statuses, but rather in terms of values and goods with which participants agree" (456). Third, despite the criticism of a lack of class base, "there does appear to be an elective affinity between a middle-class location and new social movements" (456). Finally, Buechler concludes that there is no one new social movement theory but multiple theories and he proposes a typology, an "ideal typical sensitizing construct," a heuristic tool. Buechler divides new social movement theories into political and cultural versions, which are not mutually exclusive but rather have related characteristics that overlap (457).

New Social Movements and Feminism

According to Suzanne Staggenborg (2008: 23, Table 2.1.) new social movement theories originate in large-scale social and political changes and the mobilization of everyday networks and organizational structures motivated by new types of grievances. An important feature of new social movements is their international collective identity, known as the global justice movement, which utilizes submerged networks and new types of structures, constituents and ideologies. The key outcomes are new types of values, identities and organizations using diverse cultural innovations.

Staggenborg explains how resistance to neo-liberal policies is a key factor in the development of the global justice movement (127). This movement and its allies (feminists, environmentalists, labour activists, students, community activists, churches, Aboriginal peoples) grew out of resistance to neo-liberal economic policies. The actors include the concerned citizens who organized coalitions against the Canada–U.S. Free Trade Agreement, both nationally and transnationally, those who opposed the Meech Lake Accord (Hampton 2008) and people working in environmental struggles. Coalition building increased with the formation of the Council for Canadians, which shifted the focus from Canada to the international concerns of safe water, for example. All such coalitions were concerned with extending social justice. Staggenborg thinks that submerged networks are critical to the success of the global women's movement, as well as many other initiatives, such as cultural and political activities "connecting issues of sexism with interlocking oppressions of race, class, and sexuality in cultural and political projects" (85).

Staggenborg calls third-wave feminism the global women's movement because it focuses on international issues, including violence against women and reproductive rights (81–87). The global women's movement includes transnational women's networks formed via the U.N. and NGOs, a focus on economic issues that connect the personal with the political, a critique of policies associated with neo-liberalism and resulting economic strategies and an analysis of how "women's unpaid labour is required to compensate for cutbacks in government services and how these economic policies affected the everyday lives of poor women" (82–83). Staggenborg defines the global justice movement as a transnational movement that "began linking various socio-economic and political problems to neo-liberal policies" (127). Activists created a master frame "that diagnosed specific problems as consequences of neo-liberalism and its practice by international financial institutions (Ayres 2004, 2005)" (Staggenborg 2008: 127). Examples of strategies include the use of the Internet to raise awareness and make global linkages, raising public awareness of the poverty-enhancing effects of neo-liberal policies, and political acts using new cultural forms. Tactics such as parallel summits, blockades, teach-ins, street theatre, rallies, protests and marches provide non-violent ways in which to challenge World Trade Organisation reform and support the dismantling of capitalism. Demonstrations challenge the exploitation of sweatshop workers and promote a global living wage, ethical trading and anti-corporate activity (Naomi Klein 2001). The result is a diverse anti-sweatshop global movement forging alliances with unions, environmentalists, students, feminists and community activists to lobby against lack of workplace standards and exploitation of women in developing countries (Staggenborg 2008: 135). Staggenborg sees a difference between second-wave feminists, who initiated the idea of the personal being political, and international feminists, who expand "on this insight to connect macro-level economic policies to women's everyday lives (Antrobus 2004: 45)" (34).

The global justice movement has been successful for a number of reasons, not least of which has been the creation of international linkages that raise awareness of the exploitation of workers and the environment by international trade and monetary practices. In doing so, the global justice movement has utilized a number of political strategies and cultural forms to challenge the negative impacts of global capitalism.

This book brings together numerous strategies of resistance that women use when confronted with the obstacles of patriarchal practices. The stories, studies, and practices herein speak volumes to the courage, persistence and patience of women's resistance to the label "victim." These women resist institutional structures, social norms, and legal codes in order to change the circumstances of their lives. We found these chapters, these practices and these stories fairly surprising, sometimes shocking and always inspiring. It is our sincere hope that all who read this book will experience the same.

Notes

1. Many women still cringe when they are called "baby." During a 1984 question period exchange in the House of Commons, cabinet minister John Crosbie told Liberal MP Sheila Copps to "just quiet down, baby." Copps replied, "I am 32 years old, I am an elected Member of Parliament from Hamilton East, and I'm nobody's baby." Many women reject being infantalized because such treatment is demeaning and sexist. (Trimble and Arscott 2003: 2–3).
2. Shambhala Publications, which also produces a magazine called *Shambhala Sun*, routinely runs book advertisements on mindfulness, graceful death, practising peace in times of war and so on. It also includes articles on such legends as renowned Buddhist nun Pema Chodron, who has written many books, including *When Things Fall Apart*, on the ability of individuals to practise peace, calm and mindful attention as ways to overcome life's problems.

Section One

Introduction

Rebecca Stringer's chapter, Rethinking the Critique of Victim Feminism, provides a conceptual framework with which to analyze the debates and struggles explored throughout this anthology. Stringer challenges us to think critically about the damaging effects of neo-liberal policies on violence against women and children and the negative media portrayals of sexual assault victims, as both contribute to the backlash against gains feminists have won in both the public and private domains. Stringer acknowledges that women's agency and empowerment via a politics of identity and activism provide a clear path of challenge to the discourse of victim feminism.

The ultimate message Stringer leaves us with is the need for a multi-level resistance strategy to challenge neo-liberal policies that contribute to the stigmatization of female victims. She suggests maintaining social networks with labour groups, alliances with diverse coalitions, mobilization of global issues that intersect with the health related interests of girls and women, a focus on the redistribution of wealth and worldwide challenges to neo-liberal ideologies that blame victims. All of these strategies fit within the conceptual framework of global women's movement theories — a common thread throughout this anthology — the need to resist ideologies that represent an affront to women's gains on numerous fronts, economic, cultural, political, symbolic and social.

Chapter 1

Rethinking the Critique
of Victim Feminism

Rebecca Stringer

Throughout the 1990s feminism's relationship with the category of "victim" was subject to much critical scrutiny, as a number of popular press feminist writers generated highly publicized critiques of what came to be known as "victim feminism" (Roiphe 1993, Wolf 1993, Sommers 1994, Denfeld 1995, Walter 1998). These writers argued that, given advances in women's socio-economic status, it is no longer appropriate for feminists to talk about women as victims of patriarchy. As Christina Hoff Sommers put it, "Women today can no longer be regarded as the victims of an undemocratic domination" (1994: 260). They argued that speaking of women as victims is in any case disempowering. "Victim" is a bad word for it fails to capture one's agency, and it merely affirms the sexist idea that women are weak and passive in comparison with men. Although these arguments were made over ten years ago, they have been remarkably influential and continue to shape many people's perceptions of feminism.

My aim in this chapter is to critically evaluate these arguments. In the first section I tackle Sommers' argument that women are no longer victims in the sense of being systematically disadvantaged. I show that she can only arrive at this view by carefully disguising gender inequalities, and I argue that the main problem with her critique is that it suggests that one cannot simultaneously ascribe to a feminist worldview and critically assess feminism as a form of victim politics. I also examine the argument that victim identity is disempowering, pointing out that, although the critics of victim feminism claim to be the first to bring this problem to light, many feminists have in fact already recognized this. I explore existing feminist arguments about victim identity and question the idea that victim identity is disempowering. Using Anne McLeer's work, I argue that identifying women as victims does not necessarily entail losing sight of women's capacities for agency and resistance. In short, when feminists use the word "victim" they do not necessarily refer to a passive subject who lacks agency. Rather, as Zillah Eisenstein writes, "Feminism theorises the fact that wherever there is a victim there is a struggle over power; that there is always at least the potential for resistance" (Eisenstein 1997: 40).

Gendered Inequality: Social Reality or Noble Lie?

Christina Hoff Sommers' book *Who Stole Feminism?* is set around a contrast between two different kinds of feminism: equity feminism, which Sommers supports, and victim feminism, which she impugns. Equity feminism is a "traditional, classically liberal, humanistic" style of feminism that focuses on granting women the same citizenship rights as men, while victim feminism takes the more radical view that achieving gender equality will involve deep challenges to the gendered arrangements that structure liberal-capitalist societies (Sommers 1994: 22). Sommers argues that victim feminism has taken over as feminism's mainstream face and obscuring the fact that the agenda of equity feminism is almost complete. Gender equality has for the most part been achieved, and women are no longer "hapless victims of patriarchy" (257). However, victim feminists deny this fact and continue to represent women as victims of violence, inequality and injustice.

Sommers contends that victim feminists deny feminism's degree of success because they suffer from resentment. Resentment, she argues, is an "unwholesome passion" that serves to distort one's perception of social reality, creating a false worldview (42). In feminism's case, resentment has led to the view that society is "dichotomised into two groups politically at odds, one of whom dominates and exploits the other" and has bred "the habit of regarding women as a subjugated gender" (42). The key problem with feminist resentment is not just that it promotes the view that society is "patriarchal and misogynist" (222) but that it leads feminists to "fabricate atrocities" to match their distorted worldview (42). Over several chapters of her book Sommers attempts to show that key feminist issues, such as domestic violence, rape and the gender pay gap, are neither compelling social problems nor indicative of ongoing gendered asymmetries of power. Rather, they are "noble lies" wrought through resentment (188). In order to neutralize these issues Sommers rivals feminist accounts of them with alternative explanations in which they appear as gender-neutral, as exaggerated by feminists or as biologically based and therefore impervious to political challenge.

With regard to domestic violence, Sommers refers to a study that found that women as well as men commit domestic violence (Gelles and Strauss 1990, cited in Sommers 1994: 194). On the basis of this finding, Sommers argues that it is inappropriate to treat domestic violence as a gender issue. Because both male and female spouses commit and are subject to such violence, this violence ought to be regarded as a gender-neutral "pathology of intimacy" (200). In making this argument, however, Sommers strategically de-emphasizes certain other findings from the study she cites — namely that in cases of domestic violence women are significantly more likely to sustain physical injury and need medical care, and that women are significantly less likely to cause physical injury. In this case, then, Sommers' tactic for countering what she sees as the distortions of "gender-specific analysis" (255) is to ignore rather than acknowledge the significant gender differences that are in evidence.

Sommers pursues a slightly different tactic with respect to the issue of rape, where it is not possible to deny that women are overrepresented as victims of rape and men are overrepresented as perpetrators of it. To negate the feminist view of rape as a form of sexist injustice, Sommers offers the gender-neutral explanation that rape is "caused by criminal violence, not patriarchal misogyny" (223) and is perpetrated not by men but by "people who are wont to gratify themselves in criminal ways" (225). For this reason, rape should be treated not as a pernicious feature of patriarchal gender relations but as "just one subvariety of crime against the person" (226). Further to this, Sommers argues that by using an "expanded definition of rape" feminists have manufactured false evidence of a "rape epidemic" (220). In Sommers' view, definitions that recognize that rape can occur between people known or related to one another and which establish that "any sexual intercourse without mutual desire is a form of rape" (220), in-spire women to make false rape complaints. Impugning the idea of date rape, for example, she writes: "By such definition, privileged young women in our nation's colleges gain moral parity with the real victims in the community at large" (220). Genuine rape victims, she argues, can be found "on the streets of downtown Trenton," not in "an office in Princeton" (220). In other words, Sommers wills a return to traditional rape law, where, as Susan Estrich describes, the only form of rape treated as law-worthy is "rape involving extrinsic violence (guns, knives or beatings) or multiple assailants or no prior relationship between the victim and the defendant" (Estrich 1987: 4). Determined to roll back feminist-led rape law reform and using the time-honoured argument that women who claim they have been raped are lying, Sommers argues for re-instituting the traditional definition of "real rape."

As with the issue of rape, Sommers is unable to deny the statistical reality of the gender pay gap. Despite the fact that many countries have incorporated the goal of gender equality into their labour legislation while female labour par-ticipation rates have risen exponentially, the world remains bereft of a national economy in which women as a group earn as much income from paid employ-ment as men as a group (UNICEF 2000: 131–32; see also Rose and Hartman 2004; Stringer 2006). Rather than deny this reality, Sommers again offers an alternative interpretation of it, but this time not a gender-neutralizing one. According to Sommers, feminists are wrong to treat gender pay gaps as evidence that labour markets are still set up to systematically discriminate on the basis of gender. Instead, the gender pay gap "naturally results" from women's childbearing role and cannot therefore be regarded as "discriminatory" (Sommers 1994: 241). Here Sommers turns to a classic anti-feminist argument: responsibility for women's unequal status rests with female biology and accordingly is impervious to politi-cal intervention. The female reproductive body, rather than the sphere of paid work's aggregate failure to fully and equitably accommodate women who have dependent children, becomes the locus of the problem, suggesting an inevitable distance between female sexual specificity and successful liberal individuality.

Sommers explains that in the North American context gender pay gaps appear because women "choose to move into and out of the workforce during childbearing and child-rearing years," thus bringing less "experience" to the workplace and gathering less remunerable merit (241). But in this attempt to recast the gender pay gap as a product of individual work/life preference, Sommers distorts social reality to the extent she claims victim feminists do. At Sommers' time of writing, women were the sole, primary or co-equal earners in more than half of American families. With the decline since 1970 of the breadwinning wage, women have emerged as the new providers: their income from paid work is indispensable rather than disposable family income. In the absence of assured government income support such as childcare subsidies and paid parental leave, and since the transition from welfare to workfare, the majority of women cannot afford the choice between paid work and childrearing that Sommers implies is available to all women. If they do not work, or fail to manage the competing demands of paid and unpaid work amidst rising living costs and declining real wages, they are punished with poverty — and this is the main reason why 30 percent of all female-headed households in the United States live in poverty (Roesch 2004: 16).

In her chapters on victim feminism's purported fabrication of atrocities, Sommers does not so much build a cohesive equity feminist worldview as steadily depart from feminist explanation altogether. She repeatedly downplays indicators of gendered asymmetries of power, offering a series of gender-neutralizing conceptual makeovers: spousal violence becomes privately dysfunctional intimacy; rape narrows to a symptom of criminal pathology; gender pay gaps are first naturalized then presented as freely chosen by women. Over the course of these ministrations, feminism's political ground steadily contracts, its key issues either downsized or made redundant. There is also a great irony at work in Sommers' book — even as she impugns feminists for representing women as victims, she herself repeatedly turns the category of "victim" to her own uses. Sommers situates herself as the representative of new populations of victims (genuine victims): "the true victims of abuse and discrimination in our society" (56), whose experiences purportedly are trivialized by feminism's "false victims"; men, whom she portrays as under siege by the "feminist establishment" (274); women who feel alienated by victim feminism; and, finally, women who have been "indoctrinated" into victim feminism's resentful worldview while attending women's studies "re-education camps" (116).

Ultimately, Sommers' critique of victim feminism fails to convince. Rather than offer a vigorous rethinking of feminism as a form of victim politics, Sommers gives us barely disguised anti-feminist rhetoric. Although her attempts to debunk feminist concerns are at times ingenious, her characterization of contemporary liberal-capitalist societies as free of gendered inequality and injustice draws a long bow indeed. Perhaps the most disappointing aspect of her account is that it creates the impression that one must subscribe to anti-feminist views in order to question feminist dealings with victim identity. As we will see in the following section, this impression is false.

Victim Identity and Disempowerment

In addition to arguing that the woman-as-victim construction is inappropriate given feminism's degree of success, critics of victim feminism make the argument that victim identity is in any case disempowering for women (see Wolf 1993: 225–30; Roiphe 1993: 50–82; Denfeld 1995: 58–89). They argue, in effect, that feminists invite women to regard themselves as vulnerable, passive victims where they ought to be inspiring women to regard themselves as strong, capable agents. While this argument may seem entirely reasonable, it fails to acknowledge a certain conundrum: it is the case that feminists should recognize and inspire women's agency, but it is also incumbent upon feminists to bring to light the victimization women do experience. How can feminists shed light on victimization without speaking of women as victims? We will see that the answer lies with examining what is meant by the word "victim."

The critics of victim feminism make the argument that feminists neglect agency as though for the first time, when many feminists have already acknowledged this problem. bell hooks points this out in her book *Outlaw Culture*, where she responds to Katie Roiphe's critique of victim feminism:

> By cleverly calling no attention to the work of powerful feminist thinkers who have continually critiqued the very excesses she names... Roiphe makes it appear that her ideas offer a new and fresh alternative to feminist dogmatism. In fact, her book draws heavily upon and restates critiques that have been continually voiced within feminist circles, yet voiced in those circles in a manner that in no way ridicules or mocks the seriousness of feminist agendas. (hooks 1994: 104–105)

As hooks suggests, it is indeed possible to critically interrogate feminist dealings with victim identity without losing sight of feminism's political purpose and crossing into anti-feminism. And hooks herself can be listed among those feminist thinkers who have already raised the victim problem. Her 1984 essay, "Sisterhood: Political Solidarity Between Women," offers one of the earliest and most systematic critiques of victim identity in feminist politics. hooks makes three distinct criticisms of feminism's woman-as-victim construction, each of which points to a different respect in which this construction can be disempowering for women. First, she argues that second-wave feminists created a political framework in which the respective categories "women" and "men" are sharply drawn as "victim" and "enemy." This framework served to marginalize rather than interlock with anti-racist politics and class struggle, which call upon women and men to work together, and also served to disguise "the fact that many women exploit and oppress other women" (hooks 1984: 44). Second, hooks argues that victim identity in itself is "psychologically demoralising": "Women who are exploited and oppressed daily ... cannot afford to see themselves solely as 'victims' because their survival depends on continued exercise of whatever personal powers they possess" (45). Third, hooks contends that feminism's woman-as-victim construction "directly reflects male supremacist thinking" in the sense that it can serve to affirm rather than challenge the idea that women are the "weaker sex" (45).

In her work on feminist anti-violence campaigns in contemporary India, Ratna Kapur (2002) points out a further respect in which the woman-as-victim construction can be disempowering for women. Kapur observes that feminist politicizations of violence against women have had the unintended effect of bolstering the paternalistic law-and-order agenda of the Hindu Right. Successful feminist arguments for recognizing women's right to freedom from violence as a human right have been translated by the Hindu Right into amendments to the criminal law that render women as vulnerable subjects who require protection by the state. Kapur observes that while these amendments "touch on issues that are of concern to women, there are no corresponding proposals to promote women's civil rights, mobility, freedom, bodily integrity, or substantive equality" (27). Kapur's concern is similar to that voiced by Anna Yeatman in her work on feminist concepts of power. Yeatman warns that when feminists enlist state intervention on behalf of women's rights, the rights-bearing status that is won "may be a qualified one, namely one that exists only to the extent that it is reconcilable with the idea of state-sponsored patriarchal protection of women" (1997: 149). For Yeatman, patriarchal protectionism is at odds with the effort to constitute women as self-governing agents. In her view, feminists need to ask the state not to protect, but to *respect*, the personhood of women (152).

Given the compelling arguments these theorists make, we may well agree that feminists should abandon the woman-as-victim construction. Kapur suggests feminists conceive of the subject of feminist politics not as a victim subject but as a "resistive subject," observing that "it is important to foreground the moments of resistance demonstrated by women in their different subject positions" (32). This move is similar to that of rape crisis workers who refer to women who have experienced rape as survivors rather than victims: "Survivor rhetorically establishes that one has been victimized, yet also implies that one should be recognised for overcoming the often debilitating effects of sexual victimization" (McCaffrey 1998: 278). Adopting alternative terms is indeed a viable strategy, but in my view it is equally viable for feminists to specify what "victim" means in the feminist sense. Critics of feminism's woman-as-victim construction presume that the word can only ever describe a non-agent — a subject to whom power, capacity and resistance are perfectly unavailable. As Kapur puts it, the victim subject is "thoroughly disempowered and helpless" and "cannot accommodate multi-layered experience" (10, 6). But in her work on feminism and victimology Anne McLeer (1998) has shown that the word "victim" is open to other meanings and connotations.

Victimology is a branch of criminology devoted to studying the criminal-victim relationship. As McLeer explains, victimologists contribute to the study of crime by "increasing knowledge about the victim, rather than the perpetrator... the relationship between criminal and victim is thus seen to be mutually informative" (42). Importantly, victimology's focus on the victim does not imply victim-blame. Blaming the victim serves to "*deflect* agency from the criminal" while victimology serves to "*explain* the agency of the criminal" and to provide "a neutral and elucidative construction of victim subjectivity" (43–44, emphasis added). Because the role victims play in events of victimization "varies from passive to quite active" (44), victimologists offer a definition of the word "victim" wherein the victim's capacity for action, resistance and prevention is posited as variable, and the word is dislodged from any necessary tie with either pole of the active/passive dichotomy. The victim is not prohibited from agency in this definition; yet to retain the sense in which victimization involves abrogation of agency a third term is introduced into the equation: "subjectivity." Adopting this language in the following passage, McLeer indicates that within the victimological framework the victim/agent dichotomy is preserved and, in view of the complexity of victimization, reworked:

> Although the victim was the "done-to"… she is not automatically presumed to lack subjectivity in this situation. The relationship between criminal and victim of a crime is posited as having a more complex configuration than that of subject-object, doer-done-to dualisms… term "victim" in the language of victimology contains an understanding of an active subjectivity that does not imply the helplessness and lack of resistance implied by the term in other discourses. (42–43, 51)

McLeer's key interest is in radical victimology, which moves beyond individual instances of crime to allow "institutions and classes to be considered within the existing parameters of victimology" (45). Radical victimology is suited to feminist theorizing, argues McLeer, because it offers a way to investigate systems of gender oppression while foregrounding the various modes of negotiation and forms of subjectivity women take up within these systems. In short, the victimological framework offers precisely what Kapur and others see as lacking in the victim subject: the ability to bear witness to agentic resistance and to accommodate multi-layered experience.

McLeer's work indicates that it is possible to adopt a complex and flexible conception of the victim subject rather than jettison the word "victim" from the feminist lexicon. In my view there are two main reasons for taking up this alternative. The first has to do with the role the language of victimization plays in feminist arguments for social and political change. Feminism tends to press against forms of violence, inequality and injustice that are not immediately recognizable as forms of victimization, but rather are regarded as benign, normal, natural and therefore impervious to change. Recall, for example, how Sommers casts the gender pay gap as natural and freely chosen, in order to render gendered economic inequality beyond the reach of political change. The logic of Sommers' argument is: "no victimization is taking place here; hence there is no possibility or need for change." But a form of victimization *is* taking place: that women as a group garner significantly less income on average than men as a group indicates that the sphere of paid employment still privileges men, and does so at women's expense. The objective of using the language of victimization in response to an argument such as Sommers' is not to open a window onto suffering and helplessness. Rather, it is to point out the need for political intervention and change. So the first reason for taking up McLeer's strategy is that the language of victimization is key to feminist efforts to make certain configurations of power visible, in order to open up the possibility of transformation.

Second, I believe there is value in continuing to use the term "victim" in the contemporary moment, shaped as it is by the global politics of neo-liberalism. Since its emergence in the 1970s neo-liberalism has posed a direct challenge to the array of collective political movements — including feminism, anti-racism, the disability rights movement, the lesbian and gay rights movement, union movements, and welfare liberalism — that have sought cultural recognition and economic redistribution for marginalized and disadvantaged social groups. To counter the achievements of these movements and in order to downsize the sphere of public and state responsibility, neo-liberalism promotes a doctrine of individual responsibility for individual socio-economic fate. This doctrine disappears socio-economic relations and forces, representing economic inequality and social disenfranchisement as individual failings rather than collective concerns. Neo-liberalism presents victims as self-made: victimization is not the result of an eliminable form of inequality or injustice, but of bad choices and irresponsibility on the victim's part. As Kathy Laster and Edna Erez explain, "In the neo-liberal world, victim status must be avoided at all costs since to require assistance and support suggests a lack of enterprise and application" (2000: 247).

The key achievement of the neo-liberal campaign to replace collective struggle with strong individualism has been its stigmatization of the victim subject and, relatedly, its rendering of collective political movements as threatening the proper workings of market meritocracy. These notions are what political theorists call legitimating discourses: they help to secure the legitimacy of neo-liberalism as a mode of governance. At present neo-liberalism is under threat owing to the fact that it has overseen a vast upward redistribution of wealth and historically unprecedented degrees of inequality between rich and poor (Harvey 2005). In the face of this threat neo-liberal stigmatization of the victim subject is bound to intensify. My view is that those engaged in collective struggle need to move in the opposite direction: the task of resisting neo-liberalism calls upon us to track its generation of inequality, but also, and crucially, to *de*-stigmatize the victim subject.

Section Two

Legal Challenge/Reform and Resistance

This section underscores both legal practices and resistance strategies that are used in legal arenas around the world by women who refuse the label "victim." Originally conceived as the only emphasis for this book, it was clear in examining the range and variety of work submitted that further emphases were warranted. In this section, Rebecca Bromwich, Suzanne Bouclin and Doris Goedl provide examples from different parts of the globe of the ways in which women's collective resistance strategies impact on challenges from individual legal cases dealing with international child abduction, the working rights of erotic dancers and the effects of war/rape/violence on women.

A deeply moving example of the need for legal reform is highlighted by Rebecca Bromwich's critique of the *Hague Convention on International Child Abduction*. Bromwich indicts the Canadian state for complicity in woman and child abuse by not protecting women from their abusive former partners. Bromwich points to the patriarchal underpinnings of the custody provisions in the *Hague Convention*, which these fathers use to force mothers to return their children to an abusive home. Bromwich shows how the *Convention* stigmatizes the seemingly irrational actions of mothers who seek to protect their children. She provides compelling reasons to challenge the way the international treaty has been interpreted in Canada, broadening the frame of reference to global immigration issues.

Beginning with an analysis of how neo-liberal policies pushed women out of low paying jobs into the sex trade, Suzanne Bouclin provides a micro-level look at how sex workers in Canada organize for changes in labour practices. Female erotic dancers formed a pan-Canadian alliance against unsafe working conditions. This action not only challenged societal assumptions about dancers as victims, but it presented women dancers as labourers with collective rights to the same protections around working conditions as any other labour force. Erotic labourers engaged in discussions around health and safety issues, better working conditions, violence against women and sexist policing. One of the main issues the national alliance took on was lapdancing because of the potential for sexual exploitation and unsafe working conditions.

Doris Goedl shows us how, although the Dayton Agreement was ratified in 1995, years of war in Croatia and Bosnia and the disintegration of the former Yugoslavia have left women who had been sexually assaulted virtually invisible. These female victims were denied recognition in the reconstruction project. Doris Goedl challenges the tired stereotype of the sexual assault victim-as-participant through the lens of trauma. Beginning with large-scale social issues — war and nationalism — she explores the gendered nature of women war victims and their grievances.   By providing a political context to the nationalistic policies that supported the traumatic events of rape and torture, Doris Goedl firmly places the personal into the political. She demonstrates that there can be an effective women's lobby, which can impact the work of the International Criminal Court and the U.N. In this chapter, we see examples of a genuine effort to listen to women's stories and address and heal the pain by developing everyday networks of women's groups, by developing a women's caucus in the U.N. and through organizing against nationalist policies and ideologies. Doris Goedl shows that institutional forms of justice are often inadequate for resolving the specific harm of sexual torture and trauma. Truth and reconciliation forums are most effective when they go hand in hand with formal justice initiatives. International and domestic trials are simply not enough.

Chapter 2

Flight

Woman Abuse and the Hague Convention

Rebecca Jaremko Bromwich

At thirty-six, the woman in my law office, a petite blonde Irish woman with a lilt to her voice, is a mother of six and a grandmother of two. Her face is attractive still, though it bears, on her cheeks and eyes, scars from her husband's violence. She has fled her home country with those four of her children who remain minors to seek refuge from the religious laws of Ireland, which do not protect her or her children from her husband, even though the Canadian police, on her arrival, compiled physical evidence and statements about their sexual abuse by him.

Later, another woman, this time dark haired, also soft-spoken. Hailing from Bangladesh, she came to Canada as a landed immigrant after an arranged marriage and now remains here with her son. Diminutive and traditionally dressed in splendid colour, she repeats over and over again that she is a lesbian. Because she can say it here, in the quiet of this room of our own, this legal space that we have appropriated. Her husband has returned to Bangladesh. While she had been living there for some months with her child and husband, she would like now to stay in Canada. She tells me she cannot confess her sexual orientation to anyone who might bring the news to Bangladesh, where her mother and sisters might be killed out of reprisal for this disgrace.

These women come from different religious, ethnic, racial and socio-economic backgrounds. They differ in almost every way, including how they have experienced violence. However, they have in common the facts that they have both been accused of abducting their own children and both are survivors of violence at the hands of their accusers. As such, they have been both "victimized" and blamed in legal discourse. As I learned later, after conducting legal research, these women are hardly alone in their predicament. As early as 1993, American researchers were noticing that women who "abduct" their children across international borders are often also fleeing abuse. That year, Geoffrey Greif and Rebecca Hegar published a study dealing with 368 parents whose children were abducted by the other parent. In the majority of the cases they studied, they made the surprising finding that the "abducting" parent was the mother. They also found that domestic violence tended to be a major feature of these parents' marriages (Greif and Hegar 1993).

In this chapter, I look at Canadian experiences respecting woman survivors of domestic abuse who flee that abuse with their children. I discuss how these women, by "abducting" their children to protect them from abusers, are often resisting oppressive legal regulation. I look at the *Hague Convention on the Civil Aspects of International Child Abduction* (1980) and Canadian caselaw that has developed under it from the perspective of how this body of law often fails to address the realities of woman abuse. I provide examples of how a lack of recognition of domestic violence in *Hague Convention* cases, where women cross borders with their children to flee from their abusive intimate partners, puts women and children at risk.

The *Hague Convention* itself is problematic for several reasons. It is written in a manner that is "gender blind," meaning there is no reference made or relevance given to whether it is a male or female parent abducting the child. This does not reflect contemporary Canadian law, which has been changed to protect women against partner abuse. It was not written in contemplation of the possibility that a mother's "abduction" could be in the best interests of the child.

Also problematic is the body of caselaw, both from Canada and elsewhere, dealing with hearings under the *Convention*. In many cases, courts have disregarded allegations of woman abuse, holding that they are irrelevant to the determination of whether a child should be returned to the petitioning parent. To be consistent with Canada's refugee law and domestic family law, when Canadian courts are called upon to do hearings under the *Hague Convention*, an effort should be made to afford women protection from woman abuse, or at least, such hearings should not be made available to abusers as means to forcibly return women to abusive and dangerous situations.

I look at how women who have been cast as "victims" of domestic violence challenge the dominant discursive processes and social imagery of our legal system. Such "victimized" women take possession of legal space by making arguments under the *Hague Convention* (U.S. Dept. of Justice 1995: 3). They resist regulation by oppressive laws by fleeing jurisdictions where woman abuse is condoned. I see their self-help remedy of flight with their children, often mischaracterized as abduction, as a form of women's resistance against unjust and oppressive laws. I argue that this form of resistance can and should be protected under the *Hague Convention*.

I practice as a lawyer, predominantly in the areas of family, immigration and refugee law. An intersection between these areas of practice occurs when victims of domestic violence, either in Canada or elsewhere, cross international borders. Their voyaging may be voluntary. Too often with my clients, it is not. As a practising lawyer, I do not conduct statistical data analyses. I represent clients, and in the course of this representation, do legal research. The research on which this chapter is based comes from four sources: documents such as international agreements and domestic laws, previous "precedent" cases, legal scholarship and, finally, experience dealing with clients.

I meet with clients who take the initiative to call upon me for help. My clients come from three main sources: private referrals, legal aid referrals and women's shelter duty counsel work. Private clients are women who call me directly and pay for my services out of their own funds. Legal aid clients come to see me after first attending the offices of Legal Aid Ontario, where they are granted a certificate for free legal representation if they are determined to financially and otherwise fall within Legal Aid's budgetary guidelines. My third source of clients is women's shelters, where, acting on behalf of Legal Aid Ontario, I periodically give advice to women in crisis. The primary purpose of such duty counsel services is to provide onsite, urgent advice for women with emergent family law crises. However, there is a secondary purpose to such advice, in that it connects women in need of legal services with a lawyer with whom the intention is to build a rapport and an ongoing solicitor-client relationship.

It is said that woman abuse knows no socio-economic status or race. While I do not have statistical information about the demographics of my sample population, I have found this anecdotally to be true. The woman survivors of abuse with whom I meet hail from across a broad spectrum of social classes and racial and ethnic heritages. They tend to be of child bearing years, often as young as their late teens or early twenties, but I have seen some women in their later years only now emerging from decades of abuse. What they have in common is their gender, though not necessarily their sexual orientation or gender identity.

The women with whom I come into contact in my practice are not by any means a random sample. They are exceptionally courageous and resourceful, often taking subversive, self-help action, crossing borders, using deception to secure themselves and their children from physical and sexual violence and possible death. By virtue of the fact that they have asserted themselves by resisting abuse and oppressive legal regulation, they may represent a determined minority of a much larger group of women who were unable or unwilling to take similar steps. Further, the women who come to see me have demonstrated a faith in legal processes by seeking my help, and their experiences will be seen and considered by women in abusive relationships who are deciding whether to seek help.

What is inspiring for me in this area of practice is not the idea that I can rescue these women. That is not the point; it is about my clients' own agency and individual autonomy. These women inspire me. Cast as victims, they challenge the dominant discursive processes and social imagery of our legal system, and particularly of the *Hague Convention*, by taking possession of legal space and by the subversive act of their flight from abusive partners and legal systems that support abusive relationships.

Woman Abuse: An International Problem

It is well documented that woman abuse is a problem of disturbing magnitude in Canada, as well as internationally. According to Status of Women Canada, half of Canadian women (51 percent) have been victims of at least one act of physical or sexual violence since the age of sixteen (2004: 11). Canada is not alone in having to contend with the pandemic of woman abuse. International statistics also speak to high numbers of women being battered each year. For example, one United States study indicated that each year, one million American women suffer nonfatal violence by an intimate partner (U.S. Dept. of Justice 1995: 3). This is in addition to the women killed by their partners. Too often, violence against women results ultimately in homicide of the female partner (see Crawford and

Gartner 1992). Overwhelmingly, the aggressors in these relationships are male. Further, victims of female perpetrated domestic violence are considerably less likely to experience more serious forms of violence (Canadian Center for Justice Statistics 2005: 14–16). Woman abuse is a gendered problem, with patriarchy and power at its roots. Race, class, sexual orientation and ability intersect with the experience of abuse in ways that compound the vulnerability of women who are not easily identified as "able" and "white" (see Razack 1994). Further, the extent to which state protection is available to women who have suffered abuse at the hands of their intimate partners is highly variable internationally (UNICEF 2000).

Where women are abused, children are at risk. Isolation and threats against children are key tools in the arsenal of many woman abusers (Domestic Abuse Intervention Project 2008). So is the use of institutions and laws that elevate men as superior to women. Abusers are helped by systemic complicity and overt co-operation in nations and regions where woman abuse is tacitly, or openly, accepted. Even where abusers do not seek deliberately to harm the children of their partners, a growing body of research now shows that witnessing domestic violence itself harms children (Suderman and Jaffe 1999; Bala et al. 1998).

Women who cross borders with their children may do so for many reasons that are interrelated with abuse. When they do so, they may be subjected to accusations by abusive partners of abducting their children. Unfortunately, abusers can use the *Hague Convention* to force return of their children to them and indirectly force return of their spouses. The *Convention*, an international treaty, has been directly incorporated into Canadian law, affording persons with custody "rights" to children a recourse to have children returned to, or retain children in, their country of "habitual residence." This determination is fact-specific and hinges on two questions, (1) the "settled" purpose of the parents and the children spending an (2) "appreciable time" in the country alleged to be the state of habitual residence. There are some exceptions to this rule, including most importantly a narrow exception that allows for consideration of "grave risk of harm" to children.

Legal Protection against Woman Abuse

Canada's family and refugee laws are imperfect, but over the past twenty years or so, they have been significantly revised in order to protect women against domestic violence. The laws of other countries, including the United States, have similarly shifted over the past few decades (Weiner 2000; Leto 2002). Out of a growing awareness of woman abuse, driven primarily by feminist political action, our laws have changed to protect women and their dependant children from structures of rights and property that have historically facilitated their subordination and oppression. The following is a brief discussion of ways in which Canada's refugee and family law systems now seek to recognize and protect against, violence against women.

Family Law

Much as wives were their husbands' property, children once belonged to their fathers like chattels (Mason 1994). However, children are no longer legally the property of either of their parents; no one has "rights" to custody of a child under Canadian law. It is the child's right to live in accordance with his or her best interests.

Custody of children is a separate legal notion apart from the question of where they will live. Custody is a concept relating to legal authority. Whenever custody and access issues arise, the court must determine the application by reference only to the needs of the child. Courts have broad discretion when making custody orders, with the sole test to be applied in determinations of appropriate custody arrangements is the "best interests" of the child(ren), as is set out in the *Divorce Act* (s. 16(8), s. 17(5)). The "best interests" test applies both under the *Divorce Act* to custody disputes ancillary to divorce and to custody disputes in relation to children whose parents are not determining arrangements ancillary to a divorce under provincial statutes like Ontario's *Children's Law Reform Act*. On the one hand, this test has been criticized as notoriously indeterminate, allowing judges almost *carte blanche* in doing as they see fit respecting custody. On the other hand, the indeterminacy of the legal test allows judges to look at the lives of children in their entirety and to consider gendered issues of violence against women in making custody and access determinations. Section 16(6) of the *Divorce Act* confers this discretion on the court, empowering it to grant custody or access for a definite or indefinite period and subject to any such terms, conditions or restrictions as the court thinks fit.

As Julien and Marilyn Payne (2006) note, the "best interests of the child" is a holistic notion encompassing the physical, emotional, intellectual and moral well-being of the child. The court must look not only at the day-to-day needs of the child but also consider the ramifications of any decision to the child's longterm growth and development.

Matrimonial fault, historical problems between the parties or other aspects of conduct by either party are not in themselves relevant to the determination of custody or access in relation to a child. For example, Ontario's *Children's Law Reform Act* (CLRA) provides that custody and access are to be determined without reference to past misconduct by the spouses against one another (s. 24). Such conduct is only relevant if it bears upon a party's parenting ability. This is also set out in the *Divorce Act* (s. 16(8), s. 17(5)).

As Simon R. Fodden is careful to point out, the list of factors that are relevant to custody and access determinations set out in the CLRA is not exhaustive; other considerations can be legitimately within the contemplation of the court (1999). A relatively recent case discussing what factors are to be considered is the Nova Scotia decision of *Roberts v. Roberts*, where it was made clear that custody and access cases require an integrated assessment of all relevant factors and circumstances in order to determine the best interests of the child.

In the relatively recent leading Alberta case of *Calahoo v. Calahoo*, factors to be considered in determining the "best interests" of the child were set out in some detail and included the following:

the provision of the necessaries of life, including physical and health care and love; stability and consistency and an environment that fosters good mental and emotional health; the opportunity to learn good cultural, moral, and spiritual values; the necessity of setting realistic boundaries on conduct and fair and consistent discipline in teaching appropriate behaviour and conduct; the opportunity to relate to and love and be loved by immediate and extended family and the opportunity to form relationships; the opportunity to grow and fulfill his or her potential with responsible guidance; to have optimal access to the non-custodial parent in order to encourage and foster a good relationship; to be with the parent best able to fulfill child's needs; and the provision of an environment that is safe, secure, free of strife and conflict, and positively guides the child in development. (*Calahoo v. Calahoo* citing *Starko v. Starko*)

Where there are no glaring problems with either parent's ability to care for the children, three factors will be of great importance: preservation of existing arrangements to afford the children stability in their living arrangements, which parent was the primary caregiver during the parties' marriage and a disinclination of the courts to split the siblings (see Payne and Payne 2006).

Notably, domestic violence perpetrated by one parent has come to be recognized as a glaring problem with that parent's ability to care for the children of the relationship. It has been found in a growing number of cases that domestic violence on the part of a parent negatively impacts on children, even where the violence is not directed towards the child. Increasingly, witnessing domestic violence is understood by Canadian courts to be harmful to children (see Bala 2000). Thus, while domestic violence cannot be considered relevant to the "best interests" test as "marital fault," it is relevant to the best interests of the child and is considered frequently as a significant, often determinative factor, in deciding with which parent a child will live (see Bala 2000).

Refugee Law

Refugees are a subgroup of a broader category of displaced persons. A "refugee" is defined under the *Geneva Convention Relating to the Status of Refugees* (1951) as a person a outside his or her country of habitual residence who has a well-founded fear of persecution and who is unable to access the protection of that country, or to return there, for fear of persecution. The majority of refugees are women. Like men, these people are vulnerable and need protection, but they also face gendered problems. Women fleeing their abusers may become refugees. In many countries, legal and governmental regimes either continue to support, or by inaction fail to stop, woman abuse. Such political systems are complicit in the abuse suffered by women, who must cross international borders to seek protection (UNICEF 2000). Or, women may voluntarily flee other forms

36

of political oppression in their countries of origin accompanied by their abusers. Alternatively, women may leave their families and communities as a result of coercion by their abusers. Women who cross borders with their children when fleeing abusive intimate partners may not necessarily fall within the parameters of the definition of refugee. For example, if, as Canadian citizens or permanent residents who have been habitually living abroad, they have a right to remain here, they will not be considered refugees.

In its inception the *Geneva Convention*, a multilateral international agreement much like the *Hague Convention*, provides no grounds of sex or gender on which refugees can be granted protection from persecution. Women can be found to be refugees under the *Geneva Convention* for the same reasons as men. Usual grounds for protection are threat of persecution because of race, religion, nationality and political opinion. Being gender-blind, this international treaty is, like the *Hague Convention*, also blind to the particular problem of violence against women.

The definition of who is a refugee was primarily designed with men in mind. It does not address problems uniquely faced by women. However, in 1993, long after the *Geneva Convention* was signed, Canada was first among many countries that began to address the particular needs of woman refugees. The Immigration and Refugee Board (IRB) prepared guidelines for woman refugee claims and expanded the categories to cover women as a group that can be protected (Immigration and Refugee Board of Canada 1993).

So now, while they still cannot do so in many countries, in Canada, in addition to being able to claim refugee status for the same reasons as men, women can be found to be refugees for reasons relating to their gender. For example, a woman who fears abuse at the hands of a man from whom her country's government is not able, or willing, to protect her can make a refugee claim on this basis. Also, women can be found to be refugees if they fear repercussions in their country for breaking rules only applied to women. For example, if women are compelled to wear a certain type of clothing, style their hair a certain way or participate in an arranged marriage, and they fear punishment for breaking these rules, they could be considered refugees.

Despite the fact that our incorporation of gender issues into the determination of refugee claims in Canada is not by any means a perfect system, it nonetheless provides a useful example of how concerns about violence against women can be made visible and considered in the context of a determination of rights under an international agreement that, like the *Hague Convention*, is gender blind on its face.

International Child Abduction: The Hague Convention

As noted, the primary means by which nation states have come together to protect children against international abduction is the *Hague Convention*. The *Convention* is an international, multilateral agreement intended to prevent abduction of children across international borders, to facilitate return of abducted children and to protect the rights of custodial parents. As a piece of international law, it is to a great extent a success story, being implemented and enforced in many signatory countries.

More specifically, the objectives of the *Convention*, as provided in Article 1, are "to secure the prompt return of children who have been wrongfully removed to or retained in any Contracting State" and "to ensure that rights of custody and of access under the law of one Contracting State are effectively respected in the other Contracting States." Article 12 provides that where a child has been "wrongfully" removed to or retained in Canada, an order will be made for return of the child to the country of his or her habitual residence. In Canada, the *Convention* has profound and far-reaching implications because it has not only been ratified but has also been incorporated into domestic law.

The *Convention* operates in the following manner where an abduction is alleged. Article 12 provides the parent left behind with the remedy of having the "abducted" child forcibly returned to him or her where it is found that a child was wrongfully removed from that parent's jurisdiction pursuant to Article 3. A hearing will be held in the country where the children are found to determine whether or not the child has been wrongfully removed and whether or not the remedy of return should be granted. The burden of proof to show that there has been a breach of Article 3 is on the party bringing the application, the petitioner. Where a child is found to have been unlawfully removed or retained, it will be said that a *prima facie* case has been made for return of the child to the petitioner parent.

The onus then shifts to the respondent parent to defend his or her action in removing the child. Return will not be forced in all circumstances; the respondent parent does have defences available. The application must have been made promptly upon the child's removal. Article 12 allows that, if the child has been settled in the jurisdiction to which he or she was removed for in excess of one year, he or she will not be forcibly returned to the petitioner. Article 13 allows a court hearing a *Hague Convention* application a discretion not to return a child when that child is of sufficient age and maturity to express his or her opinion and indicates a desire not to be returned. More significantly from the perspective of women fleeing abuse, Article 13 (b) allows that the child will not be returned where the respondent can show that this would place the child at a grave risk of harm. This "grave risk of harm" exception could conceivably be interpreted to include the harm a child will suffer when he or she witnesses domestic violence, as is recognized under Canadian domestic family law. As such, this defence could be pursued by a domestic violence survivor to defeat the remedy of return.

As mentioned, the *Hague Convention* has been incorporated into Canadian domestic law. In Ontario, for example, section 46 of the *Children's Law Reform Act* incorporates the *Convention*. Although they are to bear in mind treaty obligations, Ontario courts must apply Ontario law in interpreting the phrase "habitual residence." This is done by reference to section 22 of the CLRA, as was made clear in the decision *Medhurst v. Markle*, which is discussed in more detail below.

The significance of the remedy of return provided by Article 12 of the *Hague*

Convention in the lives of women who have fled abuse, as well as in the lives of their children, must not be underestimated. As Merle Weiner emphasizes:

> The remedy of return uniquely disadvantages domestic violence victims who have abducted their children — it reverses the accomplishment of the victim's flight by returning the child to the place from which the domestic violence victim has just fled. The remedy puts the victim's most precious possession [*sic*], her child, in close proximity to her batterer either without her protection (assuming she does not return with the child), or with her protection, thereby exposing her to further violence. (2000: 634)

Problems with the Hague Convention

The *Hague Convention* has several features that call into question its ability to deal justly with "abductions" by abused women of their own children. First, as mentioned previously, the *Convention* is gender blind in its language. Both parents are formally equal under the *Convention's* articles, a fact that also blinds legal discourse around the *Convention* to the gendered problem of woman abuse.

Second, beyond failing to appreciate the gendered nature of their circumstances, the *Convention* was clearly not written with abused women in mind. It is drafted in contemplation of a malevolent abduction by someone, a parent or otherwise, with either a direct intention to harm the child or a disregard of the child's best interests. Such an abductor might be a parent seeking to subvert custody rulings made against him or her or might be a third party with the intention of exploiting the child. The *Convention* does not primarily contemplate the situation, which I have repeatedly encountered, where the removal of the child has been committed by an abused mother specifically in contemplation of the child's best interests. Debate surrounding the signing and ratification of the *Convention* referred to the looming spectre of international trafficking in women and children and the notion of a male abductor taking a child by force. Also highly publicized were cases of American or Canadian parents left behind. Left virtually out of the discussion is the notion of flight by a woman, with status to remain in Canada with children, from an abusive partner hailing from a jurisdiction unwilling or unable to protect her or her children from his violence (Weiner 2000).

Third, the *Convention* rests on patriarchal notions that are out of step with Canadian domestic family and refugee law. Concepts underlying the protection conferred by the *Hague Convention* are not drawn from one particular legal system. For example, the crucial matter being protected, being parental "rights of custody," does not coincide with the notion of custody under Canadian law, but is defined within the structure, definitions and purposes in the *Convention*. These definitions emerged from discussions between representatives of nation states, many of whose family law regimes still protect paternal rights of property in children. As discussed above, the notion that anyone can have a "right" to custody of a child is discordant with Canadian family law, which has been quite deliberately amended to remove the notion of property in children. Consequently, the enforcement of the *Hague Convention* under Canadian law results in a fundamental inequality whereby children "abducted" across international borders are treated very differently from those taken by a parent within Canada.

The gender blindness of the *Convention* is also discordant with the IRB guidelines discussed above with reference to Canadian refugee law. We are left with a situation where women who have strong claims for refugee status on the basis of domestic violence and who would almost certainly gain custody of their children under the domestic "best interests" test, can face the spectre of harassment and coercion in the form of applications by abusive partners for return of their children to countries where the women's victimization by abuse has been ignored and even permitted.

The *Convention* is intended to afford protection of children when an aggressor seeks to traffic in children and to afford protection from harm they will likely suffer as a result of parental "abduction" (Freeman 2000). However, balance must be struck between seeking to protect children from harm they may suffer as a result of a malevolent abduction and the harm they will almost certainly suffer if they are forced to remain under the control of abusive parents, the harm that will arise if they are not "abducted." All states have an interest in protecting women from domestic violence and children from the negative effects of witnessing that violence.

Hague Convention applications by abusive partners are likely to be successful; the *Convention* as currently interpreted forces many domestic violence victims to return their children to their home country. In light of this, it would be beneficial to amend the *Convention*. Nonetheless, however problematic it may be, the *Convention*, concluded after years of drafting and negotiations between many nations, is something we must, at least for now, acknowledge. The language of the *Convention* is sufficiently indeterminate, like many laws, that it has been used in abusive ways, but it also could be used differently. Like most laws, it is written in a way that allows it to be used well or badly depending upon the interpretation. A more emancipatory interpretation of the *Hague Convention* is possible. To explain this, I provide caselaw below elucidating the courts' current interpretation of the *Convention*.

Interpretation of the Hague Convention in Canada

While amendment of the *Convention* would be ideal, it may not be possible for a long time, and it might not be necessary. Interpretation of the *Convention* has developed differently in countries other than Canada and the U.S., where it is interpreted in similar ways. While elsewhere it has grown in potentially promising directions, it is beyond the scope of this chapter to discuss in detail domestic *Hague Convention* caselaw from jurisdictions other than Canada and the U.S. However, the importance of the manner in which the *Convention* is interpreted to its impact as well as of the proposition that the wording in itself is sufficiently indeterminate so as not to dictate outcomes are confirmed in the writing of Marisa Leto (2002). Leto takes the opposite position to Weiner, who argues that the *Convention* should be amended to address the predicament of abused woman "abductors" and their children (Weiner 2000). Leto, looking at international caselaw from several jurisdictions, argues that, as interpreted in certain countries other than Canada and the U.S., the *Convention* already relies on a "best interest of the child" standard that is largely subjective and allows judges to make discretionary decisions that may in part be motivated by "gender biases." Made clear by Leto's criticism is the flexibility of the treaty's drafting. If, in other countries, the *Convention* is already being read in a manner that makes issues relating to gender and the best interests of children relevant, the same perspective could be taken in Canada.

Two aspects of many Canadian decisions in *Hague Convention* hearings are particularly problematic. First, the narrow interpretation the courts often give the exception for "grave risk of harm" prevents the court from looking at allegations of domestic abuse by the petitioner, and as such flies in the face of custody determinations under Canadian domestic family law. Second, the negative treatment and significant weight courts give to "deception" by the respondent parent presents a further obstacle for women who have fled their abusive partners.

Canadian cases on the *Hague Convention* are hearings that take place in Canada where an allegation is made by a parent that one or more of their children have been wrongfully retained here or abducted from another jurisdiction. It is difficult to interpret this caselaw from a gendered perspective for several reasons. By virtue of the formal equality enjoyed by litigants under Canadian law, detailed analysis of cases would have to be made to determine patterns. My anecdotal understanding of the gendered experience of woman survivors of abuse is that this legal blindness to race, class, sexual orientation and ability serves to prevent the court from "seeing" the systemic nature of the barriers women face. A detailed statistical analysis of the embodied identity of respondents and petitioners in Canadian *Hague Convention* proceedings, similar to that conducted in the United States by Grief and Hegar (1993), would certainly be useful but is beyond the scope of this chapter. Space and time constraints as well as the nature of my legal research necessarily limit this discussion to the analysis of "leading" cases, recent Canadian decisions that outline the current state of our common law where allegations of abuse are made.

An especially salient example of the restrictive meaning given to the "grave risk of harm" defence in Canada is *Medhurst v. Markle*. The *Medhurst* decision is also important because it is a "leading" case, meaning the statement of law set out in the decision has been approved of and applied in numerous subsequent decisions. In *Medhurst*, a father sought to have his child returned to Germany under Article 8 of the *Hague Convention*. Notably, the father in *Medhurst* was ultimately successful, but at trial, the father was unsuccessful, even though it was found that the child's habitual residence was Germany. The trial judge found that the proceedings were an abuse of process as the father's real purpose in making the application was to force a reconciliation with his wife, who had, in effect, left the country to get away from him. On appeal, it was found that this was an error of law. The Court held that the three conditions determining whether a child is to be returned to Germany were that the appellant had custody "rights" to the child, that the child was wrongfully removed or retained, and that the child was habitually resident in Germany. As a result, the child was returned to Germany, leaving the respondent mother with a difficult choice, either to remain in Canada, where she herself would be safe from her former partner's abuse and leave the child at risk of harm in his control, or return to Germany to be near her child and seek to ensure the child's protection.

Significantly, although it did not find such a situation, the Court in *Medhurst* also confirmed that any determination of the fate of a child under the *Hague Convention*, pursuant to the text of the agreement, does remain subject to a finding on a balance of probabilities that there is a grave risk that the return of the child would expose the child to physical or psychological harm or would otherwise place the child in an intolerable situation.

Medhurst presents an affront to those of us who work consciously to help women extricate themselves from situations of abuse. Clearly, the husband in the matter was able to use the *Convention* as a tool to control and continue abusing his wife. Also unfortunately, from the perspective of the best interests of the child, where the case involves allegations of violence by the parent applying for the child's return, the threshold for this "grave risk of harm" qualification has thus far been very high under Canadian jurisprudence. As is shown by *Medhurst*, violence against the child's mother by an abusive spouse is not considered. *Medhurst* also demonstrates a further problem with current interpretation of the *Hague Convention*: the husband was, in practical terms, using it to perpetuate his control over, and force a reconciliation with, his wife. Despite Article 13(d), which clearly intends to protect children from "grave risk of harm," on the basis of the blatant disregard of spousal abuse allegations in *Medhurst*, abusive partners can use the *Convention* as a tool in their arsenal of abuse.

It is important to note that not all Canadian judges have failed to see the relevance of domestic violence committed by a petitioner father to the appropriateness of the *Hague Convention* remedy of return. In a 1999 Ontario Court of Appeal decision authored by Madam Justice Rosalie Abella, *Pollastro v. Pollastro*, where a respondent Canadian mother brought substantial evidence of the American petitioner father's alcohol problem and long history of physically abusing and harassing the mother, the Court found that the child would be placed at a "grave risk of harm" and refused to return the child to him. The decision allowed that the victimization of the mother by the father was relevant as it impacted on the child's best interests; physical or psychological harm to the parent on whom the child was totally dependent would harm the child.

For those of us who work to support women in their efforts to resist abuse and oppressive legal regulation, the *Pollastro* decision is a welcome and highly useful decision. However, *Medhurst* continues to be followed after *Pollastro* was decided and courts continue to interpret Article 13(b) narrowly. It is significant that an abundance of evidence of severe abuse causing injuries over a long period of time was tendered by counsel for the respondent in *Pollastro*. The mother was able to produce documentation of her injuries from a physician in the petitioner's home country and obtain third party witness reports of the abuse and resulting injuries. In many situations, a woman's flight with her "abducted" children may be undertaken before years of brutalization take place. I argue that a body of evidence of abuse as large as that tendered in *Pollastro* should not be necessary to meet the "grave risk of harm" test. This is particularly important as, while Reesa Pollastro was abused in the United States, where there is some progressive recognition of the problem of domestic violence, in the case of many women, victimization takes place in a country where circumstances prevent her from thoroughly documenting the abuse.

Another Ontario Court of Appeal case, where a mother made spousal abuse allegations against a *Hague Convention* petitioner father, that came shortly after *Pollastro* was *Finizio v. Scoppio-Finizio*. *Finizio* is a good example of the evidentiary difficulty set out above. In that decision, the Canadian mother contended she had been physically assaulted by the Italian petitioner father by being "punched in the face" on at least one occasion. Here, the Court did not find the domestic assault to meet the threshold of "grave risk of harm." Despite the evidence of physical assault on the mother, the Court found "no evidence that the husband has ever done anything to harm the children" (*Finizio v. Scoppio-Finizio*: para 30). The children were ordered returned to Italy.

A more recent leading Ontario Court of Appeal case than *Pollastro* on this question is *Jabbaz v. Mouammar*. The *Jabbaz* decision makes clear that the "grave risk of harm" test is still being given a narrow interpretation by Canadian courts. In *Jabbaz*, a mother resident in the United States allowed her former husband to take their child to Canada on the understanding that the child would be returned to her once her life stabilized. There were no allegations of domestic abuse by the father, but the statement of law provided by the Court as to the scope of the "grave risk of harm" test remains applicable to cases where abuse is alleged. At trial, the Court held that, while the habitual residence of the child was the United States, it would place the child at "grave risk of harm" to be returned there. On appeal, this decision was overturned. In the *Jabbaz* decision, Rosenberg J.A. stated:

> The circumstances in which a court may refuse to order the return of a child under Article 13 are exceptional. The risk of physical or psychological harm or, as alleged in this case, an intolerable situation must be, as set out in Article 13, "grave." The use of the term "intolerable" speaks to an extreme situation, a situation that is unbearable; a situation too severe to be endured. (*Jabbaz v. Mouammar*: para 23)…
>
> Unlike virtually all other child welfare statutes, the test under the Hague Convention and Article 13 in particular is not framed in terms of the best interests of the child. The court to which the application is made under the *Hague Convention* is not concerned with determining which parent should have custody of the child using the best interests of the child test. (para 24)

Problematically for woman abuse survivors, at paragraph 39 of the *Jabbaz* decision, Justice Rosenberg went on to strongly suggest that decision-makers should not import "public policy" notions into their interpretation of the *Convention*. He wrote as follows:

> I repeat the observations of Chamberland J.A. in *F. (R.) v. G. (M.)* at para. 30 that the *Hague Convention* is "a fragile tool and any interpretation short of a rigorous one of the few exceptions inserted in the Convention would rapidly compromise its efficacy." That means that courts should be very wary of grafting new public policy exceptions on to the *Convention* in the face of the very clear public policy represented in the *Convention* itself.

Deception and Abuse

When a woman flees her abuser with her child or children, she will more likely than not deceive her partner to some degree in doing so. This deception may be necessary for her to safely escape and may be a crucial element in facilitating her resistance against the abuser as well as against a regime that condones, or is otherwise complicit in, domestic abuse. This deception, however, may lead to a finding against her in a *Hague Convention* proceeding. It has been found in Canadian caselaw that deceptions by a parent that facilitate his or her abduction or retention of a child in violation of the *Convention* can prevent the country to which they were removed, or where they were falsely retained, from becoming their "habitual residence." It is also arguable that the test for habitual residence calls for consideration of the parents' "purpose" in coming to a country and should be considered in "all of the circumstances." For example, one case where this was found was the Manitoba decision of *Belton v. Belton*. In *Belton*, a father removed his daughter from the United States, where they had resided with her mother, on the pretence of visiting his parents in Canada. The mother made an application for return of the child to her under the *Hague Convention*. She was successful, the court holding that the daughter's habitual residence was Tennessee, where she usually resided. She did not lose her place of habitual residence merely by moving to Manitoba. The wife did not acquiesce in the daughter remaining in Manitoba and took steps as soon as she reasonably could to oppose the husband.

Because of the rules of precedent and because the *Convention* is gender blind, the *Belton* case can be used by counsel for abusive petitioners where a female "abductor" has fled domestic violence to successfully argue that deception by the fleeing parent should prejudice her claim to retain the child with whom she has crossed into Canada.

Conclusion

The *Hague Convention* is, in some respects, an impressive piece of international law. Unlike many multilateral treaties, it is being actively enforced. It deals with a high level of effectiveness with the sort of international child abductions it was intended to remedy: abductions by parents seeking to gain advantages in litigation, abductions by parents seeking to circumvent lawful custody orders and third party abductions by parties seeking to exploit children. However, the *Convention*, especially as currently interpreted in Canada, can easily be used to harm women and children when its remedy of return is invoked by a father who has abused the child's mother and from whom she has fled in search of safety for her herself and her children. This situation is all too common. When it takes place, the *Convention's* remedy of return jeopardizes the mother's safety and the child's best interests.

It is frustrating to deal with the situation I see too often, where women who have taken the initiative, courage and risks to flee their abusers to another country with their children are, just as they start to be hopeful that they are safe in this new country, turned back by abusers using the *Hague Convention*. The Irish client I describe above, for example, gave up and returned to Ireland, refusing to defend a *Hague Convention* application, afraid of the spectre of police forcibly returning her children to their father. As is shown by the caselaw above, Canadian courts do not protect abused women from use by their intimate partners of the *Hague Convention* as a tool of abuse and, in failing to offer such protection, become complicit in that abuse. To be a just law, the *Convention* should provide women forced by their abusers to flee to Canada with an opportunity to have their matters heard here. The current gender blindness of the *Convention* and the Canadian laws that make it enforceable here, together with the body of caselaw that has been decided under it in Canada, makes our state complicit in woman abuse and a party to harm of children.

I see my job as a lawyer as one with creative dimensions. I try to find ways to work within existing laws to make them emancipatory, to assist in women's resistance. Ideally, the *Convention* will be amended. Until then, particularly on the basis of the *Pollastro* decision, there is scope to better protect women using the *Convention* as written. Judges need to start accepting the "grave risk of harm" exception under Article 13(b) in more cases, taking the lead from the Ontario Court of Appeal in the *Pollastro* decision, and to start using it as a way to "see" domestic abuse. For them to do so, lawyers need to advance this argument more often on their clients' behalf.

It is not only the courts who could assist with ending Canadian complicity in the abuse of women who are accused by abusive partners of "abducting" their own children. As is shown by the example of the guidelines put in place by the Immigration and Refugee Board with respect to woman refugees, politicians could set out policy guidance for interpretation of Article 13(b). Of course, wherever political action is possible, this puts an onus on the public at large to lobby government for change. Justice demands that the courageous women whose resistance against abusers and systems that support abuse takes the form of flight across international borders are met at their destination with our support.

Chapter 3

Bad Girls Like Good Contracts

Ontario Erotic Dancers' Collective Resistance

Suzanne Bouclin

In most Canadian jurisdictions there has been a shift in the labour performed by female erotic dancers from visual entertainment (stage dancing) to more individualized services (lapdancing) (Frank 2002). This requires additional physical and emotional investment from dancers and renders them more vulnerable to sexual and economic exploitation (DERA 2002). Given their ambiguous employment status, dancers also lack access to employment protections and common law remedies. This is compounded by the stigma associated with their work and the fine line dancers walk between legal and illegal sex acts. In light of the aforesaid conditions of constraint, some dancers have organized to craft more meaningful choices for themselves.

This chapter first provides an overview of the feminist methods and theories that guide my research on dancers' collective resistance. I then outline the efforts of Ontario-based dancers to respond to unfair labour practices, arguing that affiliations have emerged as a venue through which women can exercise agency and subvert the oppressive structures of their workplace. I go on to discuss the barriers marginalized and stigmatized workers face when attempting to organize. I conclude that, in conditions that foster individualism and competition, support systems for dancers can lead to sophisticated political and legal campaigns to change the erotic industries.

Methodology, Methods and Theoretical Frames

This research project was conceived in 2002, when I attended a Stigmatized Labour Support Network (SLSN) meeting and met members of the Dancers' Equal Rights Association (DERA). In light of the marginalized and stigmatized nature of the Canadian erotic dance industry, a history of the women working within it is not readily accessible. As a result, my core findings draw upon semi-structured interviews with five primary and five secondary research participants. The former are DERA members: current and former dancers in their mid-twenties to their mid-thirties, who identify as English-speaking and white and who live in Ottawa. Two are in long-term relationships; two are single-parent heads of households; four were experiencing financial difficulties at the time of the interviews. Secondary informants include an SLSN member (a nurse providing outreach in clubs), two former dancers, a legal studies professor and a labour organizer. Finally, I also engaged in considerable correspondence via e-mail with women in other jurisdictions who are championing the rights of sex trade workers through STELLA (Montreal), the International Union of Sex Workers

(England) and the Exotic Dancers' Alliance (U.S.). I collected information on four Ontario-based groups: Canadian Association of Burlesque Entertainers, Exotic Dancers' Alliance, Association for Burlesque Entertainers and DERA. Members of these small, fairly homogenous affiliations share a commitment to changing labour practices. However, the approaches taken by these groups have not always resonated with the broader dancer community, as they tend to focus on the needs of a privileged minority of dancers (white, young, English-speaking and who have some formal education). While these limitations do not render their activism fatally flawed, they do speak to the generalizability of my findings.

In terms of theories, this research is influenced by feminist re-readings of the concept of resistance. Briefly, during the early eighties a debate emerged among North American feminists around the rhetorics of choice/constraint as they related to the sex trades (Bell 1987; Chandler 1999). More recently, these binaries have been challenged for being caricatured:

> The simplistic binary constructs that my culture gives me to interpret these events, passive victim versus active agent, do not encompass my experience. I was both and neither, something different, something to be located in the underlying play of differences between the dichotomy of victim and agent. (Ronai: 1999: 126)

A recurring project in more recent feminist theorizing has been to move away from binary categories to emphasize how women resist oppressive systems that regulate their lives. Feminist postmodern/poststructuralist theorists deconstruct the unitary notion of the female subject and accentuate the shifting nature of identity (Alcoff 1991; Butler 1990; Cixous 1983). This is reflected and reproduced in more recent readings of erotic dancing, which, for example, can be personally and financially rewarding, but may also be experienced as exploitive and oppressive. More likely, the work of an erotic dancer is located between these two extremes (Bouclin 2004; Bruckert 2002; Egan 2003; Sanchez 1997), and dancers individually and collectively negotiate choices for themselves within their workplace. In this context, resistance refers to tactics or strategies that individuals employ in order to contest the conditions of constraint in which they exist. Indeed, dancers do engage in everyday individual acts of resistance within the Foucauldian (1976) understanding of power and agency. For instance, not unlike waitresses and flight attendants, there is an expectation reinforced by employers and customers that dancers will engage in emotional labour (Hochschild 1983; Montemurro 2001). For instance, Julie, recounts how dealing with customers is draining at times: "They try to touch you when you say not to touch you basically. And at the same time you're on friendly vibe so it's very taxing you know? And there are ones who get all depressed and tell you sob stories, you know, and you can't leave." However, with time and experience, she adopted a more "abrupt and professional" approach: upon receiving gratuities, she would "just stand up in the middle of a sentence, smile and say 'okay then have a great night'" and walk away. Erotic dancers also engage in performative defiance (Wood 2000) when negotiating customers who cross the line. Sam explains that she would adopt a highly erotic disciplinarian persona to communicate what she would and would not tolerate: "Just talk to them like puppies — good boy, sit, stay." However, the strategies available to some dancers are not available to others. Heather outlines the characteristics that might leave dancers with less space in which to manoeuvre:

> I know that some girls are afraid because… they don't have any education or another job or they don't have anything to fall back on, they're worried about supporting their families, they would be afraid of losing their jobs.

Everyday acts of resistance are to a large extent contingent upon one's cultural markers. It seems however that some dancers are cognizant of the disconnect between everyday acts and effecting changes in stripclubs. They have looked to collective strategies to bring about conditions in which they can exercise more meaningful choices in relation to their labour practices. The remainder of my discussion focuses on this collective form of resistance, which find its roots in a more traditional Marxian blueprint for social change.

Getting Organized: Dancers Resist Licensing

In 1975, the Supreme Court of Canada determined that performing nude in a cabaret theatre was not an immoral act (*R. v. Johnson*). While local ordinances on nudity varied, generally dancers could only remove their clothing down to a g-string in a manner that did not offend public decency under sections 163 and 170 of the Criminal Code. They would perform five stage shows per six-hour shift and their average weekly remuneration was $300 (Bruckert and Parent 2004). Between shows entertainers were strictly forbidden from fraternizing with customers in order to avoid being charged with soliciting for the purposes of prostitution (*Re Sharlmark Hotels Ltd v. Municipality of Toronto* 1981). Flying in the face of sanctions against nudity, clubs threatened dancers with dismissal if they did not disrobe entirely (Tracey 1997). With this and the move toward more seedy entertainment such as mud wrestling and wet T-shirt contests (Bruckert 2002) striptease emerges as a "social problem" to be controlled, mainly through municipal licensing. Dancers began to organize to challenge industry changes and intrusive regulation.

In 1978 Toronto proposed a bylaw that would require all club owners, operators and dancers to obtain licences. The city claimed this measure would protect workers, provide them with professional credibility and ensure better regulation of the industry. However, in order to obtain licences, women were required to produce medical certification that they were free of sexually transmitted infections, submit photo identification, establish that they did not have a criminal record and pay an annual fee (Cooke 1987; Johnson 1987). A group of Toronto-area dancers led by Diane Michaels organized to challenge the licensing scheme. In 1979 the Canadian Association of Burlesque Entertainers (CABE) was recognized by the Canadian Labour Council and became Canada's first and hitherto only union-backed association of dancers in Ontario. CABE went before city council arguing, according to former president Merri Johnson (1987), that licensing would push the most marginalized dancers — older dancers and those with criminal records — out of the clubs into the much more precarious street-level sex work. With the exception of having dancers' stage names on licences rather than their real names, CABE's submissions were ignored and the licensing scheme passed (Cooke 1987).

Despite this defeat, CABE remained vocal, and in 1981 it sued clubs for having barred its members from entry into clubs. In rendering its decision, the Labour Board grappled with whether dancers were employees (*CABE v. Algonquin Tavern*). CABE argued in the affirmative because of the managerial control over dancers' working conditions (attire, music, clients with which dancers interact, hours of work). The taverns argued that dancers were independent contractors and the Board agreed: dancers were not an "integral" part of taverns' business. Rather they were one of many forms of entertainment (like musical, comedic and sporting events) that clubs promoted. In short, dancers were ancillary to clubs' primary income-generating activity: food and alcohol sales. Moreover, dancers worked for a number of establishments at once and were not economically dependent on one specific employer. As a result, they were denied the safeguards and benefits afforded to employees through protective legislation (maximum work hours, minimum pay, wage protections, overtime benefits, notice for termination and vacation time). CABE was nevertheless successful on one front: the Board drew a distinction between freelancers and housegirls. Freelancers worked according to their own schedule and received no base salary, so even though they were required to meet a basic four-hour requirement, they could be considered independent contractors. Housegirls (scheduled dancers), on the other hand, received a weekly wage in addition to being required to work six to eight hours a shift; they were deemed employees. However, CABE was unable to mobilize enough housegirls to enforce their employee status (Weagle 1999). CABE therefore shifted its resistance strategy and moved from the courtroom back to the political realm. It began lobbying the municipal government to implement a bylaw requiring dancers to wear a g-string. The city responded favourably and attempted to legislate. The bylaw was unsuccessfully challenged by a coalition of club owners; its pith and substance dealt with the regulation of a business and was well within municipal authority. However, in 1985, the Ontario Court of Appeal struck down the law because its dominant purpose was regulating public morals — a matter squarely within federal jurisdiction (*Re Koumoudouros*).

CABE disbanded only three years after its inception. Amber Cooke, who worked in the industry in Toronto during the 1980s, argues that the group's favouring of the g-string law may have led to loss of confidence in its leadership, and it could "not act from a position of strength" (1987: 96). Despite its inability to present a collective voice for dancers, CABE nonetheless contributed to challenging societal assumptions about dancers as victims. It presented women as labourers working to effect changes. As well, it remains the only Ontario-based dancers' affiliation to forge formal bonds with a union.

The Shift to More Personalized Services

After CABE folded, a hiatus in organizing followed. During the eighties, there were nonetheless a number of broad societal shifts that shaped and are reflected within the micro-level of the stripclub. With the global move toward neo-liberalism, the Mulroney government emphasized deregulation of the private sector and downsized the public sector (Timpson 2001). Canada's economy suffered a severe decline, which forced working-class women from scarce manufacturing jobs to the service sector, with correspondingly low wages, little employment security and long hours (Vosko 2000). In light of these conditions, a number of (primarily white, working-class) women who met the standard of sexiness promoted within the stripping industry opted for erotic dancing or other forms of commodified sexual labour as an alternative to working for minimum wage (Bruckert 2002). With an increase of available workers, erotic dancers' labour shifted: table dances were standardized and wages atrophied. With table dancing, women would sell a one-on-one, no-contact dance for five dollars. Stage shows, while still a core element, gave way to the more personalized interactions and became a form of advertisement. With the exception of feature dancers (who tour cities and are paid at a higher weekly rate) remuneration for housegirls went from a per-show basis to per-shift basis (on average $40 a shift). According to Cooke, women were strongly encouraged to provide "hands-on entertainment rather than dance in order to make their money" (1987: 98). Dancers who refused to table dance were fined by the clubs (an egregious practice still current today) or scheduled for less lucrative shifts. Valerie found that with *de facto* mandatory table dances, women had slim options: "table dance and maybe lose the ability to choose to 'cross the line' with some customers," refuse to table dance and take the decrease in income or leave the industry altogether.

In the early nineties, the erotic dance industry underwent additional changes. First, clubs began requiring dancers to pay a ten to thirty dollar "stage fee" for every shift they worked. Clubs promoted the idea that dancers engaged in contracts for service (independent contractors) rather than in contracts of service (employees) (Weagle 1999). Management argued that they rented out the venue in which women sold titillation and company; dancers simply paid the fees for access to the club's customers. Second, owners substantially decreased the number of scheduled dancers. As Christina explains: "They just stopped putting me on schedule. I was a regular girl with four shifts a week. Then one day I go into work and there's no more schedules." Third, the creation of champagne rooms (cubicles) for personalized interactions at a higher cost (usually ten to twenty dollars) and the emergence of contact dances (lapdancing) vitally altered the labour performed by dancers. In principle, a lapdance involves a naked dancer gyrating on a patron's lap (facing him or with her back to him). In practice, the extent of contact between a patron and a dancer varies according to dancers' personal boundaries and social location, customer preference, the presence or absence of seclusion, the amount of money exchanged and club rules. Of these shifts, lapdancing has without doubt been the most contentious, and there have been considerable legislative efforts to regulate it. Specifically, in *R. v. Mara*, police officers charged two men (the club owner and manager) with allowing an indecent performance under section 167 of the Criminal Code at a Toronto tavern. Officers witnessed mutual masturbation between patrons and dancers and what appeared to be cunnilingus. At trial, Judge Hachborn found that while this behaviour may have offended community standards in other contexts, it was innocuous by comparison to the conduct dealt with in an earlier case (*R. v. Tremblay*), though, but for that earlier decision, the conduct would have likely been subject to regulation. With that, he dismissed the charges. Almost two years later, the Ontario Court of Appeal unanimously reversed that decision. First, it held that the judge had not properly applied the community standard of tolerance (*R. v. Butler*). Instead, the higher court held that lapdancing is harmful to society because it degrades and dehumanizes women, is incompatible with the dignity of each human being, predisposes persons to act in an antisocial manner and presents a risk of real physical harm to women. Second, the court found that the facts could be distinguished from those in Tremblay. In that case, the physical contact between patron and dancer was strictly prohibited and the explicit nudity took place in a booth rather than in the middle of the club. The Supreme Court upheld the appellate judgment.

Between the trial and the Supreme Court ruling, clubs began promoting lapdancing as legal; this in spite of the fact that many were being charged and found guilty of keeping a common bawdy house (*R. v. Caringi*). As one owner remarks: "Following the decision lapdancing became a popular form of entertainment at most clubs in Ontario as dancers and club owners had a judicial decision that touching between patrons and dancers would not constitute criminal behaviour" (affidavit of Mr. Koumoudouros in *OAEBA v. Toronto* 1997). Simultaneously, two anti-lapdancing discourses emerged. Some opponents of lapdancing argued that it was inherently harmful to the moral order and disrupted the nuclear family. Others argued that it was harmful to the health and wellbeing of women (Lewis 2000). Certainly, while some dancers felt that lapdancing provided them with an additional income, others felt that it decreased their ability to negotiate unwanted physical contact with patrons. Two Toronto-area groups organized in response to the Hachborn decision. It is noteworthy that although both challenged ideas about dancers' victimization they also reproduced the "harm to dancers" discourse.

Toronto Dancers Organize

The Association for Burlesque Entertainers (ABE) formed to lobby Toronto's municipal authorities around lapdancing. The bylaw campaign was spearheaded by ABE's president, Katherine Goldberg, and was backed by the provincial New

Democratic Party (Ferguson 1995). On behalf of its 200 members ABE went before city council with country-wide complaints that dancers experienced lapdancing as disempowering and were being coerced into "upping the ante." As one dancer explains:

> I remember the very first night we lapdanced... we were driving home from the club and we were crying our eyes out. We both felt like this is not what we were brought up to do. These strangers' fingers all over you... it was really nasty. (cited in Lewis 2000: 10)

In 1995 Toronto became the first municipality to ban lapdances and its bylaw was immediately challenged by a coalition of club owners. The Ontario Adult Entertainment Bar Association (OAEBA) sought an order quashing it on the basis that it was beyond the city's jurisdiction and encroached upon the federal government's power to enact criminal law (*OAEBA v. Toronto*). Two dancers intervened and argued that the ban infringed their freedom of expression under section 2(b) of the Charter of Rights and that they derived personal rewards and economic gains from the new labour practice: "I chose to participate in close contact or lapdancing for a number of reasons... I could make more money doing close contact dancing. I also enjoyed the personal contact that I developed with my customers doing close contact dancing" (affidavit of Ms. Johne in *OAEBA v. Toronto*: 651). Relying on the testimonies of ABE members, the city submitted that the law was enacted for health and safety reasons and that lapdancing increased the likelihood of violence within clubs and the transmission of infections:

> I'm not saying all exotic dancing is bad, but lapdancing and prostitution in bars is bad... I don't think lapdancing can be controlled. I urge you to get rid of it... lapdancing hurts everyone. For instance, a man fingers a girl and has a cut finger... and he gives her AIDS or venereal diseases... she goes home and gives it to her husband.... (ABE 1995, cited in Lewis 2000: 11)

The judge held that the purpose of the bylaw was in fact the protection of health and safety in adult entertainment parlours and that no Charter rights were violated (contact dancing was not a constitutionally protected form of speech). On appeal, the trial judge's decision was upheld and appeal to the Supreme Court denied.

In the aftermath of this success ABE's membership declined significantly. First, several dancers, including Goldberg herself, were banned from working at the club for their involvement in anti-lapdancing initiatives (Highcrest 1995). Additionally, its focus on lapdancing may have alienated some dancers and overshadowed other issues. As one former member comments: "No one is talking about other workplace issues such as filthy change rooms, long hours, and the whole wage structure. When we could lapdance we had some choice in how we worked" (Dawn in Highcrest 1995). However, a number of Toronto-area dancers held positions similar to ABE's. In one dancer's words: "I had enough of men saying to me I'll give you fifty bucks for a blow job... I hated the way it made me feel. So I'm actually enjoying dancing more since the ban [on lapdancing]" (in Lewis 2000: 211).

ABE folded after the Supreme Court found lapdancing to be within community standards of tolerance (*R. v. Pelletier*). But as late as 1998, members were still appearing before city councils across the country and successfully lobbying for municipal bans on lapdancing. ABE's evidence was also relied upon by lower level courts in other provinces in finding that lapdancing constituted a health risk for dancers and for patrons (*563080 Alberta Ltd*). To this end, ABE's primary strength lies in its use of an adjudicative approach, which encouraged dancers to participate and engage the courts in a meaningful way (especially interesting given the marginalizing impact the adversarial system often has on women). Finally, to date ABE is the only Ontario-based dancers' organization to actively pursue activism on a national level rather than limiting its scope to regional issues; thus its members also destabilized traditional stereotypes about dancers by presenting themselves as pan-Canadian labour rights advocates.

Around the same time as ABE's inception, another Toronto group began to organize. In 1994, a woman working in the region initiated a series of regular meetings between dancers, health workers and government officials to strategize around health and safety issues relevant to the industry. The result was twofold. First, a pilot program was implemented in three stripclubs; once a month a public health nurse would go into clubs to do intake with dancers. Primarily, the nurse would provide methods for minimizing the risk of transmission of disease, e.g., best methods for removing dried semen, blood and other bodily fluids from furniture and props (EDA 2001). The program emphasized that it was not dancing in and of itself that rendered women vulnerable to infections, but the nature of their labour practices and work environments (Lewis 2000). Second, a group of dancers received funding in 1995 to form an association, the Exotic Dancers Alliance, to champion erotic dancers' rights (EDA 2001). Mary Taylor, EDA's first executive director, had been active in trying to change dancers' working conditions for several years. In fact, in 1992, Taylor and thirteen other dancers "marched in G-strings, bras and little coats" to a Scarborough area bar to denounce a club's decision to raise deejay fees from $10 to $20; they negotiated management down to $15 (Hendly 1999). Ms. Taylor left the industry when lapdancing became an occupational requirement: "Everybody has their line they've gotta draw... I didn't like it in the end and I would only go to work out of desperation when I needed to pay bills" (in Snug 2000: 1). Shortly thereafter she became involved with EDA and helped draft its mission statement with the objectives of building solidarity among dancers, developing programs and services and ensuring fair treatment of dancers within the judicial system (EDA 2001).

EDA was successful at generating public attention around issues of concern to dancers primarily through workshops and burlesque shows that demystified the industry (Reid 2001). They also attempted to raise awareness around violence against women and systemic sexism within policing. For instance, they approached reporters to cover a story about a Toronto-area dancer who had her head smashed against the wall by a gang of young men. When the police arrived they did not offer the woman assistance, but counter-charged her with assault for biting her assailant in self-defence (Reid 2001). The association's primary networking and information-sharing tools were, until recently, its website and monthly newsletter, "The Naked Truth," through which dancers could access basic legal information and links to social services. In the first volume (2001) EDA printed a list of demands for better work places (lockers, ventilation, doors on bathroom stalls and cleanup of the unhygienic conditions). However, lack of funding led EDA to shut down both of these services and even disconnect its phone line. However, since June 2002, it has made use of an Internet group as a means of increasing communication among dancers. Members discuss issues from legal questions and coping with coercive managers or patrons, to beauty tips and advice for interpersonal relationships. The interactive and informal format allows dancers to engage at their convenience and to post their opinions with anonymity. However, its easy access means that customers and club owners can also log on and dancers may self-censure for fear of being banned. That said, contentious questions do arise, especially around lapdancing and other sex acts that occur in clubs. For instance, one member, known as Dancer on Tour, posted the following on October 14, 2004, in an attempt to spur on collective action by "real dancers":

> I am proud to be a "clean" dancer who does everything to prove to the world that not all dancers are whores… It's a shame that there are so many dancers [who] are more interested in "cut-throating" each other than pulling together to get better conditions and a fair wage or at the least an abolishment of "fines" and "stage fees."

Clearly, in objecting to lapdancing, dancers sometimes overlook other relationships of privilege and exploitation that further complicate women's decision to engage in certain labour practices. In other words, the anti-lapdancing discourse produces and reproduces hierarchies among women occupying different social locations. Moreover, while interactive communication technology holds the potential to bring about new affiliations between dancers as well as attract a more diverse constituency to the discussion, it is limited to women who have access to the Internet and may exclude more marginalized women who are most vulnerable to exploitation: poor women, older women and women for whom English is not their first language.

At its peak EDA's paper membership was at less than twenty (Hendly 1999). Because the EDA was labeled an anti-lapdancing organization by owners and managers, most members have been banned from a number of clubs (Prittie 1999). Further, in 2000, Ms. Taylor left EDA due to infighting. In her opinion, power had become centralized, communication among members had broken down, and some dancers were more concerned about getting media attention than continuing to struggle for better working conditions for dancers (Personal communication). Rhonda Collins, a health care practitioner, has taken the helm. Under her direction EDA has forged greater alliances with social workers, community groups and the police in efforts to improve dancers' working conditions and general health (Thesenvitz 2002). Most recently EDA supported a joint licensing effort between itself, the Peel Region's Health Department and the local police. Unlike CABE, EDA feels that the long-term aim of licensing could ultimately be a self-regulating system whereby dancers themselves would administer the licenses and city council and police would be able to access the database of files when necessary, in cases of missing women for example (Weagle 1999). However, dancers have consistently been against licensing and fear that it will result in greater regulation of women rather than increased protection.

Lewis and Maticka-Tyndale (2003) found that the most successful work done by EDA at its peak (in the late 1990s) was outreach in clubs in conjunction with local health units. To this end, they argue that the approach favoured by EDA was more service oriented than a grassroots model of organizing. Unfortunately, most of its service provision has been abandoned and it seems to have moved toward a pro-regulation approach. The emergence of EDA should nonetheless be read as a success. First, until recently, EDA's leadership and membership was always limited to current and former dancers, which enabled it to maintain its credibility as a legitimate voice within the dancer community. Second, whereas ABE engaged in more politicized action and challenged legal regulation and oppressive labour struggles within a courtroom setting, EDA centered its action around service-provision, information-sharing, coalition-building and the creation of support networks, which may have effected a more direct impact on dancers' everyday lives.

Ottawa Dancers Resist Lapdancing

While normalized in clubs since the nineties, it is only with the Supreme Court's ruling in Pelletier that lapdancing was deemed legal (*R. v. Pelletier*). Pelletier owned a club that enforced strict touching rules: patrons could touch the dancers' buttocks and breasts only and only in the context of a private dance in a champagne room. In 1997 two undercover police officers visited the bar and purchased lapdances. The dancers did not offer additional sexual services, nor did they permit the officers to touch them in a manner that would breach club rules. Nonetheless, Pelletier was charged with bawdyhouse offences under sections 197 and 210 of the Criminal Code.

The judge held that these acts were not indecent and that the club, under Ms. Pelletier's constant supervision, enforced strict rules to which both dancers and patrons complied. The Court of Appeal reversed the acquittal and entered a conviction with a fine. That decision was overturned by the Supreme Court in 1999. It determined that the trial judge had thoroughly considered all relevant factors in analyzing the community's standard of tolerance and made no error of law in his application of that test. With this ruling, lapdancing was effectively legal, subject to municipal ordinances banning it. Since the early 1990s, the city of Ottawa had a bylaw in place that prohibited lapdances. As in other jurisdictions with similar proscriptions though, the bylaw had never been systematically enforced and by the late 1990s all Ottawa area clubs offered lapdancing (DERA 2002). According to my participants, some dancers were in favour of the new industry practice and felt it was a sustainable way to increase their income, though most emphasized the economic motives that position women who want to work as erotic dancers with little alternatives: "It's a harsh reality. They really don't think they have a choice — if they want to make money. In a strip club right now you have to get touched if you want to make money" (Raye Ann). Others experienced increased vulnerability to economic exploitation and sexual or physical violence. It is the latter concern that spurred Samantha Smyth, a former Ottawa-area dancer, to found the Dancers' Equal Rights Association (DERA).

According to Ms. Smyth, lapdancing has become the defining feature of the erotic dance industry and has resulted in "the abuse, mistreatment and exploitation of women working in [Ottawa]" (DERA 2002: 1). DERA's objective is to further dancers' labour and human rights; it was incorporated in 2000 and received its first grant from the United Way in 2001. Drawing upon the work of previous such groups, DERA's specific goals include the promotion of health and safety standards in clubs, the harmonization of municipal regulation of clubs and the eradication of *de facto* mandatory lap dancing (DERA 2003). Its approach is unique in that shortly after mobilizing it forged a coalition with service providers, health care workers, lawyers, academics and students in order to increase DERA's visibility and to help counter the stigma of being an organization of "deviant" workers. The SLSN was formed in March 2002 to assist DERA in achieving its objectives and to provide resources for DERA members and other women working as erotic dancers. While SLSN's members come from divergent backgrounds, most advocate the decriminalization of sex work and are all working toward the destigmatization of erotic dancing. As with DERA, the SLSN's key spokesperson is Ms. Smyth. In many ways then, DERA and SLSN can be viewed as two halves of one organization: the former is exclusive to dancers and provides a safe space for information-sharing; the latter is comprised of community groups who are working with dancers in order to effect changes within the industry. Some DERA/SLSN initiatives include public education (speaking at conferences, organizing roundtable discussions between government officials and community members), coalition-building, political lobbying, establishing a dancer support group, fundraising and promoting in-club health programs (based on the EDA model).

At the fore of DERA's more recent activism is its work to establish clear labour practice guidelines and to harmonize Ottawa's adult entertainment bylaws. In 2004 the city of Ottawa met with various stakeholders including DERA and after considerable discussion proposed a bylaw that would have required clubs and dancers to obtain licences (upon the provision of photo identification). DERA opposed municipal licensing because of the risks inherent in providing governmental bodies and club owners with personal information (and specifically whether or not a dancer has a criminal record). As Sam explains:

> If you've been convicted of prostitution and you don't want to be a prostitute anymore where else are you going to get a job? I think she should have the right to choose not to be a prostitute.

A public health nurse working with DERA adds that licensing will be used as a "tracking device" that will further marginalize dancers:

> People don't get licensed for nothing. There has to be something in it for them. So what do women gain by being licensed. Healthcare? Decent wages? No. It's just a way to keep track of the women.... I see the ultimate goal as protecting men. It's so that the guys that go to the clubs know that they are clean so they know that they are not taking anything home to their wives.

Despite being against licensing, DERA agreed to endorse the bylaw so long as other key concessions were made, namely, a strict no touching/no lapdancing policy implemented and elimination of champagne rooms. City council accepted their arguments and removed licensing from the agenda. Yet, in August of that same year, it passed a bylaw eliminating champagne rooms in order to prevent lapdancing and other forms of sex acts from occurring between patrons and performers.

In June 2005, club owners, managers and dancers associated with the nine Ottawa clubs applied to have the bylaw quashed (*AEAC v. Ottawa*). They claimed that DERA did not represent their interests and the city was wrong in relying on the evidence its members put forth. They added that the city had not undertaken empirical studies to determine whether lapdancing posed a serious risk to the health and safety of club attendants. A number of dancers deposed that they had never engaged in sex acts with customers and that they were unfairly portrayed as vulnerable and in need of protection.

Judge Hackland of the Court of Justice dismissed the application and held that the city was reasonable in relying upon DERA's submissions as representative of the interests of performers. The objections to the law mirrored those expressed by DERA, namely increased regulation of women. Basing his judgment on the *OAEBA v. Toronto* decision, Justice Hackland found that the no-touch provisions were within municipal jurisdiction and did not violate the Charter. The decision is currently under appeal and may well find itself before the Supreme Court within a year.

This is a substantial success for DERA, which managed to gain momentum and mobilize community members in spite of considerable backlash from clubs owners, who not only banned members from their clubs but who threatened to fire any dancer who voiced opposition to lapdancing. This may help to explain the reality that despite its success, as with the other erotic dancer affiliations I have researched, DERA has experienced difficulties in recruiting members. To date, estimates of membership vary from five to ten current and former dancers, in spite of an estimated 750 currently working in Ottawa clubs.

Barriers to Organized Resistance

The groups I examined draw their legitimacy primarily by virtue of their "insider claims-maker" status (Best 1987). That legitimacy is subject to challenge though when we consider that their membership rates has been and continues to be relatively low. What follows then is a discussion of the barriers to mobilizing dancers.

First, dancers are highly independent and autonomous and for the most part view themselves as self-employed. As such, attempts to collectively lobby around labour issues may not seem relevant. My findings support the research of others (Bruckert 2002; Cooke 1987) who have found that for many dancers, the energy required to organize does not seem worthwhile:

> It's difficult for them to make a commitment.... A lot of dancers are like that. It's difficult to approach dancers at work because a lot of them [are] just there to make money and they don't want to talk about, or get into this stuff at work. They just want to make their money and do their thing. (Heather)

For a number of dancers, particularly those who see their labour as pleasant, short-term and lucrative, maintaining the status quo is more important than getting involved with dancers' affiliations, advocating broader changes within the industry or assuming the working-class militant persona (Sangster 1997). As Raye Ann explains: "The girls don't care. They don't care. This is the way it is. I'm not going to be here very long. Don't care. Don't want to know." This may be due to the perception from dancers that they stand to earn a better income through gratuities from lapdancing than through minimum wage and table dances (Heather). To this end, dancers need incentives to get organized. For instance, Christina argues that were clubs to eradicate lapdancing, dancers would need to receive something in return, namely, increased income:

> If they got rid of lapdancing, I think that the price of regular non-touch dancing should be upped. A lot of the $20 dancers are not going to want to go down to $10 a song — that's a fifty percent [decrease] each song and that's always going to be going through their mind.

Second, many of the key spokespersons no longer work in the industry. Heather, an active DERA member, is keenly aware that because of this, the group risks becoming "out of touch" with dancers' day-to-day work experiences:

> We need to know more what they want. Sam and I aren't in the clubs anymore. We need girls who are actually working in the clubs right now so that we know exactly what's going on, what they need, and what they want.

Third, dancers do not want to be associated with the group for fear of reprisal by owners and, specifically, of losing their jobs. As noted earlier, this concern is not unfounded given that the women at the helm of all four Ontario-based organizations have been banned. In short, those dancers who are highly independent or who view their work, in its current form, as an enjoyable and viable means of making a living, are difficult to integrate into a collective resistance strategy. That said, these findings should not be read as suggesting that dancers' affiliations are not legitimate voices. Instead, they contextualize the activism in which they engage and highlight the reality that even within subversive forms of organizing some voices overshadow others.

Conclusion

The object of this inquiry has been to document and to tease the potential of dancers' affiliations as a venue for collective resistance. My findings are framed within the understanding that erotic dancers are labourers who operate within constraints: poor working conditions, limited access to labour protections and collective bargaining mechanisms, social marginalization and stigmatization. They are also often subject to hostile state regulatory practices. However, dancers exercise agency through their collective efforts to reshape labour practices that they have determined, limit their individual choices. Documenting these attempts in Ontario, and discussing the extent to which formal resistance enables dancers to craft better working conditions, contributes to the growing literature on the striptease industry. Despite their near absence from historical records, Canadian women, and working-class women specifically, have a long history of collectively resisting oppressive systems of class, race and gender in order to promote their fundamental human rights under Canadian law. Through a feminist lens that centres labour and resistance, mine is an attempt to engage with the paradigm shift in theorizing around women working as erotic labourers from seeing them as either "sex radicals" or "victims." Instead, I grapple with more nuanced readings of women's labour and their occupational choices and ability to resist exploitation as something that is fundamentally influenced by their individual social location. What I have learned is that despite limited resources for formal organizing, Ontario-based erotic dancers have consistently mobilized in response to particular labour concerns and sometimes even in an attempt to fundamentally change their work environments. They have found that in order to respond to changes in the way their work is organized and in industry standards, they must work together so that they can make choices about how to earn a wage. For instance, Sam argues that getting organized can assist women in gaining the support needed to resist the stresses of their working life, overcome feelings of powerlessness and fight for better treatment by club owners and managers:

> There are strengths in numbers. It gives a big sense of empowerment… A lot of women don't even know they have rights. [DERA aims to] educate each

and every single dancer on what their rights are, what they can say no to, and eventually set up standards and guidelines that reflect the dancers.

Without doubt, by rejecting notions of individualism and competition, groups like EDA and DERA are collectively resisting conditions of constraint. They have assisted dancers in subverting stereotypes encrypted upon their occupational choice and provide a space in which they can emerge as workers rather than victims.

Chapter 4

Be Active, Be Emancipated
Women's Responses to Violence and War

Doris Goedl

We no longer can subsume all women under the sprawling canopy of "victims" nor all men under the category of "militia fighters." (Enloe 2004: 104)

Political and social instability have characterized conflicts in all parts of the world of late. Depending on the form of political change, like the downfall of military regimes in Central America, the end of apartheid in South Africa or the collapse of communism in Eastern Europe, we see different forms of transition. In Europe after World War II, there was a period of relative stability until 1989, when political and socioeconomic changes and upheavals started in former socialist countries. Some countries, like Poland and Hungary, achieved transition in a more or less peaceful way. In other countries, such as the former Yugoslavia, political change became violent and resulted in war and genocide. This genocide was the first in Europe since World War II, and women were especially targeted for sexual violence. For a certain period of time, public awareness was focused on women rape victims in Bosnia, but there was little awareness about women's active responses and resistance to violence and war.

Using the disintegration of the former Yugoslavia as a case-study, focusing especially on Croatia and Bosnia, my work analyzes nationalism, war and genocide using a gender perspective. This gendered focus is of importance as most of the recent conflicts in the world are grounded in nationalism and often include violence and genocide. Examples are Bosnia (1992–95), Rwanda (1994) and more recently Darfur.

The fact that women took an active part — although to a lesser extent than men — in nationalistic politics is well documented, at least in feminist theory and gender studies (Koonz 1991; Böltken 1995; Gödl 1998). In this chapter I discuss the effects of nationalism on women during war and their resistance through community-based activism. Using the political notion of trauma I outline the role of international organizations such as the Women's Initiatives for Gender Justice (WCGJ) in the U.N. and the role of vengeance and forgiveness in the aftermath of war and genocide. I show how women's efforts to overcome their status as war victims (via the Centre for Women War Victims [CWWV]) and build civil society are impacted by domestic and international law.

My analysis focuses on individual memories, perceptions and meanings of violent disintegration. This approach allows a closer look at the gender dimension of these processes. In the case of the former Yugoslavia women were specifically targeted as members of an ethnic group. During the demise of communism in Yugoslavia the question of ethnic identities returned to the political discourse. Questions of ethnic identity — above all as part of setting oneself off from other ethnic groups — began to assume increased significance. Thus, the connection between the newly created states and nationalism began to return to the focal point of political consideration. With the outbreak of armed conflicts we were confronted with politically induced violence against women and children, whereby the rape of women was used as a military strategy to destroy ethnic group identity and to decimate cultural and social bonds. Women were forced for political reasons to undergo traumatic events such as rape and violence. In Bosnia, this was especially traumatic because, in many cases, women survivors experienced the killing of family members, flight under terrible conditions or rape by people who had previously been neighbours. One women activist spoke about her experiences in July 1995, when Serbian military groups forced the removal of the Muslim population from Srebenica. The majority of the mass killings took place between July 12 and 17, during which time 7000 to 8000 men were forcibly separated from their families and exterminated (Bogoeva 2002).

On 11th July Ratkom Mladić's troops forced us to leave Srebenica. Everything was very chaotic. Grenades came from all directions, people were torn in pieces. My son went away and I was away so that we didn't say goodbye to each other. I called after him to wish him good luck. This was the last time I saw him. Then they started to get people separated. They led my brother away. The next night was horrible. There was loud crying and shouting, as people were slaughtered. It was night, I couldn't see, but these cries were terrible. The next morning we were deported with buses. There were some men, they held a gun on the neck of my husband and took him away. It took me several years to identify his corpse in a mass-grave. They led away every male person, the boys, young men and the elder ones. I entered the bus and was paralyzed. I couldn't feel anything. I didn't think anything, I was feeling numb, just doing what was ordered. On our way we passed dead bodies, observed executions along the road-side and had to face that military men entered our bus and took away young women. (female interviewee from Bosnia)

This violent disruption of social bonds in small entities (like villages and factories) is accompanied by a loss of confidence and trust, with many psycho-societal consequences for the individuals involved (Stiglmayer 1993; Drakulic 1995; Broz 2004).

One might ask why Croatia and Bosnia are the focus of my analysis. In 1991, when the war in the former Yugoslavia began, public attention in most Western European countries was focused on "militia men" fighting each other and on the strong nationalistic rhetoric of the political elite. But little was known about the strong movement of women's groups against nationalism and war. In 1994, when I was attending a conference about war and the involvement of men and women, I got in touch with the remarkable work of women's groups and activists all over Yugoslavia. After finishing my talk, one of the Croatian activists approached me and asked if I would like to work with a group of self-organized women, to teach them psychology, psychotherapy and socio-political aspects of war traumatization. After negotiating with Women for Women, a German non-governmental organization (NGO), for financial support (travel expenses and translation), I agreed to work with a group of eight women. Then, there I was, on a cold day in January in 1994, on my first arrival in Zagreb, the capital of Croatia. And I continued to come back, every eight weeks until 1997, when the German NGO stopped the financial aid for the project. After the Dayton Agreement was signed many of the Western countries quit their support and a lot of projects came to an end.

Over the years I gained a deep insight into the activities of different women's groups across the former Yugoslavia, and I was deeply impressed and moved by the remarkable work they did. In a certain way I became part of this political culture. Therefore I wanted to know more about women's and men's roles in transition, war and post-war society. With a grant from the Austrian Research Fund (FWF) I came back to Slovenia, Croatia and Bosnia-Herzegovina between 2001 and 2003 to investigate the perspectives of men and women on the violent disintegration of their former country. With Vesna Kesić, a colleague from the CWWV in Zagreb, we conducted approximately sixty interviews with men and women who were engaged in different local and regional NGOs, across Slovenia, Croatia and Bosnia-Herzegovina.

The Effects of Nationalism on Women

According to Yuval-Davis (1997) nationalist projects focus on genealogy and origin as their major organizing principles. Being born into a certain national collective, as in an ethnic group, one becomes a full member of this group. For a better understanding of this concept I emphasize the link between these two ideas. In the case of the former Yugoslavia the project of nation-state-building was embedded in ethnic nationalism, which led finally to war, ethnic cleansing and genocide. The central role of women in this process is related to their biological role as reproducers and their cultural role as "cultivators of the boundaries of ethnic-national collectives and their ideologies" (Korac 2004: 252). I use the example of Croatia to show how the concept of nation is connected to certain female and male images.

Immediately after independence and the founding of Croatia in 1992, the young nation was in the process of losing the war. At that moment, the nationalistically oriented public began to employ an aggressive language: "Croatia the Motherland" became "Croatia the Fallen Woman" (Kesić 2000: 20). Croatia, Kesić explains, went through a moral collapse since only women surrender to their fate without a struggle. Women were seen as the embodiment of the nation and also represented the borders of the nation, which made them "ethnic markers" in nationalist ideology. Depicting women in their national symbolic function shows how quickly the symbol of woman enlisted in the service of politics can change: from virgin, to mother and provider of sustenance, and finally to fallen woman, a whore. This also symbolically shifted responsibility for the military defeat from the men to the women. The potential for violence began to grow as a result of such symbolic processes of transformation. However, at least since the political changes in the early 1990s, there were no Yugoslav women in the former Yugoslavia; rather, there were representations of national women, mothers, sisters and daughters. The women who were others — for instance, Serbs or Muslims — were subordinated to a national stereotype and were physically, psychically and sexually attacked. "Women's bodies became first symbolic, then real battlefields, on which all kinds of wounds, discrimination and violence can be inflicted" (Kesić 2000: 21). Within this context, sexual violence against women can be described as an example of "genderizing nations" or "genderizing ethnicity." Sexualized violence was not treated by the political and military elite as an act of violence committed by men upon women, but rather as a nationalistic offence (Jalušić 1994: 119–28). Thus, the nation was raised to the status of victim, and — as a last resort — its masculinity had to be restored. Such a rape metaphor constitutes an important form of preparation for the ensuing national wars. But this also enables us to see — at least partially — that "the female (constitutes) the specific Center for the overall organization of nationalistic and racist thought in the violently waged confrontation surrounding the reconstruction of masculinity/ the patriarchy" (Jalušić 1994: 125). Positioning the image of the raped woman on the level of the highest form of violence — on a national basis — was always a precursor to, or a means of justifying, excesses in the society. In the early eighties, when protests for the status of autonomy in the province of Kosovo became violent, the media started to report some rape-cases of Serbian women to justify the military intervention in the region (Jalušić 1994).

Ruth Roach Pierson, who deals primarily with the question of the gender perspective in the formation of nations and/or in the emergence of nationalisms, examines the gender-specific extent of violence. Scholars in the fields of cultural studies and gender studies, like Blom, Enloe and Yuval-Davis, have investigated the representation of nations through women, and their social scientific analyses have attempted to explain the differing participation of women and men in the construction of nations.

> The understanding of nationalism as a gendered phenomenon indicates gender-specific involvements in nation building and in the construction of national identities, even as it demonstrates how "woman" symbolized "nation" — in this case nations struggling to find themselves and become independent. (Blom, Hagemann and Hall 1999: 6)

Two things can be brought to light with this approach: first, the fact that one element that belongs to national defence is the will and the wish to die for the nation; "this became the extreme heroic form for this suturing of the individual and the nation together" (Eley 1999: 29). Women also wanted to join the military to fight for their homeland. For example, when the war broke out in Croatia in the early 1990s, a young female student, who was already safely in Germany, came back to fight the war in the Croatian army, "for my homeland," as she stated. And she wasn't the only one. Thus, women were actively included in military forces and were not only the victims of patriarchy, violence and war. When the mass media promoted national homogenization, images of young, beautiful women in Croatian uniforms became symbols of the young nation. On the other side, in embodying their nation, women who survived sexual violence during the war were turned into metaphors: "A raped Croatian women is a raped Croatia" (CWWV 2003: 11). Women were portrayed as victims and their bodies were used to inscribe nationalist state-forming projects.

> On the other hand, militarization of men goes along with a familiarization and privatization of women. The emerging nation may have been militarized and masculinized, but it was also familialized, construed as a patriarchally and hierarchically organized folk family. Within that family, women, embodying the canon of female virtues, found their properly subordinate and dichotomous place as defined by the new bourgeois gender order. (Pierson 1999: 46)

One women activist in Ljubljana puts it this way:

> *Certainly the reconstruction of femininity is purely that the women have to be at home, having children and so on. Concerning the ideology it is much worse than before. Then they started to talk about the role of women, that they should give birth to little Slovenes. This was really scarring. (Female interviewee from Slovenia)*

We can see that women are represented as the authentic body of national tradition, embodying nationalism's conservative principle of continuity. Women are brought into the national/ethnicized political discourse as "biological reproducers of members of ethnic collectivities, and as reproducers of the boundaries of ethnic/national groups" (Anthias and Yuval-Davis 1989: 3).

Second, women were depicted "participating centrally in the ideological reproduction of the collectivity and as transmitters of its culture, as a focus and symbol in ideological discourses used in the construction, reproduction and transformation of ethnic/national categories" (Anthias and Yuval-Davis 1989: 7).

Dealing with these kinds of nationalistic state-forming projects, women focused their attention on silent warning signs of political change, especially in the decisive shift in national ideology, such as the nationalistic use of female bodies in both real and symbolic ways. When women's groups across the countries started to fight against nationalism and war, they were accused in public of being witches, traitors and not feminine. And when the war ended in 1995 with the Dayton Agreement, "women war victims, whose quantity had been used as a means of manipulation and competition by the nationalist regime in Croatia, disappeared from the public eye and the 'honour' and privilege was awarded to men, the warriors" (CWWV 2003: 11).

There is little public acknowledgement of war crimes in Croatia, where there is a national policy of forced denial (Drakulic 2005). The remarkable work of different women's groups, during and after the war, across borders and ethnicities, is neglected by the political elite. For example, in 1998, when the Croatian Women Human Rights Groups, B.a.B.e. (Be active, be emancipated), received the U.S.–E.U. Democracy and Civil Society Award for their work to foster democracy and civil rights, the diplomatic community of Zagreb, some members of civil society and numerous journalists attended the ceremony, but no members of either local or regional governments were in attendance.

This deliberate political denial creates great obstacles for peace, reconciliation and social stability in the region. This is of great importance as the work and success of the International Tribunal for the former Yugoslavia (ICTY) depends on the political will of the governments in Croatia, Bosnia and, of course, Serbia. But as many examples show, there is a strong national resistance to extraditing war criminals, especially in Croatia and Serbia. In these countries, the accused are treated as national heroes, not war criminals. For example, when the case of Mirko Norac, a Croatian military officer who committed crimes in 1991 against Serbs in Gospić, was tried for committing war crimes in spring 2001 before the Croatian chamber of The Hague, war veterans held a national protest demonstration attended by more than 70,000 people (Drakulic 2005). This way of dealing with the past not only denies memories and experiences of victims during the war, it also channels memories into the establishment of a main narrative, which creates the historical background of one "national truth." The consequences are tensions and conflicts within and across the new nation-states (Gödl 2007).

Women's Response and Resistance to Violence and War

My experiences in the socio-psychological educational project for war traumatized women in Zagreb (1994–97) compelled me to take an activist perspective. In the beginning of the 1990s there was a remarkable growth of women activists in anti-nationalistic and anti-war movements. Women wanted to show their unwillingness to accept a political power that interfered and affected their personal lives. When the war in the former Yugoslavia started in 1991 in Slovenia, several women's groups protested in Ljubljana and Zagreb. In 1992, when the first reports of mass rapes and sexual violence against women in Bosnia-Herzegovina reached public awareness, again women protested. They finally gained international attention and financial support from international organizations for their projects involving refugees, war traumatized women and human rights education.

Let me discuss one example of women's wide-spread activities to help and empower women war victims to overcome sexual violence, trauma and victimization. The CWWV emerged out of the anti-war campaign in Croatia (1992) in Zagreb. Besides providing socio-psychological services for refugees in the camps, the work in the Centre included human rights and peace education. With the increasing awareness of sexualized violence against women in Bosnia, the Centre focused its attention on the situation of women in the refugee camps across the country.

Some of the women were not raped but deeply traumatized by the disappearance and death of their family members or close relatives. Many of them have been witnesses of the worst possible brutality. In these circumstances identifying particular groups (like raped women, women without rape experiences or ethnic belonging) would be an insufficient response to women's experience. (CWWV 2003: 29)

The decision to work with all women, not only with those who experienced sexual violence, was partly due to the social mores in the region, where women who have been raped are stigmatized. Pointing the finger with special programs would lead to further traumatization. The approach of field workers in the CWWV was orientated within the women's communities to help women to exchange their experiences, to give support to regain control over their lives and, if needed, to provide special services. The socio-psychological work in the CWWV was based on a political notion of trauma, which is of great significance to this analysis. The political approach to trauma is different than the clinical concept, which is mainly orientated toward post-traumatic stress disorder (PTSD) rather than the political circumstances in which the trauma took place. If the political aspect of the trauma is neglected or denied, survivor victims feel a personal responsibility for what happened to them.

The Political Importance of Trauma

In the case of the former Yugoslavia, people were emotionally attached to the ideology of brotherhood and unity, which was interrupted by violent disintegration through war and genocide. All my interviewees, and also some political leaders, expressed the unexpectedness of the war, a reality that was then experienced as trauma (Mesić 2004). In this context, women suffered gendered violence: they were raped by their neighbours. This kind of destruction of personal and social connectedness is referred to as "extreme traumatization."

> This type of traumatization is marked by a certain way of carrying out power in a society, meaning that the sociopolitical structure of society is based on the destruction and wiping out of some members of this society through other members of the same society. (Becker 2000: 37)

This approach allows the individual traumatic experience to be brought into the frame of the political circumstances that give rise to the traumatic events. We can, rather than simply focus our attention on the individual, focus instead on the political context. Doing so makes it possible for female victims to understand that the traumatic event was not a personal failure, but had to do with violated political circumstances. To take this approach seriously, it was necessary to merge the personal and the political during the socio-psychological/therapeutic treatment. In this context, the experiences of war and terror could be seen as a central assault on the dignity of men and women, leading to a loss of confidence in their world.

Against this background we can underscore that the work in the CWWV was based on a political concept of trauma. The conscious decision not to single out one special group, but to work with all women, embedded in their cultural and social backgrounds, was a significant step in the politicization of individual trauma.

> We also have realized that women are great survivors. They have numerous strategies for survival, display great resilience, and make real attempts to overcome their trauma. Community life and group support is certainly one of the best resources at their disposal. (CWWV 2003: 36)

This political understanding of traumatization brought both experts and the women activists to some public protests. In December 1992, on International Human Rights Day, different national and international women's groups organized a women's demonstration against sexual violence and war rapes. The women's groups wanted to achieve the recognition of rape as a war crime by the international community. As my colleague Vesna Kesić told me, this protest in 1992 was the first and the only one in Zagreb. In organizing public protests, women activists demonstrated the important shift from individual experiences of a targeted victim to experiences of collective action. As a direct consequence this role-model led to the empowerment of women. Many of them were no longer seeing themselves just as victims, but also as strong and, to a certain extent, powerful activists.

Women's Role in the International Community

When the political elite of the U.N. worked on the legal and political framework for the International Criminal Court (ICC) women were active in advocating women's rights and gender issues. A group of women founded the Women's Caucus for Gender Justice (WCGJ) for "strengthening advocacy of women's human rights and helping to develop greater capacity among women in the use of the International Criminal Court, and other mechanisms that provide women avenues of and access to different systems of justice" (WCGJ 2005: 1). The initiative grew in 1997, when a small group of women human rights activists realized that the preparatory committee for the establishment of the Court did not include women's concerns. Based on the work of previous women's caucuses, the WCGJ formed around the women's world conferences in Vienna, Cairo and Beijing. These women activists focused their work on the integration of a gender perspective into the definition of crimes against humanity and war crimes (WIGJ 2005). The group worked to achieve widespread participation of women in education, law, justice and the judiciary in all regions of the world

The Women's International War Crimes Tribunal in Tokyo is a good example of popular education on women's human rights (*ICC Women's News* 2000). This "tribunal sought to prosecute those who are responsible for the Japanese Imperial Army's sexual enslavement of over 200,000 women from more than ten Asian countries" (*ICC Women's News* 2000a). In the beginning of the 1990s women from Asia began to break the silence about their war experiences of sexual slavery and other atrocities they suffered under the Japanese military in the 1930s and 1940s. Thirty-five women who survived the "comfort women" system testified in person or by video before the Tribunal and demanded an apology and compensation for their sufferings. By giving public evidence of the sexual slavery of women, the Tribunal brought a suppressed part of the national history to the surface. Testifying before the Tribunal, these women became — decades later — activists of their personal history. "We want justice. We want the Japanese government to take responsibility. What we are saying is the truth. We didn't come here to lie. We come here to tell the truth" (*ICC Women's News* 2000: 24). The Tribunal's actions created much public debate about "approval" or "denial" for this part of national history, as did the right wing parties in Japan (*ICC Women's News* 2000: 24). These parties still denied the existence of the comfort women system during the war and demanded that the Japanese government not take any responsibility for these war crimes.

Three points come from this analysis: 1) Seeking truth and justice for women needs the interplay between several actors: international women's organizations, national and regional women's activist groups, and women who are willing to rewrite their personal history of abuse as victims and become activists. 2) Dealing with the past under a gendered perspective causes not only public debates but raises also questions about "national truths." As the example of the Tokyo Tribunal shows, the official version of the past no longer represents the only historical "truth." 3) Opening of the past via suppressed memories interferes with the official narrative and leads in many cases to a national fight over history.

Post-War Societies and Civil Society Building

"We wanted democracy. Now we had to do development work, with all our knowledge, potential and of course socialist tradition," said the Croatian Women Human Rights activist Vesna Kesić in an interview with the author for an Austrian newspaper in 1998 (*Volksstimme* 1998: 11. This statement brings civil society in its widest sense into the realm of policy debate and practice and should have absolute priority in post-war societies. Ten years after the Dayton Agreement the newly emerged nations of Slovenia, Croatia and Bosnia faced many problems. Aside from unresolved economic and political issues, there was a need to deal with old and new nationalisms, as well as with various psycho-societal problems.

The Dayton Agreement had a special impact on women's groups and projects, which faced insecure financial support and public neglect, leading to major transitions inside women's organizations. As a result, the CWWV in Zagreb started to shift their attention from providing services to lobbying and raising awareness for women's rights. The activists started organizing public protests, for example, the "sixteen days of activism against sexual violence." They also monitored elections and organized forums, roundtables and radio broadcasts, and started an education program on women's human rights. In 2003, activists from the CWWV edited a jointly written volume, *Women Recollecting Memories*, to celebrate ten years of remarkable work. They made a public presentation of the volume in Zagreb to show their strength and power, and sent a strong message that they are part of civil society, even under the worst political conditions.

Understanding civil society as a living arena of social actions and interactions, as a coalition of (instead of a distinction between) institutional and cultural spheres of society, I want to emphasize the contribution of the CWWV in the process of civil society building in post-war Croatia. Together with different women's groups, across borders and ethnicities, their activities became a crucial arena for the development of democratic values such as ethnic tolerance and gender equality. These values became very strong in the activists because they emerged through experience, through participation and involvement in processes of democratic change. Using excerpts from my interviews with women activists in the former Yugoslavia I underline the importance of women's activism in democratization processes. Because of their experiences as activists, these women represent a huge potential in civil political culture. As group members they embody a high level of interpersonal trust and a readiness to deal with political conflict more through compromise than through coercion or violence. Even though they were strong mediating forces building in post-war society, few women reached decision-making ranks: neither in the vast bureaucracy of humanitarian operations, in post conflict management nor in the new "democratic societies." In analyzing my interviews with male and female NGO activists across the borders of former Yugoslavia a specific kind of gender difference came to my attention. While most men became involved in the work of NGOs for political reasons, like becoming an important part/position in the new civil society, most women became active for reasons like fighting for women's human rights. Whereas most of my male interviewees talked about political, societal and economic changes in post-war society, many female interviewees were primarily focused on issues of peace, forgiveness and reconciliation. Let us listen to the voices of three women, one from Sarajevo, one from Banja Luka and one from Baranja.

I seek justice towards a single person. My father was killed near the mosque, which means somebody selected him because he was a Muslim. As far as we know, it would be possible to trace back this killing. Yes, I wanted them to be punished. If I could figure out who killed my father I would seek justice and the indictment of this person. But otherwise I don't have anything against the people (referring to the Bosnian Serbs) because that would be irrational. You can hate a concrete person, but not a whole nation. (woman from Sarajevo)

When the Bosnian Serbs took over Banja Luka, the police raided and looted flats and houses of the Muslim population. First, the police came to the house of my grandparents and expelled them with force. They were old, stayed their whole life in this house, and now had nowhere to go. Afterwards, the same happened to my parents. I was the last in the row. When they came to my flat, the police officer took his gun on my head and forced me out of my flat. Later, I lost my job too. But I didn't leave the city because this is what they wanted us to do – to become an "ethnically cleansed" city. After the war I saw this police officer in a coffee shop and my first reaction was revenge. But then I realized that if I would react in this way, the process of forgiving could never begin. And I didn't want to spend the rest of my life hating a whole nation. I ordered a coffee for this police officer and he came to my table to ask who I am. I told him the story and he started to recognize me. I said, 'I could look in your eyes before and I could do the same now.' He lowered his eyes and asked me to forgive him. That is what I did! Since this time, peace has become real for me. (woman from Banja Luka)

At the end of the war I was working in the ambulance of the hospital in Baranja (East-Croatia). An old man was brought for treatment and he asked me if I would know who he is. I denied, but when he mentioned the name of his wife I started to recognize him. He was in jail because during the war he and his wife (both Serbs) had killed sixteen Croats in a very perfidious way. They searched the birth register, figured out the Croats and went to visit them for coffee, and then they killed them. I asked him for the reasons and he answered: "I did it for my people." Then he asked me if I will still give him medical treatment. To be honest, for a second I thought I could kill him and nobody would know. But then I said, yes, of course. This is my duty as a medical doctor. He was taken by the UNPROFOR and is now in a jail in Serbia to wait for his trial. (woman from Baranja)

This last statement refers to one of the main problems of post-war judiciary, the interplay between local courts in Croatia, Bosnia and Serbia, and the Hague Tribunal. Local courts are strongly biased in that they reluctantly extradite members of their own ethnic group. In contrast to the Tokyo Tribunal, the ICTY was established outside the former Yugoslavia and therefore the Tribunal had to deal with problems of the interplay between international and domestic law. Even when the democratic governments that replaced the former authoritarian regimes in Croatia and Serbia made efforts to reform their judicial system, we faced limited public support for war crimes prosecutions, especially against members of the ethnic majority. Effective and fair prosecutions were possible only if governments were seriously willing to commit themselves to create the conditions necessary for criminal accountability.

In recent years, government support for domestic prosecutions of members of the ethnic majority has gradually increased in Bosnia-Herzegovina and Croatia. Government officials in Serbia and Republika Srpska have either opposed or grudgingly supported the work of the Hague Tribunal. Official policy in Serbia states there is support for domestic prosecutions, but there is no concerted effort to arrest fugitives. Instead, the authorities try to convince them to surrender voluntarily, as the prosecutor of the ICTY, Carla del Ponto, stated in a press release (Office of the Prosecutor 2004). The hollowness of their support is evidenced by the fact that there have been few domestic trials in Serbia and virtually none in Republika Srpska. "It remains the case that nine years after Dayton, the authorities of Republika Srpska have not apprehended a single individual indicted by the ICTY" (Office of the Prosecutor 2004: 2). In 2002, the Hague Tribunal announced its intention to refer all cases — but not involving the main political and military figures from the Yugoslav wars — to the national courts in the region, with the exception of Serbia.

There is a legitimate concern that countries like Serbia, which is not willing to arrest indicted war criminals, will either not be interested in, or capable of, trying alleged war criminals domestically. The networks which support persons accused of war crimes are so powerful that they can interfere with the judicial proceedings, including intimidating witnesses… or even threatening the stability of the country. Both in Serbia proper and in Kosovo, aggressive nationalist rhetoric is being used in smear campaigns against the Tribunal and its Prosecutor. (Office of the Prosecutor 2004: 3)

This comprehensive statement of the chief prosecutor refers to another problem of the ICTY — the ethnic bias of the tribunal. Based on trial monitoring, Human Rights Watch has concluded that bias by the judiciary has influenced trials in Croatia, Bosnia-Herzegovina and Serbia. Looking to Serbia it became clear what it meant: In the past three years only Serb defendants had been prosecuted by Serb judges and prosecutors. The only cases in Republika Srpska involve defendants of Serb ethnicity, which exacerbates the ethnic bias (Human Rights Watch 2004). Besides ethnic bias on the part of judges and prosecutors, the key obstacles for fair and effective trials include poor case preparation by prosecutors, inadequate cooperation from the police in the conduct of investigations, poor cooperation between the states on judicial matters and ineffective witness protection mechanisms.

In the end, Carla del Ponte tried to find an answer for the question about the achievements of the ICTY. "Although significant progress was achieved, it has to be stressed that a number of obstacles which are outside of the Tribunal's control may still derail the completion strategy" (Office of the Prosecutor 2004: 1). del Ponte addresses two important obstacles to achieve completion: The lack of cooperation of the states in arresting and transferring to The Hague people who have been indicted, and the failure to find important culprits like Radovan Karadžic and Ratko Mladic. del Ponte urged the governments of Croatia, Serbia and Bosnia-Herzegovina to take responsibility in bringing these fugitives to The Hague.

Besides problems with the judiciary in post-war Yugoslavia, the ethic bias and enduring nationalism within the legal system is a huge problem in building civil society in these countries. As we can see, the politics in Croatia and Bosnia serve the interests of the dominant ethnicity, which tries to exclude minorities. Dealing with long-term consequences, important questions like distinct citizenship statuses and ethnic belonging are still not solved. The case of a female factory worker from Srebrenica who is now living in Sarajevo, the capital of Bosnia, as a refugee, deals with the status of a non-citizen. "I'm still an expelled person without rights," she said in the interview.

In the Republika Srpska I don't have the same rights like the Serbian population, and in the Croatian-Muslim Federation I don't have rights, because I'm not a citizen of the federation. To seek justice, I'm working in the organisation Mothers of the Enclave Srebenica and Zepa. Besides fighting for our status as citizens, we do a lot of work on the disappeared (to register, identity and bury them) and try to help their families. (female interviewee from Bosnia)

What are the conclusions out of these narratives? I think the stories told by these women in Croatia and Bosnia show the importance and meaning of justice on a personal level. Besides international efforts in dealing with war crimes, these women want to give testimony, to face their perpetrators and seek out justice on an individual level, so that they can then start to forgive. These narratives also show very clearly that there are different levels of truth and reconciliation: the ICTY as a huge international framework (like the narrative from Sarajevo), the domestic level of judiciary (like the narrative from Baranja and Sarajevo) and the efforts of individuals. Only the latter can forgive, because forgiveness is something between human beings and needs the facing of victim and perpetrator (like the narrative from Banja Luka). Furthermore, these narratives show not only the connection between justice and peace, they also break with the prejudice of the "ancient hatred" in the Balkans. If truth is based on justice and if there is a process of public acknowledgment of what happened, then truth and reconciliation can be more than rhetoric. These narratives are good examples of what I would describe as the "victim-activist tandem": Victimized by political circumstances these women became politically active as a remarkable way out of the cycle of victimization. Even though "the status of women is horrible," as one woman from Ljubljana stated, she doesn't think that their status in the previous system was better.

I just think that women had better access to jobs. They could provide for themselves. In that sense they were more independent because they had their own money. They got jobs, they were employed. Actually in this sense they were equal. They didn't need men to provide for them. Okay they had this double burden, because the ideology didn't change. It was the patriarchal ideology but even though they had the chance to survive on their own. But on the other hand for expressing opinions, for doing whatever you want, for having plural thoughts, to fight for the thoughts, to have the equal saying, that is something what I appreciate a lot; the liberal political freedom. (female interviewee from Slovenia)

Conclusion

Civil society building in war-torn societies has to confront past crimes and massive human rights abuses. According to Priscilla Hayner, "The concrete needs of victims and communities that were damaged by the violence will not be addressed through such prosecutions (like The Hague), except of course in providing some solace if the perpetrators are successfully prosecuted. The institutional or societal conditions that allowed the massive abuses to take place – the structures of the armed forces, the judiciary, or the laws that should constrain the actions of officials, for example – many remain unchanged even as more democratic and less abusive government comes into place" (Hayner 2002: 11). Even though there are efforts on an international and less on a national level, the example of Croatia and also Bosnia shows that post-transition justice is rare and has to deal with a violent past. Confronting this past involves facing victims and perpetrators of the previous regime and addressing the damage done to women, men and communities. Investigating and acknowledging the truth about the violent past could be reached — as examples all over the world demonstrate — through "truth commissions" with a victim centred approach. Collecting and publishing thousands of testimonies is for many victims the "first sign of acknowledgment by any state body that their claims are credible and that the atrocities were wrong" (Hayner 2002: 16). However, even testimonies evoke some controversy: do they only deal with past crimes on an institutional (collective) level? And, if so, what are the effects on the victim (individual) level?

I think the political efforts inventing the ICTY were important steps towards justice and peace. Although there is some criticism, I agree with Jonathan Bass, who wrote that this kind of legalism will never make up for the lives lost, but legalism is all we have now (2000). It does not make up for the losses, but the level of international and national law and justice is important for recovering from individually experienced trauma. The interplay between political circumstances and violent individual experiences is the focus of attention and therefore becomes crucial for truth and reconciliation processes. In working with victims of political violence it is very important to make them understand that the traumatic experiences of rape or torture are not a personal failure, but have to do with political circumstances. Therefore it is necessary that political and military leaders as well as other perpetrators take responsibility for what happened. Convening trials to seek the truth is an important step towards peace and justice. But post-war societies like the former Yugoslavia need more than international and domestic trials. To overcome the past these societies need an open dialogue between the political elite and non-governmental organizations in order to move towards peace, justice and democracy.

Madeleine Albright states: "Justice is essential to strengthen the rule of law, soften the bitterness of victim's families, and remove an obstacle to cooperation among the parties.... It will establish a model for resolving ethnic differences by the force of law rather than the law of force." (statement at ICTY May 28, 1997, in Bass 2000: 284). If we believe, that peace in post-war societies has different layers (like economic stability, some kind of prosperity and perspectives for the future), justice has to be seen as "a parent to peace." I would like to see the Hague Tribunal as a parent to peace in the former Yugoslavia, mainly because the treatment of the past through international and national law shapes not only the present, but also the future of entire post-war societies. Trying to come to terms with truth and reconciliation can be described as a narrow route between processes of remembering and forgetting, but it has to be taken. Whereas nations have to deal with their past on a collective level, victims and their families have a moral right to know and to gain security about their rights and justice on an individual level. The interplay between both can finally lead to peace and reconciliation, but it will take time.

Section Three

The Politics of Resistance

This section traces collective resistance strategies beyond law to public fora, in terms of political protest, institutional policy and practices of therapists dealing with sexual assault survivors. The politics of resistance are both of an individual and a collective nature in this section, but all point clearly to the need to highlight the situations of women's resistance in various Canadian settings. In this section, we find chapters by Carole Roy on the Raging Grannies, Norma Jean Profitt on sexual harassment in the university, and Linda Coates and Penny Ridley on the representations of victims of sexual assault by psychotherapists.

Utilizing strategies gained from the protest cycle of the 1960s and 1970s, the Raging Grannies is an international network of older women that uses old-fashioned civil disobedience methods to influence public social change. The Raging Grannies challenge the stereotype of the grandmother as passive, while at the same time forming alliances with other social justice networks to address global concerns such as health, the environment and women's issues. The Raging Grannies use the tactics of the court jester, entertaining to raise social awareness and providing satirical playfulness to make "fools" of the justice system. Using "in your face" humour the Raging Grannies challenge stigmatized identities. Its collective identity, as that of older women with grievances, airs new types of issues using national and international networks. As well, the Raging Grannies are concerned with the intersections of "racial equality, social justice and witnessing for peace." The Grannies connect women from diverse backgrounds and provide new types of identities for older activist women. Their activism includes singing songs of protest in public while wearing outrageous costumes, lobbying for change, writing letters to government and corporate executives, performing acts of civil disobedience and cultural innovation. The Raging Grannies provide an "intergenerational web of resistance" by challenging the generalizing neo-liberal stereotype of all protestors as young, ignorant, unorganized and individualistic, and do it all with a great sense of *joie de vivre*.

Documenting the effects of patriarchal violence on the body and the mind, Norma Jean Profitt outlines the tensions of individual and collective acts of resistance within the university context. She questions the effectiveness of such resistance in the face of tactics such as internal reviews of sexual harassment cases. Utilizing the frame of trauma and dreams-as-consciousness, she stands at the periphery of two opposing contradictions. As a sexual harassment officer she wants to bring feminist values to her work, yet perceives she is met with resistance within the paternalistic university, which attempts to downplay the existence of abuse of power within its walls. Not only must sexual harassment officers support individual complainants, they often find themselves in the contradictory situation of challenging organizational structures that maintain sexism, racism and homophobia. In providing examples of contradictions in stated institutional goals, Profitt uses personal narrative to document social oppression and outlines the institutional barriers that keep her from doing her job. She suggests new types of supportive feminist networks, structures, constituents and ideologies, yet also finds that making a difference seems to be elusive when faced with the challenge of institutional resistance.

Linda Coates and Penny Ridley raise the issue of violence against sexual assault victims who are pathologized through the therapeutic process. Coates and Ridley challenge victim blaming ideologies to show that ignoring victim resistance, concealing violence and obfuscating perpetrator responsibility contribute to victim blaming. Using an innovative process involving examination of the discursive and interactive view of violence and resistance from the perspective of therapists, they show that therapy in action is a form of social control. The authors challenge diagnoses of sexual assault victims that are pathologizing and victim blaming. The authors also challenge victim precipitation models that blame sexual assault victims. In so doing they challenge the all encompassing victim identity so often constituted via medical surveillance of sexual assault victims. In revealing their findings they propose a new type of grievance against the global practice of pathologizing sexual assault victims. Lifting this challenge to the international level Linda Coates and Penny Ridley note the importance of contextualizing this new form of "thought control" in previous imperialist practices.

Chapter 5

The Raging Grannies

Outrageous Hats, Satirical Songs and Civil Disobedience

Carole Roy

The Raging Grannies are a growing social protest movement of (mostly) older women who create mischief to right wrongs. Their approach is unique and their techniques range from singing satirical lyrics to humorous actions to civil disobedience. With creativity and daring they insist on being heard and rebel against the invisibility older women often experience. The Raging Grannies seek peace and justice, matters that deserve the best of human wit, creativity, courage and protest. The Raging Grannies create songs and actions to make their point, challenge conventions and stereotypes and, at times, engage in civil disobedience. Nineteen years after they started in Victoria, British Columbia, more than seventy groups of Raging Grannies keep an eye on current issues across Canada, the United States, Greece, Japan and Israel. Usually law-abiding, these women become newsworthy when they step over the line and get arrested. Such actions challenge the judicial system and society as a whole to take notice of their views. It is significant that women well into their senior years engage in civil disobedience, a measure that conveys the urgency of their concerns and their determination to express their views. While the law is often portrayed as immutable, to defy it consciously and willingly reflects an understanding of the law as a social construct. Martin Luther King Jr. and African Americans during the civil rights movement in the United States, South African activists under Apartheid, Gandhi and Indians all carried out acts of civil disobedience and showed that law and justice are not always synonymous: in such cases, the law must be opposed. While there may be consequences for those who break the law, such actions allow a wider public to question a law that may contravene decency, fairness, justice or dignity. At times, protests, including civil disobedience, result in changes, a legacy the Raging Grannies value as they sing that without the struggles of the past, there would be no vote for women, no schools for the poor and kids would still work in mines (Hadrill 2000: 6).

An examination of the Raging Grannies allows us to gain greater understanding of the contributions of older women to social justice movements and a greater appreciation of the role of humour and civil disobedience in collective resistance. Through their creative approach the Raging Grannies redefine protest and aging, and make it problematic to label protesters as young and inexperienced idealists, or older people as passive, conservative or disinterested. This chapter explores the Raging Grannies' defiant spirit and sizzling resistance through songs, spirited actions and civil disobedience. This article is from material gathered for my doctoral research on the Raging Grannies: I conducted forty-six interviews with thirty-six Raging Grannies from twelve groups from Halifax to Victoria, reviewed collective files of three groups and personal files of six Raging Grannies, read 600 songs and examined media reports. Welcome to the flair and pizzazz of these meddlesome crones!

Spirited Women Defying Invisibility

The original group of Raging Grannies formed in 1987 in Victoria, British Columbia, in response to visits of American nuclear warships and submarines to the local military base. Concerned with the threat to health and environment such visits posed, these women joined the local peace group but, as two original Grannies suggested, found themselves faced with sexism and ageism (Doyle 1998; McCullough 1991: 18). Determined to explore alternative ways to reach out and communicate their concerns, a small group of older women took to the streets and discovered that humour was engaging: people leaned in to listen rather than hurried away. There was brilliance in linking grannies with "un-motherly" public rage, concepts rarely, if ever, associated. Humour is based on the juxtaposition, and collision, of frames of reference not usually associated, which makes people stop and think. The idea that grannies care enough to rage, challenges the image of older women as sweet and inoffensive, and invites us to expand our definition of care to include expression of anger at injustices. To connect rage, power and self-determination with women expected to be polite and loving is jarring and attracts attention. The name embodies the Grannies' ability to use paradoxes and ambiguities, a skill they have honed to superb mastery. The need to show their outrage at nuclear ships persuaded those opposed to the idea of rage to move beyond the stigma attached to women's anger. Granny Doran Doyle was inspired by Mary Daly's suggestion that rage was not a stage, not something to get over, but rather a transformative force. The original Raging Grannies were also inspired by Margaret Laurence's assertion that as we get older we should become more radical, not less so:

♪♫A Granny's Life for Me,
A fancy hat and a walking cane
The courage to speak when the world's in pain...
The wisdom that comes when we're growing old
More interests and friends than our arms can hold...
Personal freedom at last has come...
(Tune: *Fox and Cat from Pinocchio*. *Raging Granny Carry On Songbook* 2000: 199).

What we grandmothers are doing with our lives, the problems we face now, the present true state of our relationships, the issues which we might raise as important — our priorities — are not considered interesting. These are never the subject of poems or political analysis by younger women. If they do break this rule, they are often punished by a rebuff from publishers who believe that "old ladies don't sell." (Copper 1988: 11)

Granny Joan Harvey has her own idea of why invisibility afflicts older women:

> Middle age women become invisible because they're not seen as possible sex partners, so men and women start to ignore middle age women, menopausal women, and post-menopausal women. Older women are completely transparent and invisible: you try to go anywhere to do something, and you can stand there for hours and you're not there.... "Well, the only way we're going to get anyone to notice us and pay attention is to dress ridiculously. Now that we have your attention, listen to what we have to say. (Harvey 2002)

Rather than dressing to pass incognito or deny their age, the Raging Grannies claim their age with loud shawls and flamboyant hats. Divesting themselves of an "artificial notion of decorum," they make fools of themselves and, in the process, highlight the stereotypes where the goal is to regiment and control, according to Moira Walker, briefly a member of the first group (M. Walker 1998). In the *Canadian Theatre Review*, John Burns suggests the Grannies are reversing "cultural expectations by empowering themselves within a society which belittles their experience and point of view" (1992: 21). Baba Copper writes:

> The old woman finds herself captured by stereotypes which drain her initiative and shatter her self-respect. The... Wicked Old Witch with unnatural powers, the Old Bad Mother with neurotic power needs, and the Little Old Lady, ludicrously powerless, cloud the individuality of every woman past sixty. Since childhood all of us have been bombarded by systematic distortions of female aging in fairy tales, legends, books, movies, plays and TV.... Ageism rationalizes the discarding of old women. (1988: 14–15)

In images and print, the elderly are often absent or misrepresented. Older women are seen as amiable, weak and defenceless pensioners, bag ladies or "adolescent mentalities in aged bodies on TV sitcoms" (Bell 1986: 1). These are unjust and inaccurate labels. Studies of representation of elderly people in the media suggest they are underrepresented or misrepresented in commercials, serials, drama productions and youth literature (Ketchner 1999: 93). Older women rarely appear in films, and when they do they are almost always shown as "less friendly, having less romantic activity, and as enjoying fewer positive outcomes than younger characters" (Ketchner 1999: 93). Since what we see and do not see affect our perceptions, Ketchner believes this leads to thinking that the elderly existence is insignificant.

According to Ford and Sinclair, feminists have also been slow to recognize the experiential and theoretical importance of old age and its impact on women (1987). Second-wave feminists focused their demands on questions relevant to young women, such as reproductive issues, child care, opportunity in education and work and balancing careers and intimate relationships. In the early 1980s,

Nett claimed that gerontological research took place within the "male paradigms of the academic disciplines, especially of sociology and psychology" (Nett 1982: 203). Arlene T. McLaren suggests that portrayals of elderly women greatly underestimate the contributions they make to society (1982: 213). As recently as 1999, Scheidt, Humpherys and Yorgason found that older people, especially women, were still identified with characteristics of "dependency, disease, disability, and depression" (1999: 278). Patriarchal society loses interest when women move beyond reproductive years, while aging men are seen as gaining maturity: "For a man, the signs of great age, the wrinkles, the lines, the heavy paunch suggest character, fortitude… maturity and celebrate his engagement with life. For a woman they signal obsolescence" (Wilkinson 1992: 105). Ritcey suggests that it is not biology but social constructs that perpetuate the experience of old age for women (1982: 220). The disregard for age makes youth the normal human condition. To grow old in a society that places importance on speed, productivity, efficiency and increasing material wealth through work and competition means older people are devalued. Old age is often assumed to be a negative experience in spite of the diversity of personalities and circumstances. In the process of aging one may gain or lose but with ageism the elderly are always losing (Copper 1988: 3). By their name the Raging Grannies claim their age and by their actions they offer us an opportunity to question assumptions associated with age as they boldly defy labels and stereotypes. They contribute to a new interpretation of old age and help us reclaim "old" as "sagacity, kindliness, wisdom, generosity, even graciousness and beauty" (Cottin 1979: 1).

In her attempt to defeat adversity and stereotypes, the figure of the Raging Granny transcends limits through jest (Burns 1992: 22). In contrast to what is expected of polite and proper older ladies, basically to be an amiable, silent and unobtrusive presence, the Raging Grannies dare to be seen misbehaving, as in ♫♫ "Grandmothers' Squawk":

> The Raging Grannies squawk
> And do much more than talk
> 'Cause there's so much work to be done
> There's the question of peace
> While weapons sale increases…
> Our leaders of course
> Show no shame or remorse
> Supporting the slaughter called war
> So we'll bitch, rage, and roar even more
> Till we change our country's course
> They say hi-tech war is good for trade
> But notice how craftily
> They chop and slash from our social economy…
> Hungry kids are a bloody shame…
> Let's all rock the ship of state

Together we can challenge our rage…
(Tune: *Grandfather's Clock*. *Grannie Grapevine* Summer 1996: 8)

Informed, strong and unafraid, the Grannies dispel the passivity anticipated of older women and provide an image of modern crones:

> While the archetypes of the Virgin and the Mother were consolidated into the Christian figure of Mary, the feared archetype of female age, the Crone, was eradicated…. Thus the "wise, willful, wolfish Crone" was female power and danger in its most potent form: in patriarchy, she had to be erased. (Copper 1988: 58)

Crone time used to be a time of freedom from conventions: it is

> only the hag that rides free… which is why she is feared, ostracised, tortured and murdered. Or worse, she is deformed into a stereotype — the easier to recognise and discount her. But the old woman, the crone, is that aspect of womanhood that is no longer controlled; she is the self that flies free. (Wilkinson 1992: 103)

The Crone survives lacks of all sorts, including freedom, but refuses confinement and crosses over labels and divisions, essential tools of patriarchy (Beadle 1986). In *Trojan Women*, Gwendolyn MacEwan shows that an unquestioning loyalty to a bankrupt culture, especially one that is built around the paradigm of stereotypic gender roles, is deadly. But MacEwan also shows that it is the figure of the crone who is the freeing agent; the old woman (who knows all the past and who is willing to call the present into account) is able to accomplish this because she moves beyond patriarchal rules. And because she is more free than most of us it is the old woman who is righting our stories (Wilkinson 1992: 107).

To reclaim the Crone is to claim strength, vision, vulnerability, and insights. Gatherings of hags "have embarrassed and harassed the powerful into responding to their demands… have refused to be silenced by a thrown bone, or discouraged by the lack of female support or impressed by belated congratulations" (Wilkinson 1992: xiv). The Raging Grannies are crones, proud to create disturbances and, if possible, some embarrassment for authorities.

Resisting with Imaginative Actions

Millions of long-living women scheme to change the world. (Ruth Harriet Jacobs 1997: 301)

Aside from offering resistance to the stereotypes of aging, the Raging Grannies reclaim agency by joining in political resistance. The Raging Grannies have crashed commissions, hearings, official visits and open-house events on American (possibly nuclear) warships. Such actions expressed their resistance to uncritical acceptance of what society is told and their refusal to be contained in locations where the public's presence is not tolerated in spite of the fact that some of the places and events that are out-of-bounds are highly relevant to the public. For example, disrupting official visits by politicians or commissions is courting the disapproval of authorities. Their colourful irreverence and unpredictability forces those confronted with their unexpected actions out of the complacency of well-oiled roles and procedures and make them interesting for the media. These actions contradict the idea that little "old ladies don't sell" (Copper 1988: 11).

One action that took place in New Brunswick in July 1998 challenged the notion of older women as irrelevant, conservative and overwhelmed by modern times. In an action titled "Closets Are for Brooms," Fredericton Raging Grannies marched around their city hall to demand that the homophobic mayor and council rescind their decision to ban the local Gay Pride Parade. Their action generated letters to the editor, and ultimately the mayor and council reversed their decision, finally stepping into the twenty-first century. With humour and creativity the Raging Grannies challenge the notion that protests and political actions are humourless angry events, as well as the stereotypes of sweet little old ladies that are benign, irrelevant and can be dismissed. The Raging Grannies' behaviour provides a positive example of transforming anger and despair into actions and ways of expressing commitment and determination.

When Humour Is Not Enough

Grannies are generally respectable and concerned citizens. They have joined groups, signed and collected petitions, lobbied elected officials, written letters to the editor, to premiers, to the prime minister, demonstrated and marched for decades. In order to express their commitment with even more determination some have also engaged in acts of civil disobedience and have consequently been arrested. One action generated much interest. During the escalating threats of war in the Gulf in 1990, some Victoria Grannies resurrected their World War II uniforms and marched to the local Armed Forces recruitment office to volunteer for a tour of duty. Having lived long lives, they thought it unnecessary to risk their grandchildren's lives for oil and felt ready for the mission: since the officer could not discriminate on the basis of age, he had to plough through the paperwork in spite of the fact that these new applicants were silver-haired (*Times-Colonist* 1990). A photograph of their action graced the front page of the local newspaper the next day, providing Victoria citizens with one more chuckle. Fifteen years later in August 2005, the Raging Grannies in Tucson, Arizona, walked into their local U.S. Army recruitment centre to volunteer for Iraq. They were arrested and charged with criminal trespass, and the charges were later dropped. News of their action attracted media attention all over the world and galvanized the Grandmothers' Peace Brigade, formed by New York Raging Grannies and Grandmothers Against the War, to repeat the action on October 17, 2005, in New York City, where eighteen older women were arrested after the soldiers at the recruiting office locked the door and went into hiding! A ninety-year-old blind Granny was handcuffed by the police as per the rules!

This act of civil disobedience and how the Grandmothers were treated reveal the inability of the law and law enforcement to act accordingly to the perceived threat of a situation. It encourages citizens to question the law that makes it acceptable to have soldiers and Iraqis killed for oil, but illegal for a group of elderly women to express their position in a non-violent protest. The inability of the law to discern what is just from what is legal is revealed. In April 2006, the women of the Grandmothers' Peace Brigade were acquitted after a trial at the criminal courts of New York that lasted one week. Enlisting actions were done by other groups of Raging Grannies and other Grandmothers Against the War all across the United States on February 14, 2006, in an effort by Grannies to bring attention to the lies recruiters used to enlist young people in the army, often youths struggling with poverty. This time, staff in Army recruitment centres, when not in hiding behind locked doors, were generally affable, although one soldier admitted he had been instructed not to engage with the Grannies. Darci Marchese from WTOP Radio in Washington, D.C., reported the arrest of Grannies who tried to enlist in their local Army recruitment centre in Silver Spring, Maryland (Marchese 2006). Jean Athey sent the following statement by Silver Spring Grannies about their motivation for their action:

> Grandmothers, heartbroken and enraged over the enormous loss of life and the terrible injuries in Iraq, plan to enlist in the military. They state, "The old make wars and the young die in them; today, on Valentine's Day, we are demonstrating our love for this country and its young people by enlisting in the U.S. military. We vehemently oppose this war; our action is not a show of support for our military action in Iraq. But if someone must die, let it be us, not the young. Our hearts are broken already. Too many have died. Too many have been maimed. Enough. End the war now." (Athey 2006)

By defying the law, Raging Grannies reclaimed the right to freedom of expression, a fundamental right in a democratic system. The fact that some recruitment offices had been told not to engage with the Grannies yet not to prevent their visit, reveals the recognition from military authorities that the image of grandmothers being arrested is not beneficial for military forces short of recruits and trying to suggest to the public that they are there for protection. It gives dissenters much visibility and breaks the image of unity and consensus for the war in Iraq, which authorities like to portray as reality. Grandmothers have credibility and cannot easily be accused of being starry-eyed young and inexperienced idealists as they have lived through many events, including wars, and have learned from experience. This tactic, unusual for older women, makes them newsworthy and more of a threat as they attract attention. Civil disobedience and crossing the legal line with consciousness and discipline communicates to others that the Grannies are determined and committed; it can also reinforce their own dedication to the cause. This is an example of resisting the law as well as the stereotypes of older women, who are supposed to stay quietly home and be easily dismissed.

Doran Doyle, Lois Marcoux, Anne Pask and Jean McLaren were the first Raging Grannies (Victoria) to tread on the legal line when they took part in the Grandmother Peace Action at Nanoose Bay in August 1988. This action was a symbolic attempt to reclaim Winchelsea Island for peaceful purposes (Evasuk 1990: B3). Winchelsea Island, located in the Georgia Straight (B.C), is the centre of the Canadian Forces Maritime Test Range (CFMTR) at Nanoose Bay and is used by the U.S. military to test underwater weapons, which can later be fitted with nuclear components. This brings U.S. warships and submarines, potentially nuclear powered and/or nuclear weapons–capable, into British Columbia waters. The Raging Grannies were arrested and charged with criminal trespass on Department of National Defence property, an offence carrying a penalty of $1,000 fine or up to one year in jail (Lightly 1989: 15). The charges were later dropped, possibly an indication that the government did not want to prosecute these otherwise respectable older women. For some Grannies, civil disobedience was a risk. Upon return to Victoria, Marcoux was ostracized by the leaders of the Girl Guides group she and her daughter belonged to as she had broken the law. Even though charges were later dropped and she was never convicted of wrongdoing in a court of law, as far as the Girl Guides leadership was concerned, she had acted in defiance of the law and that was unacceptable. While Marcoux "felt rejected or pushed down or cast aside," she is not sorry she crossed the line (Marcoux 1998). Marcoux, who came to social activism through her active involvement with the Catholic Church Social Justice Committee, found in this civil disobedience action an opportunity to re-adjust her sense of self: while she had seen herself as more of a follower, this action allowed her to realize she was "a bit of a risk taker even though you'd never know it" (Marcoux 1998).

Doran Doyle, a Raging Granny who was arrested numerous times, was also part of that first civil disobedience action in Nanoose Bay and felt "she had crossed out of the range of respectability" (Howard 1989: 14). Interestingly, Martha Ackelsberg, who wrote *Free Women of Spain*, suggests that crossing the limits of appropriate behaviour with a supportive group can be empowering and lead women "to question the appropriateness of those boundaries in the first place" (1991: 165). In 1988 civil disobedience was uncommon and there were various reactions to their action. One columnist wrote, "I'm against nuclear subs, too, but I'm not about to invade territory that is off limit to the public" (Hunter 1988: A3). The action was even controversial among peace activists. Civil disobedience reveals inconsistencies in law. In this case it demonstrated how the law is applied to six women stepping lightly on an isolated island, posing no threat to others or to the environment, while conversely it permits nuclear warships and submarines to ply the waters with such dangerous cargo or reactors.

This was the first, though not the last, civil disobedience action for Granny Jean McLaren from Gabriola Island, British Columbia. She has since been arrested eight times. McLaren suggests that police officers find it hard to arrest older women and recalls a policeman's comment to a Granny, "You're just like my grandmother, I don't want to arrest you" (McLaren 2002). While on a peace walk in Israel, McLaren was arrested and jailed:

> We had permission to walk in the West Bank and then they stopped it. There were 200 of us, 113 got arrested. They put us in jail for forty-eight hours. That was not fun. There were forty-eight women in that one jail.... Fifteen people in our room and our room was fifteen by twenty [feet].... We had one toilet in the corner.... We had no towels. They actually gave us fifteen bars of soap, and we juggled with them. And we sang. We had a workshop on self-defence and we decided we were not going to have political discussions. We just played and sang and we made it! They have to let you go or take you before a judge after forty-eight hours, so they let us go because we said, "The whole world is watching." (McLaren 2002)

The contrast between women imprisoned in crowded quarters and juggling is emblematic of a spirit of defiance that refuses to be dictated to: resistance through civil disobedience requires a willingness to assume one's moral convictions and determination to oppose unjust situations, in spite of the sometimes difficult consequences.

Five years after that first controversial Grandmother Peace civil disobedience action at Nanoose Bay the mood had changed considerably. More than 800 people of all ages and backgrounds put themselves on the line and were arrested during the 1993 summer of mass protests against the logging of the old growth forest at Clayoquot Sound, which were a few kilometres from Nanoose Bay. In that protest, Victoria Raging Grannies Ria Bos and Alison Acker were arrested and jailed for two weeks. Acker, a retired university professor, felt it was important to stand up and be counted, to "show that it's not just young people who are concerned about the future of the planet. Us old birds care too" (Birch 2001: 109). According to Acker, Raging Grannies wanted to "Break the stereotyped image that all environmental activists are trouble-seeking youngsters. As Grannies, we were concerned that the press was making it look like only a load of crazy young kids was protesting about the logging" (Birch 2001: 109). One journalist got the message as he wrote that the participation of Raging Grannies in acts of civil disobedience was "proving false the theory that radicalism is synonymous only with youth" (Howard 1992: D7). The Victoria Grannies claimed great pride in their "illustrious ex-convicts" (Woodland 1998: 85). Across the country in Halifax, Granny Betty Peterson, a recipient of an Honorary Doctorate from Mount St Vincent University, is "an eighty-one-year-old fireball" who has been "in and out of jail for protesting since the 1960s" and believes in putting her body on the line for racial equality, social justice and witnessing for peace (Greenberg 1999: 5). Her life philosophy has led her to being repeatedly handcuffed and carried away by RCMP officers. This was exemplified in 1994 when she put her "body in front of charging oil trucks" (Greenberg 1999: 5). Halifax Granny Eva Munro joked that (then) ninety-three-year-old Muriel Duckworth, a Raging Granny and a tireless peace activist for over six decades, "hasn't been in the clinker yet, but there's lot of time yet!" (Munro 2002)

The London Raging Grannies have also been involved in civil disobedience, as they showed support for marginalized youths following the Ontario government decision to pass a law aimed at criminalizing squeegeeing. The headline in the local newspaper read "Raging Grannies Take a Swipe at Squeegee Law." On February 13, 2000,

> eight Raging Grannies staged an act of civil disobedience on a busy street corner to protest homelessness and raise money for London's food bank. The guerrilla action took place just after 10 a.m.... where the rabble-rousers sang, squeegeed, distributed pamphlets and asked for donations from stopped motorists. After an hour of panhandling, the Grannies... had already raised $158.... "People have to become more aware of the homeless," said 86-year-old Florence Boyd-Graham, who blasted the province's crack-down on squeegee kids and noted that at her age, she doesn't "give a hell" about what people think of her politics. A police officer did stop to question a grannie after the action, but no charges were laid under a new law banning soliciting on public roadways that went into effect Jan. 31. "We thought we were going to get locked up," said Boyd-Graham, laughing. Michelle LeBoutillier... said the Grannies were "concerned" they might get charged, but were compelled to disobey the law because they "felt so strongly that poverty isn't being addressed in the way it should be." (Fenlon 2000: A1)

They defied the law and the provincial government by using their credibility as older women to assist youth struggling with poverty. Their gesture also made it evident that the law was aimed at a specific group. In taking part in acts of civil disobedience, the Raging Grannies express their deep desire to resist what they see as immoral, unjust or violating ecological integrity. In taking such actions, the Grannies unambiguously stand in solidarity with forces of resistance to oppression. They challenge greedy companies who see only dollars in lumber rather than the life-giving support of the forest and the government who does not allow nuclear weapons in Canada but will not ask U.S. vessels if they contain such weapons, a convenient arrangement if there ever was one! When Grannies defy the law, they claim the rights and responsibilities of citizens concerned that an egregious wrong is being committed that endangers the community or its life support and refuse to be isolated by age or fear.

Solidarity and Tear Gas in Quebec City

In the spring of 2001, many Raging Grannies joined protesters at the meeting of the Free Trade Area of the Americas (FTAA) in Quebec City, in spite of the threat of brutal reprisal by law enforcement officials. To give a sense of the diversity of protesters, media reported that "Thousands upon thousands of union representatives headed the parade, followed by an array of other activist groups that ran the gamut from communists and hardline Quebec separatists to the Raging Grannies" (Thompson 1998: A1). Joan Hadrill wrote:

> I felt very privileged as a Montreal Raging Granny to be invited to be part of the Teach-In at the People's Summit of the Americas in Quebec City with people like David Suzuki, Naomi Klein, Alexa McDonough and many from South and Central America who talked about the negative impact of NAFTA on their lives. It was very empowering to be marching with over 30,000 people there because of their opposition to Free Trade, people representing many religions, social justice, environment and human rights.... Two of our older grannies rode in wheelchairs and were photographed by people impressed by their determination and stamina. At times, we felt the sting of tear gas. (2001: 6)

The courage to go in the vulnerability of a wheelchair was inspiring, especially in light of the authorities' obvious and worrisome preparations and plans to rely on force. As Raging Granny Angela Silver noted, while they may not have been banging on "The Wall," they still had the effects of the tear gas "making them live closer to the edge than most people their age" (Silver 2002). Kathleen Foy, a frail ninety-year-old Granny who went in a wheelchair, explained that she had to defy the will of her family to go to Quebec City because it was of great importance to her. In Quebec City, Raging Grannies sang loudly and were often cheered and hugged: they happily put their mature faces into the crowd as they were just as outraged as the young protesters at what was being done (Land 2001: 2). They sang their song,

♫♫ FTAA Don't Fence Me Out!
Just let loose, no excuse for the secrecy and lies
Please don't install a Berlin wall
Where the sense of freedom dies
So I must fight for what's right while the talk commences
Face police violence, 'til lose my senses
I can't stand tyrants an'
I can't stand fences, don't fence me out!
(Tune: *Don't Fence Me In. Granny Grapevine* Spring 2001: 27)

♫♫ The FTAA Hokey-Pokey
(Chorus) And they twist it all around
That's what it's all about!!!

They have the corporations in
They have the little guys out
The NGO's are nowhere really
They're neither in nor out
They do some hocus pocus

They let the media in
If the media are good
They let the media in
If they spin it as they should
They spin the information...
(Tune: *Hokey Pockey*. Wurman 2001)

While most Grannies went along the safe route, away from the rows of police guarding "The Wall of Shame," a few elected otherwise:

> When clouds of tear gas were seen rising from the fenced-off areas above us, some decided to go and show solidarity with the younger folks. They headed up the steps towards the freshly tear-gassed area. They were warned by fleeing protesters to turn back but continued on. (Land 2001: 2)

Some Grannies suffered from asthma and others did not want to go to "The Wall," but Alma Norman, a Raging Granny from Ottawa, recalls:

> I came to Quebec City to go to the wall because that wall is an abomination and I'm here to accept my rights as a citizen. So I would like to go to the wall... [but] I won't go alone because I came with a group and I don't feel I can just walk away from the group and do this thing. And yet, it is very important to me. If I don't go to the wall, I will feel as if I have in some sense failed in my purpose in coming here.... Two of the Grannies and two others who were not Grannies then but have since joined us, decided to come with me. (Norman 2001)

While "somewhat nervous about being tear-gassed," they walked on and soon came across a group of heavily armed police in full combat gear. The police were unaccountably preventing the peaceful progress of a small group of protestors trying to make their way down a street: "The police looked more like armadillos," according to the small Grannies' band fearless leader Alma, aged seventy-eight. One "amardillo" stepped forward, fingering his rubber-bullet gun. Undeterred, the Grannies group linked arms and put themselves between the small group of protesters and the police. First they sang

♫♫ Hysteria
Hail Hysteria, Hysteria rules today...
Our leaders in their wisdom hope
To hide away from protest
Behind a ten foot barricade...
(Tune-Chorus: *Rule Britannia*. Tune-Verse: *In Days of Old*. Norman 2001)

Then [they] took small steps towards the police. Then it was, "We shall overcome," and a few more steps forward, voices cracking a little, according to the youngest, an apprentice Granny. Finally, Alma, the 78-year-old Granny leader, explained to the police that the Grannies could indeed be their mothers or their grandmothers, but that they were simply there for peaceful purposes and posed no danger. Amazingly, the police then retreated a few steps. The Granny group... made their way back down the hill. (Land 2001: 2)

Their way back was noteworthy:

> What was very moving was that, as we were going down the hill, all these young people who had been standing down the hill came up to us and hugged us and said, "Thank you, thank you, thank you so much, thank you for being with us, thank you for coming, thank you for supporting us." (Norman 2001)

Alma Norman called it a "tremendous moment of solidarity" (2001: 8). An intergenerational web of resistance was created that day, a web which extends into the future. The Grannies' presence prevented potential violence from the police towards protesters and prevented critics from making generalizations about protesters being young and ignorant (Land 2001: 2).

The Grannies expressed themselves assertively with the police. Courage and fear are contagious. Leadership is important in tense situations like Quebec City and requires determination yet flexibility. Alma Norman was no stranger to protest and her past experiences gave her perspective and courage. Always a leader, she remains active and dynamic in her eighties. In December 2001 she wrote to Prime Minister Chrétien:

> As women we have lived through at least two major wars, we cannot accept that waging war is the proper means of solving this problem.... Although a nation may use its military power to destroy an enemy militarily, armed forces cannot destroy the factors, which lead to terrorist activity.... Billions of dollars used to destroy would be better spent in helping countries deal with their on-going needs in the fields of health, education, housing and infrastructure, which help to fuel the anger and frustration which can make terrorism seem the only option. Therefore, that support for military action against Iraq or other chosen targets is both morally wrong and politically unwise. (Norman 2002)

At a protest in Montreal some years earlier she saw cameramen taking pictures of demonstrators and asked them who they were. Not happy with the response, she asked the police, who said they were journalists. Alma told them the photographers were not press since they were all dressed alike. It reminded her of Jamaica, where in the 1960s she experienced something like the Soweto riots with police on rooftops. Prior experience and a strong sense of her rights made it possible for her to keep things in perspective and resist the fear the "security" apparatus in Quebec City was meant to inspire. It is clear for Alma that confronting intimidating force is a form of resistance and is necessary if rights are to be upheld, otherwise these rights will erode. Linda Slavin, a Raging Granny from Peterborough, wrote about not going to the wall:

> I went to Quebec City because my planet is under siege. The environment is threatened, people I know are hungry, homeless, and without the most basic rights. When politicians meet behind barricades to promote the text of a commercial agreement allowing corporations to make money while threatening education, health, social services and nature, I have to be counted.... Walking peacefully with the Peterborough Raging Grannies and 50,000 others down the streets of Quebec was an energizing experience.... But, at a crucial point in the march, we were told to turn right. Traces of tear gas had us reaching for scarves soaked in lemon juice to cover our faces and, before we could assess the situation, we walked away from the barricades instead of towards them. At the steel fence were thousands of others equally concerned about our world. A few were unnecessarily violent but the state violence in Quebec was far worse: plastic bullets, tear gas, and pepper-spray linked the Canadian government to the systemic human rights abuses in many of the countries represented at the summit. Most protesters were determined to confront this insult to democracy creatively. These young people were prepared and disciplined.... They rocked the fence and the politicians while the rest of the parade walked the other way.... The state, the police, the media, and indeed some of the leaders of the People's Summit divided us. I realize now that we should have been all together... at the fence. (Slavin 2001: A4)

In spite of the efforts of security forces to scare people, Grannies were in Quebec City with their hats and their shawls, some on foot, some in wheelchairs, singing with the parade or risking tear gas and rubber bullets on a path of solidarity at "The Wall." Slavin claims the importance of solidarity in acts of resistance to the power of the state trying to discourage people from expressing their views. By participating in marches and joining younger protestors at "The Wall" the Raging Grannies defined themselves as people capable of solidarity and commitment in the face of a state obsessed with violent means of repression.

A few months later, the G-20 met in Ottawa and Grannies sang at a march where they encountered police instigated violence. Granny Ava Louwe recalled the situation:

> The police were really, really, threatening.... whole phalanx of plastic shields and black helmets, you know the Darth Vaders, and the storm troopers with their truncheons and... rifles and dogs and whole lines of them on both sides of the road.... They were looking for troublemakers, they were looking to incite trouble, and they did.... The police came into the crowd... and hauled out one or two reporters with cameras. (Louwe 2002)

While many have participated in social movements and activism before joining the Raging Grannies, for Louwe this was a new and radicalizing experience:

> A real eye-opener. I was just shocked. You could feel the energy of the police and the animosity. And the fear in the crowd, you could feel it, you could put your hand out and touch it. It was palpable. And the crowd was amazingly restrained. They [police] grabbed a young man dressed in black and a young woman and they were roughhousing her off to the side…. And the crowd said, "Let her go, let her go, let her go." The crowd stopped and I think they did let her go and then the crowd continued. But for a while I thought, "Oh my god, what are we gonna see here?" It felt to me that the crowd would have been completely peaceable but the police were determined to create an incident. Like they were there to make the crowd look as if we were all a bunch of rabble rousers, there with no purpose. They created trouble so we will lose credibility. It was shocking for me. It was almost as though the police had been set up to hate the crowd. The crowd was the enemy and they were there to make sure that peace prevailed. (Louwe 2002)

Reflecting on the experience she adds:

> I'm just getting my eyes open as to what is really happening. I find it very distressing. What I find so unsettling is that when I read letters to the editor… some of these people who wrote letters were saying, "What's with these demonstrators? What are they doing?" And I think, bless you people, don't you realise that our civil rights are being taken away and one day… you'll wake up and you'll realize you have no rights. And the people who are demonstrating are there now fighting for your rights. It's shocking and, to be honest, I have to work very hard to keep my optimism up because there are times when I feel that the ones in authority are doing a pretty good job of hiding the real undermining of our civil rights. And I have lost complete faith in what our government is doing. I think that they're all very underhanded and they do not honour the people's rights. It's shocking. We are in a democracy. That's Canada. And our rights are being taken away. (Louwe 2002)

Louwe finds herself demystifying authority and becoming aware of the brute force police sometimes use to intimidate. Her assumptions about what should happen in Canada are challenged. Active engagement provides an opportunity for people to demystify the use of force and confront contradictions between reality and the media reports. The Raging Grannies allow women from very different backgrounds to stand together, and at times, their own worldview is challenged, and their resistance is more deeply understood and internalized. Grannies seek ways of resisting intimidation and ways to support others during confrontations.

Jean McLaren, a Raging Granny from Gabriola Island, B. C., was at the march in Ottawa but had joined the Wiccan Living River Cluster and had an experience she will not forget:

> We were walking along in a peaceful parade.... All of a sudden the police just came up from a side street and started grabbing young people who were dressed in black and had their faces covered. They [Black Bloc] were walking alongside of us. It was very frightening as the police started beating them.... So we sort of surrounded them and we were standing aside and saying, "Leave them alone, leave them alone, don't touch them." And then, we sat down on the road and wouldn't move. Finally, they let us go. And we're walking along and one of the young people was right next to me and I said to him, "In all the years that I've been an activist, over 50 years, I've never covered my face or hidden or refused to say who I was." About a block later he said to us, "Will you people surround us for a few minutes because we want to take off our black clothes and put them in our packsacks!" We chanted, "Pagans support the Block," and they chanted back, "Block supports the Pagans."... For the rest of that rally they didn't wear black, didn't cover their faces. It may have been an eye-opener to them. And they danced the spiral dance with us. (McLaren 2002)

Norman and McLaren think older women can interpose themselves effectively and decrease the violence in situations, move the energy as McLaren defines it. They are effective because of their maturity, wisdom, sincerity and credibility as non-violent but courageous activists. As Halifax Granny Eva Munro said, "we're not worried about being gagged. We'll say anything, can't shut us up" (Munro 2002), and they do!

The RCMP and CSIS have noticed, and their actions may reflect the effectiveness of the Grannies' resistance. After the pepper-spray incident at the Asia Pacific Economic Conference (APEC) in Vancouver in 1997, the enquiry into police conduct revealed that the RCMP and CSIS had the Raging Grannies listed as a threat to national security, although a low threat (Thompson 1998; Mardiros 2000). Undeterred, the Grannies sang:

♪♫ These grandmothers still squawk
We don't sit on the shelf
In spite of the RCMP!
Democratic dissent
Civil disobedience
Are supposed to be a
Canadian guarantee
The cops and CSIS of course
Show no remorse
As they target old ladies such as we
While they snitch

We will bitch
Rage and roar even more
Till they learn 'bout democracy!
(Tune: *Grandfather's Clock*. Seifred 2002)

They also wrote and sang "Are you proud t' know our forces would take little old ladies on whose worst crime was singing flat a bunch of satirical songs!" (Seifred 2002)

Conclusion

As Bond and Coleman suggest, we may want to be "less concerned with charting decline and predicting outcomes and more with outlining possibilities" (Minkler 1996: 481). The Raging Grannies poke fun at people in power, communicate their progressive views on various issues, and in the process provide new images of women as elders. While little is written, experience indicates that female old age offers great potential for "radical change and self-expression . . . Centuries have passed since old matriarchs could have threatened the power of the patriarchs. Yet the conditioning against the possibility of powerful, respected, or influential old women continues" (Copper 1988: 60–61). Barbara Walker suggests that the real threat older women pose to patriarchal society may be

> the "evil eye" of sharp judgement honed by disillusioning experience, which pierces male myths and scrutinizes male motives in the hard, unflattering light of critical appraisal. It may be that the witch's evil eye was only an eye from which the scales had fallen. (Copper 1988: 62)

Like Baba Copper, some feminists are now concerned with the reinvention of images of rebellious and powerful old women (Copper 1988). Evelyn Rosenthal writes that while feminists brilliantly and devastatingly analyzed sexism, which changes our understanding of women, we now need such an analysis of ageism to uncover "similar mechanisms at work constructing the nature of old age. By investigating the lives of old women we can challenge stereotypes, critique old age as a social construction, and discover that much of what women fear about aging is not natural to old age" (Rosenthal 1990: 6). In literature, "old women have rarely been portrayed as the resourceful, productive, vital, angry and joyful women many of us are" (Wilkinson 1992: 103). In fact, Leah Cohen's research has shown that post-menopausal women "are often endowed with new energy and vitality" in spite of a society that "perceives them as declining and almost obsolete" (Wilkinson 1992: 103). Confronting "the narrow range of negative images of ageing pervasive in our culture" and seeking to "challenge and disrupt conventional story lines of women and ageing" becomes a necessity (Ray 1999: 178). By their creative and courageous resistance, the Raging Grannies defy stereotypes and at times the law, refusing the labels of stereotypes for themselves. They help ensure others, like young protesters, are also not stereotyped and labelled. Civil disobedience is only one arena of the Grannies' resistance, but an important one as few people are willing to consciously and willingly defy the law. Their willingness to take such actions conveys their seriousness, commitment and determination to express solidarity in their search for peace and justice. By engaging in various forms of resistance the Raging Grannies expand the boundaries of protest and aging while making us laugh:

♪♫ Wrinkle, Wrinkle Aging Star
Wrinkle, wrinkle aging star
Who cares just how old you are?
Your hair is grey, your dentures click
Your bosom sags, your ankle's thick
Your joints all creak, your arthritis plagues
You've got all the symptoms of Raging Age
Hurrah for Age, Age, to Hell with being beige
We won't stay cooped up in a cage
Our eyes are dim but our tongues are sharp
We go out on a limb, our wits are sharp
Yes we've got years, years and you'd better get it clear
A raging gran's a force to fear.
(Tune: *Twinkle Twinkle Little Star*. Parliament Hill Mob, *Granny Grapevine* 1995: 4)

Chapter 6

Not Tough Enough Skin?
Resisting Paternalist Relations in Academe

Norma Jean Profitt

My Story

I had been only a few years in academe and yet it is not an exaggeration to say that I could not have lasted another minute longer before departing to Costa Rica for a well-earned retreat. As I was organizing myself for the journey, I had a dream. *A woman police officer had asked me to conduct a forensic interview with a young woman who had been raped by a man whom she barely knew. Even though I am a feminist social worker with considerable experience in women's issues, I thought, "Oh no, I do not know how to ask those kinds of questions." The officer handed me a new fangled computerized screen on which to write and sat next to me, anxious for me to begin. I had a vague uneasy feeling that I knew the woman I was about to interview. The heaviness of her experience filled our waiting and I knew that I must let her speak. As I asked a few open-ended questions, I became aware of her solidity and strength. And then in a flash, I realized that the woman I was interviewing was me.* As I write about my tenure in academia, my survival instinct unfolds itself from its resting place: I would have liked my experience to be different from what it has been and I fear that I cannot distinguish that wish from what really happened. Both things exist at the same time, a consciousness of the harsh reality and a denial of it, creating a simultaneous apprehension and maintenance of hope.

I know that I must plot a strategy for my return because of my waning belief that I am making a difference in the university institution where I work. As I rest in the hammock of my soul-friend, Dellanira, in Puerto Jiménez in the Penisula de Osa in southern Costa Rica, a region that is still ecologically well conserved and without the devastation and eyesore of foreign large-scale tourist develop-ment, I try to penetrate more clearly the workings of power in the university and nail down why I am such a misfit there. Here the gentle breeze catches the platano (plantain) tree leaves and moves them about like lazily flapping elephant ears. Yellow and orange butterflies flit from tree to tree, to the bougainvillea and the hibiscus, only lighting long enough to produce a gleam in the midday sun. Drops of water captured in the hollows of the leaves of a waxy green and red leafed shrub flash like mica, waving hello, goodbye. Lifted by the wind, a broad round-tipped leaf of the platano tree stretches and opens wide, shifting yet again the patterns of light lying across its brow. A fuchsia bougainvillea blossom flutters to the earth. Birds chirp madly in bursts of song. An iridescent mint green lizard stalks its prey, lifting its legs high as it resolutely climbs the interior branches of the tree, hoping to pass unperceived, clandestine, incognito. The shadow of a branch of the pale pink-blossomed bougainvillea caresses my shoulder and I am unburdened in that moment of eternity, rocked in the cradle of life. From where do I draw the sustenance to continue?

Even though feminist theories do help me comprehend dimensions of power, as a white feminist woman I still struggle to survive and labour collectively to change damaging patterns of the university. As Anne Bishop (2005) describes in *Beyond Token Change: Breaking the Cycle of Oppression in Institutions*, universities as liberal institutions are structural entities that reflect the discrimination and exclusion present in our society and reinforce historical power relationships. Although they often claim commitments to social justice and environments free of discrimination based on protected grounds such as gender and "race," the cultural norms, values and "normal" ways of doing things often contrast with these stated institutional goals (Bishop 2005). Women's experiences with systemic discrimination and the chilly climate in academia, an institution so often oppressive to historically excluded social groups, have been powerfully documented (The Chilly Collective 1995; McIntyre 2000; Luther, Whitmore and Moreau 2001; Keahey and Schnitzer 2003a). As the old saw goes, change is slow, and I would add more arduous and costly for some than others.

In her article, "Events Without Witness: Living/Teaching Difference within the Paternalist University," Susan Heald asks: "What are the features of universities that make teaching at them differently, from a place of difference, and about difference so hard?" (1997: 39). As she observes, she, I, and other feminists across Canada have the distinct sense of being forever invisible and constantly required to adjust our work life in ways that compromise ethics, dignity and integrity. In this chapter I explore my experience in the university institution to seek a partial answer to this question and to another that, for me, is contained within: How does my personal narrative shape the way I respond to the injustice I see within its stone walls, and how do the effects of working in the university institution compound the effects of social oppression already lived?

My experience as a sexual harassment advisor for the university brought both of these questions to the fore, raising them like spectres before my eyes. Given my knowledge of "patriarchal violence" (Bannerji 2000: 152), acquired through the women's movements in both Canada and Costa Rica, I eagerly agreed to act in this capacity. Attending mostly to women affected by sexual, gender and other forms of harassment, I found meaning in providing the service that, perhaps, offered women a small oasis as they sought to end the harassment. I saw my position as a source of potential individual and collective resistance. As a feminist I could resist by serving people well with a critical analysis of patriarchal violence and power relations and I could work with others to educate and highlight the need for action on issues of harassment, discrimination and inclusion. As a member of the faculty union I could collectively advocate for the promotion of a healthy teaching and learning environment and changes to current sexual harassment policy and practice. At the end of my term, I wrote a letter to the president, reporting on consultations with concerned faculty and students, and the numbers and kinds of complaints attended. I advocated a comprehensive review of the outdated sexual harassment policy and procedures and, like others before me who had been in the role, made a series of recommendations for action and change in various ambits of the university. I received a letter of acknowledgement three months later that indeed my report had been received.

And so, of late, for survival purposes, I have been given to thinking about how to both resist the system's insidious pressures to conform and press for progressive change more effectively without so much crippling stress, anger and self-doubt. How can I protect myself from the effects of the brutalizing dynamics of the institution, hold fast to the values of feminist consciousness and resist the seeping of oppression into my lifeblood? In this challenge the lines blur between the particulars of my personal narrative and the grinding machinations of power in the university. As Jennifer Kelly points out in her discussion about withhold-ing parts of herself as a student from her supervisor, Aruna Srivastava, within a false and binary relation, it is difficult to "sort out how and where the reasons are about my personality/personal baggage and how and where they are about institutional structures and systemic inequalities and power relations" (Kelly and Srivastava 2003: 74). When these structures, inequalities and relations intersect with personal histories and the accumulated effects of oppression, what is not done is left unspoken and what is never given remains unclaimed.

To say that the institution where I work advances the rhetoric of commu-nity but does not practice it is to say nothing new. The palpability of the abyss between rhetoric and reality has a long memory trace. The underbelly of the discourse of the happy nuclear family imprinted itself on my body through my family's inability to change the patterns that locked them into being. As a watcher with keen eyes I scrutinized the politics of listening and the flow of currents of need, demand and availability. Frustration and distance grabbed for traction into understanding and connection. A curious thing happened in those early years as it surely does to some children: I felt as if I could see into what is usually left unseen, into that breach between what is pronounced and what lies behind. Later I added to that "seeing into" a repertoire of social and feminist theories that explained social structures and relations of power. Some of these laid bare the organization of the patriarchal nuclear family in white, English-speaking working-class homes in the 1960s in the Maritime provinces. And so it happens that situations in which we later find ourselves draw breath from those ancient memory traces, and from those same traces, insights into injustice draw their vitality.

I have tried hard during my time in academia to achieve more clarity about reliving old patterns of performance rooted in need, lack and want in the face of power. My attempts to have legitimate concerns heard by the institution have been mostly ineffective. Likely these appeals appeared overwrought or out of proportion to management. In a dance to outsmart peril and achieve my goal to be heard, I try to be bright and reasonable. Racing between the mind and the body, I register that it is unsafe to show anything at all. Who are these creatures that have the power to judge my worth? How does fear gain such purchase? Imagine that in my forties, in the university system, it still encircles me in every muscle and every fibre. Neon signs flash warning, alert! Before coherent speech was possible, anger and rage as responses to injustice were trapped in the flesh. They fled underground but now they spurt like molten red lava gushing from the cone of the volcano Rincón de la Vieja of northern Costa Rica. How can I live so much of my institutional life scrambling to be heard, securing little space and speaking less truth?

Keith Louise Fulton asks "What do we do with that creature knowledge so vital to our commitment to justice? We freeze it" (2003: 151). Drawing on the work of Adrienne Rich, she claims that poetic language "is a way into the stored toxic waste of our experiences, thawing our own information" (151). It "can break open locked chambers of possibility, restore numbed zones to feeling, recharge desire" (Rich 1993: xiv). Poetic language enables us "to engage with states that themselves would deprive us of language and reduce us to passive sufferers" (10). Writing thaws experience to allow for the creation of knowledge. The resultant wisdom, recorded by the "I", reaches out to listeners to connect with them in reciprocity and collectivity (Fulton 2003). Meaning-making as a form of resistance joins with the wisdom of others, swelling the ranks to action. *Unfreezing experience* infuses it with the possibility of political understanding and renewal.

Madwomen in the Academy

I have often thought that our dreams dream us. They present our lives back to us, the desires wanting to be heard, the fragments needing mending, the sense waiting to be made. Shortly after I joined academia, I had a presentiment of my experience there in a dream. *I was walking near an inlet by the sea with a group of colleagues. As we ventured onto the ice, the ice split open and one woman fell into a crack that gaped and swallowed her. I plunged into the knee-deep water while the others stood there, paralyzed with fright. I screamed to them to act: "Hang on to us!" In the dream, my real life little Linden, a superintelligent female border collie, was running around frantically trying to rescue the distressed woman. I then heard a voice say: "Get Linden to find the hurts." I doubted her capacity to do so but she did; she found people's hurts that wandered like nomads on the body and weighed down their every step upon the ground.* Sadness gathers in pods just beneath the skin, and fear flickers and dims, hiding the heart, power, and creativity within.

As I read the edited collection of essays in *The Madwoman in the Academy* (Keahey and Schnitzer 2003a), I was overcome with that rare kind of relief that I feel when I see my experience reflected in the world and know that as a feminist I am not alone in my perceptions and analyses. Contributors pass on their knowledge about that thing called the university system and its consequences for many women. As the editors so aptly attest, labouring in such a competitive, individualistic, self-serving, hierarchical system is, indeed, "madness" (Keahey and Schnitzer 2003b: 17).

Working in such a system, let alone seeking to create progressive change, produces a variety of maladies in the spirit and the flesh: "that 'not enough' space that undermines our belief in ourselves and our experience" (Keahey and Schnitzer 2003b: 16); the perpetual conflictedness about employment and survival in such a setting (Keahey and Schnitzer 2003b); the lack of "adequate childcare, flexible career paths, longer tenure tracks, and job-sharing" in a predominantly male culture that makes women's lives more difficult (Sulliman 2003: 29); the "patriarchally and institutionally produced" need for affirmation that is hard to dispel despite years of feminist theorizing (Kelly and Srivastava 2003: 64); the fragmentation of facets of the self and the separation of the intellect from the body and embodiment (Kelly and Srivastava 2003); the constant interrogation of motivations, ethically and politically, in an effort to avoid reproducing oppression rather than succumbing to the seedier aspects of academic life (Kelly and Srivastava 2003); the dimensions of re-enacting the "stereotypical suffer-in-silence role that patriarchy is so fond of" as well as "a version of middle-class liberal whiteness... in which minority peoples perform their pain for us" (Kelly and Srivastava 2003: 75).

Other authors in *The Madwoman in the Academy* attest to the biting contradictions in the university institution: living with "the promise of intellectual freedom and membership" while being subjected to marginal status in a battleground "covered with a veneer of solicitude" (Karumanchery-Luik and Ramirez 2003: 79, 82). A myriad of sensations and feelings complete this constellation of the effects of existence in racist, misogynist space: "fear in the face of authority figures who make me the sole witness to this psychic bashing, re-enacted over and over... again" (Blais 2003: 122); the silence of self-protection to prevent anyone from knowing about past sexual assaults and the powerful emotions of fear, shame and helplessness that certain situations in academia re-evoke (Donnan 2003); the subjection to ethnocentric notions, theories and modes of interaction that "lock me up in your prison house of language" (Chahal 2003: 139); the "limited ways of defining what constitutes knowledge" that cannot comprehend "those who work within frames of reference that are dialogic, inclusive, multidimensional, and organic" (Schnitzer 2003: 199). Have I recounted enough? Do I have to shout it out? The kicker is how in this vice grip we toil and trouble, hoping to make a difference, yet all the while fearing that any difference will be undone. Yes, madness is aptly described as "the defiance of unreasonable expectations and policies and the dependency upon those expectations and policies for definition and approval; the indignation and the acquiescence, resistance and internalization" (Keahey and Schnitzer 2003b: 17). The system is deadly (Shaw-MacKinnon 2003).

Power and the University

Do our dreams dream us? After a short time in the university, I would dream of being in all male environments from which it was difficult to escape: *crumbling cement buildings, enclosed parking garages, vessels of freight and passage. Inside a submarine down deep in the sea, I had no way out. A group of men came toward me and one man took out his penis, huge and erect, to wave in front of me. I so feared that he would try to stick it in my mouth. Escape was only possible if I seized the moment with patience and nerves of steel.* As if in counterbalance to those dreams of powerlessness, I dreamed of children needing my witness and solidarity. Walking the labyrinth, I follow what is written on my skin like a map to the sea, searching for traces of life and desire that pound upon the shores of some saving grace.

In my interactions with the university institution, the currents of power only sometimes directly negate: No, do this or that, you cannot do what you think is best. More often, however, I experience power as a disembodied, faceless presence, yet palpable and insidious, that sucks my energy like a chupacabra (goat sucker), preying upon every breath I take. Always it hovers just close enough to try to threaten and curtail into submission or conformity. Always it inhabits me. The power of the university institution courses through arteries and veins like lead, heavy and toxic to faith and hope. *Unfreeze experience, give life to its words.*

Susan Heald's analysis of the paternalist university offers me a way into my experience, helping me to unfreeze it, make meaning and act on it. She argues that one feature of universities that makes teaching at them so hard is paternalism. This mode of the operation of power "sets up relationships of power which at the same time deny the existence of power and make pathological any one or any thing which questions this power" (Heald 1997: 39). In this denial the product of domination and oppression — powerlessness — is rendered invisible. Under this regime, employees, treated as errant children, are made responsible for inducing the father's wrath or disfavour. Anyone who challenges his power and authority is deemed abnormal. Heald asserts that paternalist discourses, while appearing gender-neutral, benign and even benevolent, espouse a notion of community as one big happy family that "denies the possibility of competing or conflicting interests within the bounds of the university or the classroom" (40). Those who question, disagree, critique, set limits, refuse to be team players or demand rights or justice are pathologized, leaving the rules of the game intact, untouched and unexamined. She notes that paternalism displays other features: those who are subordinate act according to their obligations while those in superior positions bestow gifts, gifts that are expected to be gratefully received. Paternalist discourses also "delimit who will have the right to speak, to whom, and about what" (42). In this circumscription of speech that calls us into being, subordinates are denied the authority to define their own reality.

In my term as a sexual harassment advisor, my experience dealing with the situation of Alanis mobilized the anger and rage trapped in my flesh. Alanis, a female student, had been harassed by a male student. At the point that I met her, management and the director of student affairs had already investigated him because of a set of unacceptable behaviours on campus. Disciplinary sanctions had been imposed on him. Alanis, who clearly had been threatened, was distressed that the university had failed to adequately respond to her concerns and needs. She feared that this student would contact her again in one form or another, which, in fact, he did do. Although the director informed her that the university had resolved the situation (without any consultation with her about her experience), she had never been given any details about the conditions under which the student had been allowed to continue his studies and, more specifically, the conditions that had been set out concerning his harassment of her. Consequently, she could not return to the director should the student breach the latter conditions because she did not have the relevant information. The director of student affairs maintained that the details of any disciplinary action were confidential.

In my view, this stance conflicted with the university's sexual harassment policy and its mission statement. Although conflict among university policies may not be unusual, Alanis's situation does raise important questions about a complainant's right to information about disciplinary action that imposes conditions concerning her/his safety. Although university policies may not explicitly address this issue, sexual harassment advisors employed in staff positions often do develop informal practices that ensure that the complainant does receive such information. In this case, the academic vice-president did respond to my plea and provide Alanis with the pertinent details. While the incongruency among policies is concerning, what distressed me was that the entire handling of Alanis's situation demonstrated an insensitivity to her lived experience and a paucity of knowledge and understanding of sexualized harassment. During the investigation by the university of the offending student's actions, neither Alanis nor I were ever consulted despite the existence of a sexual harassment policy, nor had she been referred to a sexual harassment advisor. Our encounter with the university institution during our efforts to unearth an appreciation of the effects of the harassment and concern for her well-being left us with a deep sense of betrayal and bitterness. *Unfreeze it.*

It was not only in this situation that the university institution showed its paternalist character but an accumulation of separate incidents that chupacabraed my energy to push for meaningful change. Yet, that episode was enough, in and of itself, for me to lose faith and question the value of labouring in such an institution. I could not assure this woman that the university had her best interests in mind or that it would do whatever it could to create a safe environment for her within the bounds of its capacity and control. Instead I agreed with her that it would seek to protect itself and serve its own self-interests and leave us both out on a limb. Unanswered emails, orders from above to comply, the illusion of a commitment to do justice and equity. That situation of sexual harassment slid up against all the other affronts to form a raw mass of soreness. *Unfreeze it.*

That specific encounter with the university institution brought about a quickening, a hardening of some part of me. Given those other incidents, why did I, in advocating for Alanis, so naively believe that we would be seen and heard? In her article "In the Way of Peace: Confronting 'Whiteness' in the University," Patricia Monture-Angus discusses her struggle to secure tenure at the University of Saskatchewan, the consequence of a structural issue about what constitutes good native studies scholarship. Living in the way of peace, she clarifies that "It is the violation of the relationship that I have experienced as the harm" (Monture-Angus 2001: 39). Once the relationship has been violated, and then over and over again, what hope is there for repair? The harm that violates us asks, in turn, that we violate ourselves, and this we must refuse.

At a meeting of the sexual harassment committee with the director of student affairs and a member of the administration, a feminist colleague and I ask to see a copy of the training manual for residence dons in order to review what education they receive about sexual harassment and sexual assault on campus. Several students had come forth with grave concerns about how sexual assault in residence was handled. The director tells us that he will see if he can circulate this information. No one else present speaks to support our request. Surely this information is public and surely dons should have relevant and up-to-date information on community services and supports for students. After a man had sexually assaulted female students on campus, the university sent out a campus-wide email in that kind of discourse that normalizes such behaviour, inferring that it is the work of a pervert. *Unfreeze experience*. Rather than a discourse affirming women's human right to freedom of movement and the steps the university would take to improve conditions on campus, women were admonished to not go out alone, in effect policing us as women and reinforcing the myth that most sexual assaults are committed by strangers.

Under paternalism, I suppose that my duty is to be grateful for the privilege of belonging to such a prestigious institution. But I do not feel grateful. In my interactions with the university as an entity and personages within it, currents of infantilization, condescension and patronization run through gesture, gaze and discourse. Strategically placed individuals, usually men but not always, diligently uphold the law of the father, withholding, judging, devaluing, invalidating. They take up the work of policing feminist women and other rabble rousers, of keeping us in line with an arsenal of weapons such as refusing to respond or casting aside constructive criticisms of existing policies and procedures. These clones of the father, and they do have his sanctioned power, also feel licensed to mete out judgements of our psychological states, that perhaps we are too angry, emotional, revengeful, pushy or simply expect too much. *Unfreeze it*. Even among people who identify as liberal or progressive, too much critical analysis and calls for action that rock relations of power easily slide into an assessment of colleagues as possessing "poor coping skills" or "not a tough enough skin."

Unfreeze experience. Give life to its words. During the time I knew Alanis, I had the most horrible nightmare. *I was inside the sacristy of a Catholic church, where the priests ready themselves for mass. Watching from behind a thick velvet wine-coloured curtain, I saw a dead man inside a small glass casket. A priest entered the room and walked over to the casket. I could not see what he did with the cadaver but the thing was now alive, yet dead. When the priest in charge came into the room, the other priest pretended that he was putting things into a drawer. When they had both gone, the side of the glass casket slowly opened and the shrivelled, sinister thing started to climb out. He emerged, carrying a bloody sword. I watched in absolute horror.*

Paternalism binds and fetters. Powerlessness, as well as the need for affirmation, is patriarchally and institutionally produced. As a sexual harassment advisor navigating the narrows between the institution's manoeuvrings and faculty and student needs, I often felt soiled by dirty, grasping hands. Perhaps the feeling of dirtiness emanates from childhood efforts to help that I have judged to be pitifully inadequate. Perhaps it is a sense of collusion that plagues me or doubt about my own integrity or capacity to act in ethically sound ways, both, I think, generated by the institutional context and dynamics. As Deborah Keahey aptly observes, "It's just that too often the very environment of the work undermines the work being done. When the text and the context come at you from opposite frequencies they just cancel each other out" (2003: 50). While there are no clean and pure oppositional positions, where is the line where accommodation to the system begins to erode integrity? As the years pass, I fear that my resistance will be weakened and worn away to nothing and that my responses will become limited to those bland, non-committal lines that I recognize in others.

Paternalism, Patriarchal Violence and Insidious Traumatization

Dreams do dream us. *During that year I dreamed of being locked up in old hospitals, decrepit buildings, and prisons that were damp, dirty, junk-filled and claustrophobic. In one, I dreamed that I was travelling happily along a country road with Linden and suddenly the road narrowed, coming to a dead end. In front of me stood a military compound from which a man emerged and told me that we had to go with him. We walked through tunnels, gigantic buildings, open spaces and more tunnels, and all the time I feared being separated from Linden, who was becoming more and more agitated and afraid. Then the man announced that he was taking us to an emergency shelter that did not accept companion animals. "No," I said, "No, I cannot be separated from her." She was cowering, looking up at me, terrified, and I thought "I will have to stay awake the whole night long to be superhypervigilant, to make sure that he will not steal her from me." My worst thought was that he would hurt her and I would be powerless to stop it.* This series of dreams confirmed that when the workplace, as a conduit for energy that could be, that should be, life giving, fills you with anguish, something's got to give. Yet, I labour daily to breathe life into spaces and put something else, however small, however different, in its place.

In her analysis of her experience of paternalism, Susan Heald asserts: "The demand to belong to the university *as it is* and support the dominant views denies those of us who imagine and/or work toward a *different* university the right to speak or be seen" (1997: 42–43). In unequal relations of power, the unspoken expectation is that management and subordinates will strive to "understand one another" (43). However, this stance, anchored as it is in the gaze of management, assigns those in lesser positions the weight of responsibility for this striving. Rather than a failure to understand one another, Heald suggests: "It is a question of not being *seen*" (43). In her case many relevant issues, including her sexual orientation and daily struggles with incest memories triggered by workplace events, could not be made visible in the quest to be seen.

For women in academia who have experienced such forms of patriarchal violence, "paternalism… itself inherently abusive," intersects with experiences of abuse and violence to re-evoke and exacerbate them (Heald 1997: 43). In fact, the modes of power operating in the university institution replicate the very dynamics of oppression,

> denying that the abuse is taking place, denying responsibility for it, requiring/ expecting the ongoing performance of normalcy, the denial of your reality, the refusal of the right or space to speak, the creation of a culture in which your speaking can only ever be misunderstood, be wrong. (44)

The paternalist university thus provides an endless arena not only for the enactment of abusive relations but also for the mobilization of the effects of previous violation contained within the flesh.

As Bonnie Burstow clarifies in "Toward a Radical Understanding of Trauma and Trauma Work," systemic oppression and trauma are intricately connected in complex ways. Paternalist relations constitute and compound

> what Root (1992) called the insidious traumatization involved in living our everyday lives in a sexist, classist, racist, ableist, and homophobic society: the daily awareness of the possibility of rape or assault, the daily struggles to stretch insufficient wages so that the family eats, encountering yet another building that is not wheelchair accessible, and seeing once again in people's eyes that they do not find you fully human. (2003: 1308)

The forms of power that the paternalist university employs to manage us evoke long memory traces that reach from the past into the present and leave the imprints of fresh incursions upon the skin. Inscribed on the body, they break upon the pulse of life. The violence of systemic inequalities continually severs our connections to ourselves and others, tearing at the seamlessness so difficult to experience in the world.

In the university institution, exposing our differences including experiences of patriarchal violence, doubts, confusions, needs and even dreams of a better world is indeed a risky undertaking, creating an opening for the pathologization of difference.

> Paternalism asks us to accept that father knows best, that the interests of the institution supersede those of individuals, and to deny our own implication in power relations…. Paternalism pathologises difference, and pathologisation asks us to accept responsibility for all this — it is, somehow, our fault. (Heald 1997: 43)

Yet remaining silent about unjust situations and failing to acknowledge the accumulated effects of oppression is also costly and sated with shame, rage and crazy-making. In a society that still denies racism as "the rule rather than the exception" (Razack 2001: 52), questions whether women who have been raped were really raped at all, settles the blame on those "different" from the white

Anglo-Saxon Christian majority, "to keep your inadequacies and differences hidden is, at least for abuse survivors, to hook back into the shame and need to hide that abuse fosters.... Paternalism and pathologisation both erase us and ask us to erase ourselves" (45). In this process, all the structural injustices, abuses of power and patriarchal violence inscribed on the body are erased by the deadening, unseeing gaze.

Well-founded fears exist that difference will be seized upon as evidence of inadequacy, incompetence or inferiority. As Chandra Mohanty points out, in liberal education differences such as gender and "race" are also often problematically conceptualized only in terms of personal or individual experience.

> The formulation of knowledge and politics through these individualistic, attitudinal parameters indicates an erasure of the very politics of knowledge involved in teaching and learning about difference. It also suggests an erasure of the structural and institutional parameters of what it means to understand difference in historical terms. (1994: 153)

As a feminist I choose to speak about my personal and political experiences and analyses in the classroom. Sometimes such openness seems like a rash and questionable pedagogy, making myself vulnerable to the pathologization of difference, even though such pedagogical choices are a conscious way to resist discourses and relations of power.

Resistance in Academe

In my story, too, like that of Susan Heald, "nothing happened" (Heald 1997: 45), only that I as a female employee was disgruntled: a magnet, a touchstone, a chain reaction, a spontaneous combustion. For some of us in academia, though, these experiences are the norm (The Chilly Collective 1995; Luther, Whitmore and Moreau 2001). How do I continue in this place? Comfort and sustenance does come from knowing that my resistance feeds into, and is sustained by, others' collective efforts to resist and create, both organized and informal, within the university. I do know that I connect with people who turn me back to myself long enough to feel new energy and renew my faith in self and others. Another's integrity, words, writing, flow into me, and we restore each other. Solidarity can only exist if I try to own and live my wholeness and vulnerability in the space of my social location, what Keith Louise Fulton calls "an imaginary, theoretical name for how we live our lives" (2003: 153). In dominant discourse that never speaks of the violence done and then undone in disappearing acts, what else must I now know about myself and how can I continue in individual and collective struggle to resist and create something else against patriarchy's desire to erase and forget?

What must I know to resist the attempts to reinscribe patriarchal violence on my body? Reinscription is made easier by disillusionment and dashed hope, re-evoked with each enactment. In this spiral I must refuse and reframe scripts that ascribe dissatisfaction and resistance to "poor coping skills" or "a not tough enough skin."

> Survivors of violence who work in the university, I want to suggest, may be like the canary in the mine shaft. What is intolerable to us may seem like a minor annoyance to others, at least at first. There is much pressure to fade quietly away, taking our experiences up as personal inadequacies, learning to cope better with the world as it is. For feminists, the university is just one of the many sites where "the world as it is" is simply not good enough. Some can "cope" better than others, but "coping" means accepting a set of conditions which make our lives and our work simultaneously difficult and invisible. (Heald 1997: 46)

A fierce diligence is required to continually name those ties that bind and fetter from the outside and discern how they gain purchase by feeding on those on the inside. The system's modes of surveillance turn in upon the body, occupying the organs, breath and sight. Self-surveillance forestalls the recognition of disrespect, lessening the blow only for the moment but never for the long term. When old patterns rooted in need, lack and want automatically overtake my body, I must ask what hides behind them and assuage it with poetic language.

My social faith still believes that everyday acts of individual and collective resistance matter for self-respect and for signing to others that which affronts dignity; however, they do not make me whole. Drawing on the work of James Scott, Jeffrey Rubin (1995) claims that such contestations in righting the world are necessary for further resistance and contribute to the construction of counterhegemonies and multiple forms of resistance that challenge, chip away and remake power structures. Do my acts of resistance, either alone or with others, contribute in any way to changing power relations? Is it possible that some or all of these acts only reinforce the power they resist? Beyond speaking to and engaging with power, how do they add to or engender broader changes in the university institution? I want to believe that my indignation and demands chip away at power, add to the sum of individual and collective acts of resistance, and nurture grounds for other forms of political action (Rubin 1995). But these are grand claims and what if they do not?

I refuse to pathologize my responses to oppression but I do not know how to measure their effects. Nonetheless, acts of resistance in the negotiation of daily lives "suffused with domination... can be both limited in their immediate effects and far-reaching in their meaning and long-term consequences" (Rubin 1995: 252–53). Sometimes the frontier between resistance to specific unjust situations and efforts to deal with the cumulative effects of oppression become liquid in time and place. Then the clarity of my acts of resistance becomes muddled and muddied. How can I more astutely analyze both my personal narrative and the operation of power to better wield my own and contribute to mounting more finely tuned collective strategies for change?

How do I stand in front of the not-unto-life force and use my sensitivity to life in the service of, rather than experience it as a liability in, this environment? How can I use it as something valuable to read the male-cultured world of the university and its surrounds, to act from a freer place rather than one determined by survival? To read with a just and critical eye is to be called upon to act in a hostile environment. It calls attention to oneself. Is it possible to remain open without forfeiting compassion, yet become less permeable so that the erasures of the institution do not pass so easily through the cells of my skin? How can I harden myself without losing tenderness? How do I develop a shield, like Deanna Troi, to ward off violent erasures?

In desperate times I imagine academia as a path to freedom that will help me understand my needs and how to flourish. The gift that permits sensitivity and compassion is the same one that allows demeaning power to penetrate my sensibilities. With more perspicacity, can I carve out with a firmer hand and eye a space of dignity and safety through sensings, intuition and instinct? In this culture that fractures us as human beings, how do I claim my entire self, refusing to abandon, cut off and repress those aspects so necessary for life? As daunting as the task is, I will practice Keith Louise Fulton's counsel: "Everything that I do, I must do differently to embody my idea of a university" (2003: 153), "where each act mends, restores, and transforms the world" (Butler and Rosenblum 1991: 183). The terms burnout and self-care are tossed about in social work like juggling balls, but what do they offer, individualized as they are? Self-care must be a social practice of caring about and for self and others, creating networks of support and collectivizing meaning-making about our lives in academia in order to make a feminist difference.

Closing Reflections

Unfreeze experience and give life to its words. In understanding my experience in the university institution, a political framework of struggle is still very much needed. Meaning-making is a political project that entails learning to read the languages of justice and solidarity. In the feminist endeavour to make change, "collectivist knowledge production, solidarity, coalition building and a politics of resistance" are foundational practices (Bonisteel and Green 2005: 25). I now know that an important piece of these foundational practices is to politically understand how institutional structures, systemic inequalities and power relations intersect with personal histories that include insidious traumatization and patriarchal violence. Since memory traces of past experiences are wrought into muscle and fibre, they can pervade present experiences of injustice and inequity, enabling patriarchal power to gain more purchase through fear and self-doubt.

And so, in this kind of learning, my dreams dream me back to me in recurrent symbols. I have always been partial to turtles, and in Costa Rica years ago I was blessed with seeing a leatherback lay her eggs on a beach in the light of a November moon. I often dream of restlessness and unsettledness. *In one dream I was on a tropical shore and in the next moment I was "home" in the Maritimes, to and from, back and forth. As I walked with friends on the tropical shore they exclaimed, "Look at those turtles!" When I turned to look, I barely caught a glimpse of them. Then back "home" I walked the banks of a river with a friend and she said "Hey look, a turtle!" Delighted to see one, I heard a woman's voice say: "You've got to integrate the restlessness and the desire for home." Just before I left for Costa Rica for my retreat, I dreamt that I was going to see my friend Dellanira and I was taking my little girl to see her. Looking at me intently, she seemed exceptionally wise for an infant. I felt a great love and responsibility for her in this dream so solemn and serene. When the small Sansa plane began to land, I could see the beautiful long wave rich coast with leatherback turtles starting their slow, laborious return to the sea.*

Note

I would like to thank feminist colleagues for their feedback on this essay and the Social Sciences and Humanities Research Council of Canada for funding to pursue research on the interplay between the personal, the professional and the political.

Chapter 7

Representing Victims of Sexualized Assault

Linda Coates and Penny Ridley

How victims are represented has broad socio-political implications, including repercussions for therapeutic intervention. In this chapter we first argue for reclaiming the term "victim" to indicate that a wrong was done against another person and that it must be righted. Then we explain how accounts that conceal or ignore victim resistance, conceal violence and obfuscate perpetrator responsibility make it possible to blame and pathologize victims. We show how victims are represented in therapy articles, having analyzed 257 representations from twenty-nine published therapy articles for whether they presented the victim as passively affected by the violence (effects-based representations) or as actively responding or resisting the violence (response-based representations). Victims were overwhelmingly represented as "affected," that is, as passive, damaged and deficient. Finally, we present a detailed analysis of a case study excerpt to show how the account accomplishes a representation of the victim as an affected being and some problems with such an account. We argue that the acknowledgement of victims as active agents who resist the violence perpetrated against them is necessary to accurately understand violence and perpetrator responsibility and to stop victim blaming.

A central premise of this current study is that language is not a neutral medium for the transmission of information about reality but socially constitutes and transforms reality into versions or accounts. Language is central to virtually every response or intervention into violence. Professional therapists do not "objectively" identify or diagnose the problem to be worked on so much as they transform accounts of violence into suitable objects to which to respond (Davis 1986; Wade 2000). The identified problem becomes the focus of legal or psychotherapeutic action. Thus, the language used in therapy sessions not only illustrates current socio-historic trends and understandings about victims of violence, it also formulates them. It is through analyzing the language or discourse that we see social practices such as therapy in action.

A quick perusal of dictionaries, victimology journal articles and the Canadian Criminal Code reveals substantial similarities among definitions of "victim" of violence. These definitions typically require a person to have experienced "harm," "suffering" or "injury," for example, a "person or thing injured or destroyed" (Oxford Dictionary of Current English 1993), "the first ingredient for victim status is the presence of harm, suffering or injury" (Burt 1983: 262), "a victim is any individual... harmed or damaged" (Birkbeck 1983: 270) or "a person to whom harm was done or who suffered physical or emotional losses as a result of the offence" (Canadian Criminal Code: 1985: 485).

Calling someone a "victim" seems to be an unproblematic expression of common sense. A person who committed an act of violence necessarily harmed or violated another living being — often in a manner that inflicted immense physical and emotional pain. In this light, labelling someone as a victim could be seen as an act of solidarity against such injustices. Miers (1983) articulates this position very clearly in his article on criminal injury compensation:

> The process of defining someone as a victim involves an expression of values about his suffering and our reactions to it. To call someone a victim is to attach a social label to him; it is to acknowledge that his suffering is undeserved and is a proper occasion for extending sympathy for mobilizing the institutional and other arrangements that have been made to alleviate his kind of suffering. (Miers 1983: 209)

Yet, within this very article, it becomes clear that rather than a gesture of solidarity, being ascribed the status of victim is more often an act of marginalization. For example, not all victims of violence are entitled to this "mobilization" of aid. Criminal injuries compensation policies specifically exclude those victims who can be judged as belonging to particular social categories. Among those who are or have been excluded are women who had been assaulted by their husbands or boyfriends, children who had been assaulted by their parents and people who had been judged on the "basis of character" or "way of life" to have "precipitated" or "deserved" the violence inflicted against them. Such negative attributions about victims appear to be common; for example, victims are frequently criticized for having "a victim mentality" (meaning that the person's interpretations of someone's actions as hostile were incorrect) or being "a *real* victim" (meaning that the person is inappropriately dwelling on the many difficulties facing them). We see in these statements totalizing negative representations; it is as if having been subjected to violence now fully constitutes the victimized person's identity. It is as if being victimized results in a deficient person. Moreover, victim-blaming theories that posit that persons precipitate their own victimization have been central in the development of victimology (c.f., van Dijk 1999). Clearly, being ascribed the status of victim is not uniformly positive.

Some people have attempted to eliminate the negative characteristics or blame by denying their status as victim. For example, a poster from the 1985 International Women's Peace Conference featured a picture of a woman with the large caption, "No victim I." Women who have been raped or assaulted in other sexualized ways who deny their victimization can also be understood as resisting or avoiding negative social responses and exerting as much control as possible in their circumstances. By denying that she suffered sexualized violence, a woman can avoid others treating her as exaggerating the situation, lying, having caused the rape, wanting to be raped, being mentally disordered or doomed to experience long-term psychological symptoms. At the broader social level, many women use the term "survivor" instead of "victim." However, such name changes are unlikely to be widely successful in preventing the ascription of negative characteristics to victimized persons unless the underlying logic of and our role in creating such representations have been critiqued and understood. Some name changes may even be used to support negative stereotypes about persons who have been victimized. For example, a Crown prosecutor said that she opposed the use of the term "survivor" because she felt that those who used it were exaggerating the degree of danger and harm they suffered, as well as their inability to stop the violence. "You survive a plane crash," the prosecutor said, "not spousal assault." The fact that men inflict extreme violence on and even murder their spouses was ignored by this person, who is supposed to be a victim advocate and may someday become a judge.

In this chapter, we have chosen to use the term victim because we want to reclaim its meaning of indicating that a person was harmed, that violence is wrong and that victims must be supported rather than undermined. By itself, this reclaiming of the term victim is insufficient: victim-blaming attributions rely upon misrepresentations that ignore or conceal victim resistance, conceal violence and obfuscate perpetrator responsibility (the four operations of discourse). These misrepresentations tend to formulate the victim and perpetrator as affected beings but with different consequences: victims are blamed whereas perpetrators are excused. Below, we use the Interactive and Discursive View of Violence and Resistance to critique current understandings of violence and pose alternative representations (Coates and Wade 2004, 2007; Coates, Todd and Wade 2003; West and Coates 2004). Some of the main tenets of this framework are that violence is a unilateral and interpersonal act that is best understood in context; violence is deliberate; victims resist violence; and representations of violence are critical for violence research and intervention. Our position is that misrepresentations of victim resistance, violence and perpetrator responsibility lead to and support victim blaming.

Victim Resistance

Most psychological theories about violence and explanations of victim behaviour are effects-based (Wade 2000). The underlying assumption in these theories, including socialization theories, learned helplessness theories and cycle of violence theories, is that the victim is an affected being. She is cast as passively accepting violence which then triggers or exposes psychological deficiencies or disorders. Such theories seem plausible as long as they are *not* examined from a language and social interaction perspective. When such a perspective is used to examine the behaviours of both victims and offenders in context and in sufficient detail, it becomes apparent that victim resistance is ubiquitous. In fact, we argue that whenever individuals are badly treated, they resist (Brown 1991; Burstow 1992; Hydén 1999; Kelly 1988; Reynolds 2001; Wade 1995b, 1997, 2000; Zemsky 1991). Wade (2000: 95) suggested that resistance takes many forms:

Virtually any mental or behavioural act through which an individual attempts to expose, withstand, repel, stop, prevent, abstain from, strive against, impede, refuse to comply with, or oppose any form of violence or oppression, from disrespect to overt abuse, or the conditions that make such acts possible, may be understood as a form of resistance. Further, any attempt to preserve or reassert one's dignity, to imagine or establish a life based on respect and equality on behalf of one's self or others, including any effort to redress the harm caused by violence or other forms of oppression, represents a de facto form of resistance.

This statement regarding the scope of resistance is not definitive: Resistance is identified less by its physical form than it is by the meaning and situational logic of the actions from the victim's point of view.

Perhaps the most striking evidence of the ubiquity and significance of victims' resistance may be perpetrators' elaborate efforts to conceal and suppress it (Scott 1990). If victims were passive, perpetrators would not attack them when they were alone or isolated. Instead, perpetrators know that victims will resist and so they anticipate that resistance and take steps to overpower or conceal it. For example, rarely does a teenaged boy grab a girl's breasts or genitals in front of teachers, her six-foot father or police officers. Instead, anticipating that she will resist by calling out for help, he waits until she is alone or in the presence of people who are unlikely to help her, for example, his friends. When he grabs at the girl, if she knocks his hands away, he might grab her wrists and pin her arms so that she can not move them. If the girl then attempts to free herself by jerking her body back, he takes action to prevent her from escaping. For example, he might drag her down to the ground so she cannot run away. If someone could be in hearing distance, and she is crying out, he might push her face into the ground so that her cries will be muffled. Perpetrators also know that victims will oppose their actions after the assault has ended; therefore, they actively discredit victims, present their actions as mutual, carefully project positive public images and engage in a wide range of other concealing behaviours.

Victims must consider the very real possibility that the perpetrator will inflict further violence, ranging from relatively mild censure and loss of privileges to extreme brutality, to any open acts of resistance. Consequently, open attempts by the victim to stop the violence, prevent the violence or re-assert her dignity are the least common form of resistance (Burstow 1992; Kelly 1988; Scott 1990). Instead, where power inequities exist, resistance at the interpersonal level tends to be covert—that is, concealed or disguised. Victims, for example, may go limp during an attack in an attempt to minimize the severity of the violence exerted against them. Victims may seem to be passive but will in fact be engaging in prudent resistance. For example, in the movie *The Color Purple*, while publicly appearing to be deferential to her abusive husband, the main character spits covertly in his glass before giving him a drink. In extreme circumstances, the only possibility for the realization of resistance may be in the privacy afforded by the mind (Wade 2000). For example, victims have described mentally removing themselves while being raped to prevent the perpetrator from "getting into their minds," mentally saying snappy comebacks to insults or imagining a life without violence.

We argue that recognition of resistance, that is, that victims are acting upon the world rather than only being acted upon, is vital to an accurate understanding of the victim, the perpetrator and violence itself.

Concealing Violence

Research has shown that the severity, incidence and magnitude of violence against women is routinely concealed and minimized (Brownmiller 1975; Burt 1991; Clark and Lewis 1976; Coates 1997; Coates and Wade 2004, 2007; Ehrlich 2001; Ehrlich 1998; Estrich 1987; Gunn and Linden 1997). Sometimes, representations reduce or conceal the magnitude of the force used in the assault. For example, saying that "he pushed her and she fell to the ground" implies far less force than "he knocked her to the ground." The severity of the assault is often reduced by misrepresenting the acts as outside of the realm of violence, for example, rather than saying "he raped her" violence is frequently concealed by using terms that conveyed that the assault was bothersome (e.g., "molest"), an act of affection (e.g., "fondle"), playful (e.g., "it was a game") or sexual (e.g., "he had sex with her"). In fact, Lamb (1991: 250) found that academic articles on violence so effectively removed acts from the realm of violence that they "rarely projected an image of a man harming a woman."

A pervasive technique of concealing violence is to mutualize it, that is, to cast the victim as freely engaging in actions with the perpetrator (Coates and Wade 2004, 2007). For example, to describe a man grabbing a woman, holding her head still, forcing his mouth on hers and slobbering on her mouth as "they kissed" or even "he kissed her" is to mutualize it. Mutualizing descriptions misrepresent the nature of the social interaction by concealing the nature of the act and the agency of the perpetrator and the victim. Mutualizing descriptions place the acts within the domain of non-violence (e.g., sex, recreation), where the perpetrator and victim are co-agents, co-actors or co-participants. Perpetrators are not portrayed as acting upon and against the will and well-being of the victim but instead as acting with her. She becomes a partner in the joint activity. Even though the victim is cast as a participant in mutualizing descriptions, she is still assumed to be an affected being. Particularly in cases of sexualized assault, the victim is typically assumed to be passively participating. Her actions that do not fit the misrepresentation as mutual are routinely left out of the accounts or reformulated (Davis 1986). In this way, the inconsistency between the representation of the act as mutual and her actual actions are concealed. For example, accounts that describe assaults as "they were kissing" rarely include descriptions of how the victim was trying to turn her head away, crying to convey harm and protest, stiffening her body so that he had trouble pulling her close or holding her mouth rigidly closed to prevent him from sticking his tongue in her mouth. Describing an assault where a boy grabbed a girl's genitals and breasts as "they were engaged in horseplay" does not include a clear description of how the girl slapped his hands away, tried to run away or called out for help. In these accounts, how the perpetrator anticipated and overcame the victim's resistance may never come up for consideration. For example, the fact that the teenaged boy grabbed the girl's wrists after she slapped him, dragged her down to prevent her from running away and pushed her face into the ground so that her cries would be muffled are not only missing in mutualizing accounts, they are pre-emptively rendered out of place. Accounts that mutualize violence do not fully represent the extent of violence against the victim, and do reproduce or support assumptions about the passive, affected victim (effects-based representations). Two separate studies found the use of these representations to be associated with perpetrators receiving lower sentences (Coates et al. 2005; West and Coates 2004).

Obfuscating Perpetrator Responsibility

Researchers have found that responsibility for violence against women is routinely obscured in newspapers, men's magazines, academic journals, the judicial system and therapy programs, even when women are murdered (Berns 2001). Linguistic techniques such as passive voice ("she was hit by John"), avoidance of agency ("she was raped") and nominalization (e.g., "wife battery") have been identified as obfuscating perpetrator responsibility (Bohner 2001; Coates, Bavelas and Gibson 1994; Henley, Miller and Beazley 1995; Lamb 1991; Lamb and Keon 1995; Penelope 1990; Trew 1979).

One way in which perpetrator responsibility is obscured is by representing their acts as non-deliberate. Often this is done by representing the perpetrator as being acted upon by an overwhelming force that is outside of his control (Coates 1997; Coates and Wade 2004, 2007; Marolla and Scully 1979; Morgan and O' Neill 2001; O' Neill and Morgan 2001; Sykes and Matza 1957). Common explanations that cast the cause of the assault as emotion (e.g., "he lost his temper," "he failed to control his emotions"), sexual drive ("I couldn't stop myself") or many other psychological phenomena ("I just lost it") all formulate the violence as non-deliberate by externalizing the postulated cause of the violence. The postulated cause is presented as if it were outside of the perpetrator's control. Similarly, explanations that represent perpetrators' actions as being mechanistically triggered by the victim, for example, "she pushed his buttons," "she lead me on," also deny the deliberateness of the perpetrator's actions. When perpetrators' actions are presented as deliberate, their actions are concealed as arising from non-violent motivations or intentions (e.g., sexual drive, stress or emotion) and used to mitigate attributions of responsibility. For example, in Coates' research a number of men charged with raping their wives defended their actions as deliberate attempts to save or "jump-start" their marriages.

However, when examined in context, it is clear that perpetrators of diverse forms of personalized violence (e.g., sexualized violence, wife-assault, physical assault and workplace harassment) employ a number of strategies before (e.g., isolation of the victim, ingratiating behaviour, lies), during (e.g., physical violence, threats, interrogation, humiliation) and after assaults (e.g., concealing or denying the violence, minimizing the victim's injuries, blaming the victim, refusing to accept responsibility) to suppress or overpower victim resistance. When these actions are taken into account, it becomes very difficult to view these acts as non-deliberate.

The fact that perpetrators frequently seek to deny the deliberateness of their actions and present themselves as affected beings seems to stem from an intention to mitigate responsibility legally, socially and interpersonally. But perpetrators are not the only ones who obfuscate their responsibility. Similar representations are common in public, legal and psychological discourse (Coates 1997; Coates and Wade 2004; Morgan and O' Neill 2001; O' Neill and Morgan 2001). In the legal system, the use of excusing attributions is systematically related to the perpetrator receiving a more lenient sentence, particularly when the act was described as non-violent and non-volitional (Coates 1997). In fact, the language used by judges to describe the perpetrator and his violent actions were better predictors of sentence than legal factors (e.g., severity of violence, duration of attack or alcohol or drug use). Moreover, court mandated counselling was consistently for the reformulated, non-violent cause, such as anger management, not the violence. Even when men receive counselling for violence, their violence is frequently excused in the therapy sessions as non-deliberate (Morgan and O' Neill 2001; O' Neill and Morgan 2001).

Victim Blaming

Our focus here is not the nature of victims' resistance, the concealment of violence or the obfuscation of perpetrator responsibility, but how the failure to acknowledge victim resistance, expose violence and clarify perpetrator responsibility makes it possible to blame and pathologize victims. In other words, these discursive operations make it possible to turn labelling someone a victim from an act of solidarity to an act of marginalization, even contempt. One can easily find examples of such victim blaming in diverse forms of socio-political and interpersonal violence, from European imperialism to sexualized assault. Strikingly, when victim resistance is mentioned, it is frequently characterized as deficiency or disorder. For example, slaves who resisted their imprisonment and mistreatment by escaping were diagnosed as having the mental disorder drapetomania, a condition that could be managed by beating the re-captured slaves (Gould 1996). Women who refuse to be content with their husbands' abusive behaviour are recast as clinically depressed or having a deficiency in character (Anderson 1999). Children who refuse to call the perpetrators "Dad" are reformulated as having attention deficit disorder or an attitude problem.

When violent behaviour has been uncovered, but the full extent of the violence and the perpetrator's responsibility for that violence is not clarified, consideration of the victim's resistance is typically displaced. In so doing, the question of how the perpetrator attempted to suppress that resistance cannot come up for consideration, and the deliberate and unilateral nature of violence remains concealed. Moreover, the displacement or concealment of victim resistance leaves victims open to being blamed for the violence perpetrated against them. If an act was not violent but mutual, then the perpetrator was not at fault; instead, the victim is making a false claim, is a woman scorned or has disordered thoughts.

Because resistance is so frequently overlooked, particularly in its more indirect and disguised forms, victims are generally represented in professional psychological discourse as passive recipients of abuse, that is, with effects-based representations. Victims are represented as socially conditioned individuals who seek out, submit to and participate in the violence that is forced upon them. The presumption that victims are passive then becomes the foundation for causal attributions that locate the source of victims' behaviour in their psychology alone. For example, people ask "What is it about the victim that would lead her to be accept the violence that she endures?" "Why does she stay with him?" "Why does she pick guys like that?" "How could she let that happen?" and "Why didn't she tell somebody?" Such questions shift the focus away from the perpetrator's social behaviour of violence to a postulated, individualized problem with the victim. The mind of the victim becomes the focus of theories and interventions (Maradorossian 2002; Todd and Wade 2003). The victim is viewed as mentally deficient or disordered. The mental deficiencies or disorders are typically viewed as arising from or triggered by the victim's endurance of current or past violation.

The assumption of victim passivity can be used as a pretext to discredit victims and call into question the veracity of their testimony regarding the nature of the acts at issue. For example, the legal defence of presumed consent or mistaken belief rested on the notion that a lack of open and persistent resistance is equivalent to consent. The apparent lack of resistance also lends credence to the suggestion that the offender was not fully responsible for the assault because the victim did not clearly signal her refusal (Coates 2004; Ehrlich 1998). However, once the nature and situational logic of the victim's resistance is elucidated, it becomes very difficult to take seriously the suggestion that the victim accepted the violence, wanted it to occur or was responsible for it. Thus, our view is that victim blaming will occur as long as victim resistance is not adequately recognized as a basic premise, the nature of violent behaviour is not adequately understood, the full extent of the violence not adequately exposed and the extent of offenders' responsibility not adequately clarified. In short, it is likely to continue as long as we use effects-based theories of violence.

While we have articulated the above position from research and clinical experience, a study had not been conducted to systematically investigate the representation of victims of sexualized violence in clinical literature. In order to address this gap, we analyzed published case-studies for whether they represented the victims as passive, that is, within an effects-based framework, or resisting, that is, within a response-based framework (Wade 1995b, 1997, 2000; Todd and Wade 2003; Todd, 2002a; Todd 2002b). We sought (a) to gather information about the relative frequency with which therapists represent victims using effects-based or response-based interpretative repertoire, and (b) to critique representations of victims of sexualized violence.

Method

Articles for analysis were located through a search of Psyclit for published case studies that contained the words "sexual assault" or "sexual abuse." The data had been previously gathered for a study on descriptions of sexual assault in which the first author had been involved. Articles that were included for analysis in the present study all met the following criteria: they (a) contained the phrases "sexual assault" or "sexual abuse, (b) described a case study (c) and contained descriptions of victims of sexualized assault. A total of twenty-nine professional case study journal articles were analyzed.

Five articles (17 percent) were randomly selected from the sample for the purpose of developing the system of analysis. This procedure was used to ensure that any patterns or findings from the study would not be unique to the cases used to develop the system of analysis (see Coates 1997). The system of analysis that was developed required the data to be analyzed in three stages: location of relevant sections of the articles for analysis, identification of time frame and analysis of function.

First, analysts identified all representations that referred to or described the mental or physical actions of sexualized violence victims for further analysis. General descriptions of victims or sexualized assault (e.g., "long term effects of child sexual abuse include..." or "this approach recognizes that sexual abuse during childhood has implications for one's sense of self..."), and descriptions that did not characterize the behaviour of the victim (e.g., "the sexual abuse began to take place before the victim's eighth birthday, not long after the family transferred from a country town to a coastal city") were eliminated from analysis. Descriptions that characterized sexualized violence as mutual (e.g., "she described her childhood sexual abuse experiences by her uncle which ranged from fondling to intercourse") were also excluded from analysis because they were investigated in other studies (Coates, 2000a, 2000b, 2000c; Coates, Bavelas and Gibson, 1994; Bavelas and Coates 2001; West and Coates 2004; Tatlock and Coates 2003).

Through this process, all representations located for analysis characterized the victim's mental or physical actions. The process of locating descriptions for analysis was highly reliable with independent analysts, one of whom was blind (i.e., did not know) to the position taken by the authors, agreeing 98 percent of the time. Reliability was assessed across 26 percent of the articles.

Second, analysts recorded whether representations described the victim or her actions during or after the assault. Representations that described the perpetration of violence and the victimized person's immediate responses to that violence were recorded as "during." Representations that focused on the victimized person after the assault (e.g., hours, days, weeks, or years later) were recorded as "after."

Third, the descriptions located in the first stage of analysis were re-examined to determine how they formulated the victim or her actions within the context of the case study (i.e., effects-based or response-based). Analysts answered a series of questions on a decision tree to aid them in deciding upon the function of the representations. Response-based representations were those that formulated (a) the victim as proficient or agentive (i.e., acting upon the world) or (b) her mental or physical actions as resisting, opposing or countering violence *in any way*. Effects-based representations were those that *clearly* formulated (a) the victim as deficient, passive or a mere object (i.e., acted upon) or (b) her actions as symptoms, abnormal or triggered by the violence.

The system of analysis developed from the subset of the data was then applied to the entire database. Inter-analyst reliability was assessed for 12 percent of the data. Overall reliability of the analysis of function for independent analysts, one of whom was blind to the position taken by the authors, was very high (97 percent agreement).

Results and Discussion

Two-hundred and fifty-seven representations were located for analysis. The majority of representations (90 percent) were effects-based. These descriptions interpreted the victimized person or her actions as passive, ineffectual, damaged or deficient and in doing so cast her as dysfunctional. Thus, even though we would expect therapists to use representations that indicate their solidarity with the victim, they used representations that marginalized victims. For example, one therapist stated: "B. learned the victim role well... B did not know any alternative but to live as a victim." This representation casts the victim as having been passively conditioned to play a part in the violence (see Coates et al. 2005 and West and Coates 2004 for a discussion of some of the problems with representing victims of violence as participants). Her actions are merely mechanistic behaviours evoked by her past experiences. The victim's actions are so problematically controlled by her past conditioning that she passively accepts being victimized: "[B] was a non-survivor, as shown by her helplessness to end the abuse." Moreover, this totalizing negative characterization of the victim as a "non-survivor" is explicitly connected to her "helplessness" in stopping the violence inflicted upon her. In doing so, the therapist shifts responsibility for the violence from the perpetrator to the victim. The word "helplessness" bolsters the construction of the victim as passive. The term connects to the theory of learned helplessness or the idea that chronic abuse results in passive acceptance. In this way, the possibility that the victim resisted, opposed or countered the violence does not come up for consideration. Likewise, the conditions that supported the perpetrator's violence against the victim, such as inequalities in physical and social power, are not used to interpret the victim's actions, including her inability to stop the perpetrator from being violent. Instead, the victim herself is held responsible for the violence, and her deficient, psychological make-up becomes the object of intervention.

While there was a plethora of representations that cast the victim as passively affected, there was a paucity of representations that cast the victim as actively responding. Only 10 percent of the representations cast the victim as proficient, functional and mentally healthy in some way. One therapist, for example, wrote: "P. over-scheduled herself, she linked this with her history: as a child, her over-commitment was a legitimate escape from the physical danger of being at home." Here the author represents the client as actively responding to the violence committed against her. She kept herself very busy which minimized her time at home — the place where she was most vulnerable to attack. In this way, the therapist constructed the client as volitional and strategic. However, the use of the terms "over-scheduled" and "over-commitment" reveal that the therapist interpreted the client's chosen strategy to be problematic. The therapist then construes "over-scheduling" to be the therapeutic problem to be addressed in the therapy. Once again, the therapeutic problem is removed from the social context within which it is occurring — that is, the experience of being violated — and placed in the mind of the victim. If the therapist had fully appreciated the client's behaviours as acts of resistance, the client would have been formulated as appropriately scheduling and committing her time. The therapist's reliance on an effects-based theory of violence results in the problem ultimately being with the victim's mind; she is cast as mechanistically repeating a maladaptive pattern of behaviour.

The majority of representations (73 percent) described victims' mental and behavioural actions in the aftermath of sexualized violence. Ninety-four percent of these representations were effects-based. In order to test the hypothesis that a therapist would more easily recognize a victim's active resistance to the perpetrator's violent actions when the resistance co-occurred with the violent actions, we further examined the representations of the victim or her actions during the actual assault. Of these representations, a significant majority (78 percent) still represented the victim's mental and behavioural actions as affected, that is, as passively acquiescing to the attack. Thus, even in a situation where it was reasonable to expect victim resistance (and even overt physical resistance), there was a dearth of response-based representations that conveyed accurate understandings and formulations of violence.

Therapists did not often switch between the two interpretative repertoires. Authors tended to consistently formulate the clients and their actions as affected throughout the entire article. However, authors of effects-based representations sometimes formulated victims as somewhat actively responding by adopting a "coping" mechanism. Nevertheless, rather than viewing the victim as truly agentive (i.e., acting upon the world by resisting or opposing the violence), she was still formulated as an object without true agency. Her actions were merely mechanistically triggered by the violence and cast as maladaptive, dysfunctional or insufficient. For example, one therapist stated that: "powerful and overwhelming emotions were encased in a wall of protection deep inside… [this] had been a functional and effective coping mechanism." Here, the therapist casts the victim as actively responding to the violence inflicted upon her by building a "protection wall" to cope with the violence. However, the "protection wall" was now judged to be dysfunctional, indicated here by the therapist's use of the past tense ("the wall had been functional"). Having evaluated the victim's response as dysfunctional, the problem was then placed inside the victim's mind, and she became the focus of the therapeutic intervention.

Case Study Excerpt

The following analysis of a case-study excerpt is used to more fully illustrate the local accomplishment of effects-based representations as well as their consequence.

> The incest trauma had resulted in a narcissistic injury and a regression to archaic modes of defence. M. seemed to lack effective internalized systems for the promotion and maintenance of self-esteem and a stable self-representation. She coped by experiencing her own emotions and other aspects of herself as outside the self-representation.

In this short passage, the therapist's representation relies heavily on imputed unobservables (internalized systems, self-esteem, stable self-representation) that work together to discursively create the client as (a) damaged by the assaults and (b) possessing an internal (mental) deficiency. In order to support this interpretation, the author first creates a linear-mechanical, cause-effect relationship between the client's victimization and her behaviour. The trauma "resulted" in injury and regression and so currently determines the client's behaviours. Her actions are further rendered as negative by the author's characterization of "narcissistic injury" and "regression." Notice too, that the injury is not physical or emotional pain, which arguably could be seen as a consequence of assault (the decision to show this pain or not, however, would not be an effect of the assault but a choice by an actively responding victim), but "narcissistic injury." The focus has become the inner workings of the client's mind rather than the interpersonal violence. In less than a sentence, the authors have established the victim as mentally damaged.

From a background of damage, it is then possible for the therapist (and readers) to accept that any implied actions by the victim (which are suggested by the phrase "modes of defence") are not deliberate and resourceful strategies but are flawed or dysfunctional repercussions of the damage caused by the assault. The therapist bolsters the position that the victim is deficient by the use of the word "archaic," which concisely characterizes the client's mental or behavioural actions as immature, outdated or obsolete modes of defence. In merely one full sentence, the victim has been constructed as damaged and her current behaviours as dysfunctional, that is, as a manifestation of the sexualized violence. The therapist has reformulated the client from having a situated external problem (her father committed acts of the sexualized violence against her) to having an internalized cause of the problems (i.e., "narcissistic injury" and "regression" resulting from the violence). The therapist then formulates a diagnosis based upon these imputed and internalized problems. The assault is reduced to a mere precipitating or triggering factor of the real internalized cause. The focus of the therapy becomes the aftermath of the violence. The importance of the sexualized violence has been identified in terms of its postulated effects on the victim. In contrast, the importance of the victim's subjective experience of sexualized violence and her responses to this violence have been precluded from consideration.

Next, the author draws upon these discursive constructions to further develop long-term victim deficiencies. The therapist asserts that the victim lacks the "effective internalized systems" that are necessary for the "promotion and maintenance of self-esteem" and "stable self-representation." The manifest implication of this sentence is that the victim chronically lacks self-esteem and stable self-representations.

The third sentence describes how the victim "coped" with the consequences of her deficits (i.e., missing internal systems) by "experiencing her own emotions and other aspects of herself as outside the self-representation." This sentence clearly illustrates the difference between coping and responding. The violence has caused the victim to be deficient and these deficiencies now cause her to have an abnormal self-representation with which she must cope. Her coping behaviour is a passive consequence of the effects of the violence and is not a strategy of resistance employed by the victim.

In this short excerpt, the problem that M. originally came into therapy with (i.e., the incest) was reformulated by the therapist into six internalized problems: two internal forms of damage (i.e., narcissistic injury and regression) and four internal deficiencies (lacking internal systems, poor self esteem, unstable self-representation and difficulties experiencing herself). The original problem had temporal limits — the client had been victimized by her father at a particular time and place, whereas the reformulated problem has no such physical or temporal limits. The client's deficiencies are represented in such a way that they could conceivably be a life-long condition.

General Discussion

Victims typically seek therapy because they are experiencing "problems in living." In representing victims and their actions, one also formulates the reason for these problems. There was a plethora of effects-based representations of victims and their behaviours in this data. In the case-studies analyzed, the therapists systematically represented the victim's physical, emotional or mental actions as symptoms or evidence of the damage, dysfunction or pathology created or activated by the perpetrator's violence. She was a victim: passive, damaged, deficient, unskilled, dysfunctional and even pathological. It was as if she was an object that was animated by the perpetrator when he committed violence against her and now needed to be re-animated by the therapist. The victim's status as object-to-be-activated was maintained throughout the articles analyzed.

In the effects-based representations, the ultimate cause of the victim's experience of difficulty was cast as personal deficiency and the problem was located in the mind of the victim. As illustrated in the case study excerpt, victims' experiences of violence and subjugation were relegated to the past, and therefore made less relevant to understanding the client's current problems in living. These representations discursively created a passive victim whose current actions were mere manifestations or mere effects of the violent force. The question, then, was why victims were still manifesting symptoms of this force when the sexualized violence had occurred in the past. The answer: she was psychologically damaged or had a pre-existing psychological deficiency that was triggered by the violence. She, or more precisely her mind, became the problem to be addressed. She was the ultimate reason she was experiencing problems in living — not any past or current violation or subjugation. In this way, therapists reformulated a social problem (violence) into an individualized one. The problem of violence became a problem in the victim's mind.

Also, effects-based representations separated the victim's actions from the social context within which they occurred. For example, when a victim gagged while telling the therapist about being orally raped, her actions were problematized as "puzzling fits" rather than clear communicative displays of what it was like to endure this sexualized violence. Imagine the smells, the taste, the feel of a man forcing his penis into your mouth and ejaculating. Imagine trying to breathe through this rape. Can there be a better way of communicating what it was like to be orally raped than gagging? Only by examining the victim's actions within context can we make sense of these actions. However, discursively constructing the victim and her actions as affected co-occurred with the therapist de-contextualizing the victim's past and current actions.

Importantly, not a single article analyzed consistently represented victims of violence in a way that would be in line with the Interactional and Discursive View of Violence and Resistance. A few therapists formulated victims of violence as proficient, skilled and volitional at some time or in some manner. But victims of violence were never represented as uniformly volitional, proficient or mentally healthy. Instead, the few response-based representations were drowned in a sea of pathologizing, effects-based discourse. Therapists used the experience of having endured sexualized violence to fully constitute the victim's identity and her actions. Thus, rather than an act of solidarity, ascribing someone the status of victim within the therapy case studies was an act of marginalization. Victims were weak, deficient "others" who needed to be fixed by the presumably strong, proficient therapists.

The widespread use of effects-based representations may, in part, be accounted for by its apparent focus on the harm inflicted by the perpetrator. In other words, therapists, academics and others may have adopted the practice of representing victims in effects-based terminology because it appears to evince the severity of the perpetrator's actions. However, these representations replaced a careful consideration of the perpetrator's violence and the victim's suffering with the construction of a passive victim who was psychologically damaged and deficient. In this way, victims and their behaviours, and not the violence itself, became problematized. The victim's postulated damage and deficiencies became the problem to be addressed in therapy sessions. In doing so, the widespread commission of violence against women escaped being identified as sufficiently problematic. If the victim were active and not passive, or proficient instead of deficient, she would have stopped the violence or not have been or continue to be affected by the violence. If she was not "maladaptive," "helpless," "anxious" or "predisposed" then there would not be a problem. Thus, the victim was not supported. Instead, these descriptions worked to simultaneously conceal violence, obfuscate the victim's resistance, blame and pathologize the victim and reduce the perpetrator's responsibility (see Coates and Wade 2004).

It is interesting to note that violent men who drop their wives off at therapy and instruct the therapists to "fix the bitch" are relying upon the therapists to utilize effects-based representations to support their violence (Wade 1997). They are counting on therapists to view the victims and not their violence as the problem warranting social intervention.

But what if we formulate victim's actions not as passive effects but as considered responses that resist, oppose or counter violence? Then these actions, such as gagging when describing being orally raped are not symptoms of pathology or deficiencies but evidence of health and proficiency (see Wade 2000; Weaver et al. 2005). Then, it is possible to view the victim's actions, which often seem extreme when examined in isolation, as continuing because she is demonstrating or communicating her refusal to be content with mistreatment. The problem for intervention would then remain the violence, and the therapist's role would become one of support and social activism.

If this position, as espoused in the Interactional and Discursive View of Violence and Resistance, has merit, then attempting to rid the client of actions of resistance that have been deemed to be problematic is analogous to treating starvation by eradicating hunger (Wade 2000). But hunger is not the problem; it is a healthy response to lack of food. In contrast, we can treat starvation by recognizing that a person's hunger is a sign of needing food and then provide her with food. We can approach her as an active, proficient, skilful and healthy person who has been violated and so could benefit from our support, not fixing. We could engage victims in discussions and write reports about victims of violence in such a way that violence is exposed, perpetrator responsibility clarified, victim resistance honoured and blaming or pathologizing of victims is contested.

It is important to state that we are not arguing that all therapists intentionally use these terms to conceal violence and blame victims. Effects-based representations are so common that they appear to be objective descriptions until carefully critiqued. It is not necessary to take an ideological position that embraces discrimination against women to produce and reproduce social injustice. Simply representing victims within the ubiquitous effects-based interpretative repertoire tends to support such injustice. Nor are we assuming that all therapists use these terms naively. Use of terms that ignore or reformulate victim resistance, conceal violence, excuse perpetrators and blame victims is frequently intentional, as is evidenced in the discourse of perpetrators and proponents of victim precipitation theories. The representations we use to describe victims and their actions have important implications for the promotion of social justice. We argue that accurate accounts of violence and victim resistance must be a focus of social intervention.

In this chapter, we report that representations of violence in therapy are overwhelmingly effects-based. Victims are represented as passive, damaged and deficient. We argue that recognizing victim resistance as it is accomplished *in situ* can be used to contest victim blaming. When the details of the victim's responses to and resistance against violence are acknowledged, it becomes difficult if not impossible to view the violence as mutual, the perpetrators actions as non-deliberate or the victim as wanting or putting up with violence. It becomes clear that psychological diagnoses about the mind of the victim are unnecessary; her actions do not need fixing. The social problem of violence needs to be addressed.

In our attempt to re-claim the term violence, we are taking the position that we cannot theoretically or practically simply "get past" victimization. We live in a social world where people will continue to commit violence against others, particularly those with less power or privilege. If we deny victimization, we will collude with the perpetrator in suppressing resistance and concealing violence. If victimization is not recognized, victims' responses will seem extreme and pathological. Victims will continue to be blamed, and the focus of intervention will continue to be the mind of the victim. We propose that we must elucidate victim resistance, expose violence and clarify perpetrator responsibility. In this way, we can support victims by contesting victim blaming attributions and recognizing the injustice committed against them. We can use the term victim to indicate solidarity, to recognize injustice and to commit to righting that injustice.

Section Four

Resilience/Identity Formation

Identity formation as resistance is not a new phenomenon. Cultural resistance to colonialism, often described as identity politics, continues to be spelled out by authors such as Gayatri Spivak (2008). But how do identity movements occur? Isn't identity an individual politic rather than a collective movement? The next four chapters provide some answers to these questions. Cultural forms of resilience and identity formation are evident in the discussions of queer identities (Lisa Passante), resistance to mothering (Debra Mollen), the underground movement of women fleeing abuse (Karen Rosenberg) and Aboriginal women's resistance to racist and sexist ideologies (Jean Toner).

New left strategies play a role in the changing political and cultural climate in which trans-identified persons lobby for recognition. The gay and lesbian movement was built on a collective sexual identity. It used strategies and political opportunities that were a result of legal rights granted to women and racial minorities. As a result, gender identity and sexual orientation identity borrows from collective action frames that protest against neo-liberal policies, although the case study herein is an individual example.

Drawing on political and cultural opportunities, and legal recognition of sexual minorities, transgender and transsexual persons have lobbied for legal and social recognition (Mathen 2004). New forms of cultural discourses and cultural spaces have opened up for trans-identified persons such as Nikki, an Aboriginal woman involved in the sex trade and in trouble with the law. Writing from her location as a social worker with probation services, Lisa Passante grapples with the difficult job of applying a transgender specific analysis to her pre-sentence report on Nikki. Sensitive to the triple oppressions Nikki lives as a female born, Aboriginal trans sex trade worker, Passante utilizes an equal rights framework informed by law and anti-discrimination legislation valuing a politics of identity and sexual minority advocacy. In advocating on behalf of trans issues the cultural context becomes important regarding the framing of human rights issues in Canada, the U.S. and internationally.

The context in which First Nations identity is lived must be contextualized within the long history of Canada's oppression, including appropriation of land, residential schooling, banning of cultural practices and discrimination in employment and daily life. This historical context lays the basis for grievances based on historical forms of systemic oppression (Ramos 2008: 55–70). In exploring the intersecting oppression of Nikki's trans, Aboriginal and sex trade identities, Passante raises awareness, informs new types of values and identities, forces a legal organization to acknowledge trans realities and poses a new type of grievance — that of gender identity.

Lisa Passante's method of becoming an ally to Nikki is a political act; it informs new ways of processing legal clients and has the additional effect of educating the very system within which she works. In so doing Passante utilizes the global women's movement's cultural innovation and strategizing to challenge the stigmatization of those who do not conform to gender-role stereotypes. Passante provides a strong ending to this journey, which links her advocacy to feminist global women's movement strategy, starting from the ground up, dealing with grievances and new social issues, informed by feminist and sexual minority ideologies of liberation and ending in education about new forms of values and identities as well as cultural innovation.

Debra Mollen opposes neo-liberal policies that simultaneously endorse re-production and stigmatize childfree women. In resisting the dominant discourse that all women want to be mothers, Mollen proposes a new form of grievance against pronatalist and heterosexist values. Informed by identity politics and the global perception of gender role conformity, pronatalism has a strong effect on gender identity development. Women's resistance to conformity challenges the stigma of being childfree. What makes this issue a global one is the fact that there are international restrictions on access to abortion and birth control. Pronatalist ideologies impact on many areas of women's lives globally. While society pushes women to reproduce by glorifying ideologies of romantic love and marriage, parenting is given limited support. For example, in Canada there is no national subsidized daycare program.

Karen Rosenberg takes on the narrative of law as a discursive practice of power and control in her legal advocate role. In utilizing the strategy of "being *with* the law," she supports battered women in the investigation of how one might re-cast struggles with male batterers in order to "play the game" and win in the legal realm. Rosenberg challenges neo-liberal policies that assume gender neutral-ity and the availability of legal protection. While many battered women fear the legal process, yet presume that law works, the reality is that, like sexual assault victims, many battered women and children experience secondary victimization through engagement with law. The women Rosenberg worked with have had to acknowledge that law does not provide sufficient protection to children at risk. In order to survive, women have needed to find everyday networks in isolation. In her role as a legal advocate, Rosenberg documents the harrowing experiences of battered women seeking to escape oppression by disappearing from the radar of abusive partners. Challenging neo-liberal stereotypes of the "good victim," who engages with legal practices, women on the margins are punished for resisting the all-encompassing sexist and racist practices of judicial systems.

Rosenberg documents that battered women and children are not only vic-timized by male batterers, they are also victimized by the very institutions they turn to for help, namely modern institutions such as law, medicine, psychiatry, police and courts. This chapter provides us with compelling evidence of the un-derground movement of women who have been failed by institutional responses to violence against women and children.

Jean Toner's research on Aboriginal women's experiences of addiction and recovery provides a counter-narrative to racist discursive practices in mainstream recovery groups such as Alcoholics Anonymous. The focus of her work is the stories of three Native American women who talk about their resistance to medical and neo-liberal individualizing and pathologizing healing processes. Toner points out that in the face of colonization, women who use are more likely disenfranchised and experience social and economic discrimination, physical confinement by law and racism in policing. First Nations women's addiction is therefore conceptualized as a form of resistance to assimilation requiring an analysis of the intersecting oppressions of race, class and gender. In focusing on race, class and gender, Toner challenges the stigmatization and pathologizing of Native women who use drugs. Contextualizing Aboriginal women's drug use within the historical experience of genocide, colonization and resistance, Toner sees Aboriginal women's drug use as a form of agency and resistance rather than an act of victimization. The stories women tell of their resistance to status oppressions such as the destruction of their language and cultural identity by forcing them into residential schools, provides a contextual basis for understanding their drug using choices. The "spirit killing" nature of colonizing practices leads Aboriginal women to challenge the Christian basis of Alcoholics Anonymous, to talk back and to pass on their culture. This allows for a shift in self-concept from that of victim to resistance to othering. Aboriginal women in recovery resist cultural forms of violence and use creative methods to resist power and control. Toner promotes new types of values about addicted women, suggesting that woman-focused sobriety needs to take into consideration cultural specificity and difference.

Chapter 8

Queer Dispositions

A Case Study in Trans-gressing the Limits of Law

Lisa Passante

The following case study documents my experience of researching and writing a pre-sentence report (PSR) about the life of a transgender woman named Nikki. I write as a queer woman and social worker employed on a contract basis for Probation Services from 2000–02 writing PSRs and co-facilitating in Winnipeg, Manitoba. This discussion of resistance begins with an overview of the purpose of a PSR and then moves to a description of the case involving Nikki. I include my personal reflections over time and provide my current responses to the case.

Resistance is enacted in a variety of ways. For example, by virtue of living as an openly transgender person, Nikki (originally Nickolas) enacted charge of her trans heart and body in space. Seeing that Nikki's trans woman identity would be considered a risk factor in a PSR, I enacted my own ability to resist — engaging my voice, advocating for Nikki as an ally and providing the court with transgender education. As a long-time volunteer and activist in Winnipeg's queer community, I see my individual actions as resistant knowledge-making and as part of the queer social movement occurring at the time.

I use "queer" as an umbrella term to refer to sexual and gender minorities, including gay, lesbian, bisexual, transgender, two-spirit, intersex, questioning and queer allies. I prefer the term sexual and gender minorities because it is less awkward than trying to be comprehensive in a subject area that is dynamic and shifting. As well, the term highlights that we are minorities in the dominant discourse of what I call heteronormality, which dictates that heterosexuality is the only way to be sexually or romantically in relation to one's biological sex and gender identity (Douglas 1990; Rich 1983; Payne 2002; Zita 1998).

In this discussion, an example of legal practices supporting normative or differing identities will be explored in the ways in which pre-court investigations and the writing of PSRs occur. As you read, keep in mind that

> Various equality advocates have lobbied for the addition of "gender identity" as a ground of protection under human rights legislation. In our ongoing research, discussions and consultations thus far, we have become increasingly aware of the importance of pursuing and supporting this legal reform, especially considering the multi-faceted and systemic nature of discrimination born of sexist, ableist and racist stereotypes, myths and norms — and the limitations of the existing and available grounds. "Gender identity" could offer protections to those who "fall through the cracks" of existing grounds. (NAWL 2003)

The Mandate of a PSR

Pre-sentence reports provide information to the court about a person's suitability for probation in the community. Probation originated as a movement "away from the traditional punitive and repressive approach to a more humanitarian one, which attempted to mitigate the harsh penalties of earlier laws." PSRs evolved out of "pre-court investigations," whose purpose was to define the individuality of the person facing charges (Department of Justice 2000: 1).

The court requests detailed information about individuals facing charges when it is unclear they will live lawfully in the community. If a person facing charges is deemed suitable for community living with supervision, the PSR makes recommendations to the court to assist in structuring safety for that person. Recommendations include prescriptions and prohibitions (e.g., attend counselling, abstain from alcohol and/or meet regularly with a probation officer). Dispositions such as fines, incarceration and absolute or conditional discharges are not under the purview of a PSR (Department of Justice 2000).

PSR information is gathered in a series of interviews by a probation officer or an "honorary" probation officer hired on a contract basis. These interviews include in-person meetings with the individual facing charges and in-person or telephone meetings with close friends, family members and professional/work or school contacts. Data are collected across a number of subject areas, including circumstances surrounding the offences, the offender's perspective of the offences, the impact on the victim if applicable, any previous offences, family background, relationships, education, employment, financial situation, personal and social factors and responses to previous correctional services (Department of Justice 2000).

The final report provides an assessment of the person's ability to live gainfully and lawfully in the community with probations supervision and of their likelihood to re-offend. The assessment is based on the literature of Andrews and Bonta (1994) and Bonta (1996) and on associated primary and secondary risk assessment measures used by Probation Services in the Province of Manitoba (Department of Justice 2000). The literature and measures use quantitative information from studies of offences, recidivism and treatment program evaluations. The most effective treatment and supervision plans include balance in the assessment of needs and risk — higher risk indicates more supervision (Bonta 1996).

The Case of Nikki

I met Nikki when she was in the process of moving from her transgender to transsexual identity. Nikki was a twenty-two-year-old Aboriginal woman who had recently been charged with communicating for the purposes of prostitution (three charges over a six-month period) and two charges of assault of a police officer (both charges on the same night) about six months after the last prostitution charge.

We knew that Nickolas had solicited in her trans identity (i.e., Nikki). In discussion with my supervisor at Probation Services, we agreed that I would be a good fit for completing this PSR because of my relative (yet still limited) knowledge and experience with trans issues. We anticipated that the court might require specialized information regarding trans issues in order to arrive at an informed, respectful and appropriate disposition. We were also concerned about where Nikki would be sent if an order for incarceration occurred. Trans women have encountered, at minimum, a misfit of institution and at worst, violence and discrimination if incarcerated with men. There would be different, but equally challenging, experiences fitting in if incarcerated with women. These include, for instance, what name to go by, pronouns, showering, bathroom use, sharing a cell and institutional paperwork.

I first met with Nikki at a residential substance abuse treatment centre. Nikki had openly been living her female identity for a year and a half and before that sporadically for years. All of the other residents knew her in her female identity and some knew of her trans identity. Nikki shared some details about her life.

Nikki stated that she felt badly about assaulting the police officers, indicating she was high on legal and illegal substances in an attempt to hurt herself. Nikki had no previous charges to the ones under review. Nikki had contact with her mother, her two younger siblings and her step-father (who she knew as dad). Nikki's biological father had been assaultive to her mother and the family and had left when Nikki was a toddler. In spite of that young age, Nikki remembered witnessing violence.

Nikki indicated Aboriginal identity and Canadian government Indian status. She grew up in a northern Ontario reserve community, cared for by extended family members. Her mother had a substance abuse problem but there were always aunties and uncles to visit when things were difficult. The family moved to Winnipeg for employment when Nikki was a teenager. That was when "everything fell apart." Family conflict resulted in Nikki's mother drinking more, her step-father leaving and Nikki being taken into foster care. Nikki reported staying in a youth shelter for "too long," quitting school, drinking and using, and then living on the streets.

Nikki stated that she never felt like she "fit in" with her peers. She said they did not seem to understand her and they would make fun of her for dressing like a girl. Nikki reported that the only time she seemed to be accepted was when working in the sex trade. In this way, Nikki could be visible in her female identity, engage sexually with men (her sexual orientation) and be accepted at face value in the mutual transaction of sex work.

At the time of our meeting, Nikki had an endocrinologist appointment scheduled and was pursuing sobriety to access the medical assistance required for a sex change. Nikki had taken no hormones yet. She said she was interested in a romantic relationship but spoke about the challenges of finding a man accepting of her trans identity. Being a pre-op trans woman attracted to men is difficult as a long-term relationship would require disclosure and acceptance of her male body parts.

Many of Nikki's strengths appeared as I interviewed her and her collaterals.

Contacts included Nikki's mother, foster parents and a staff person at the treatment facility. They reported that Nikki shared her intelligence, expressiveness, friendliness and compassion with others. They also indicated that Nikki was hardworking, a natural leader and a good writer. Nikki said she hoped to finish her GED and had an interest in hairdressing/aesthetics, and hoped to work as a stylist after her sex change.

Location Enacted as Resistance

Nikki passed well; she decided if and when to come out as a trans person because she met the expectations of looking and acting like a normative woman (Crowder 1998). Generally, "passing" is a term used to describe the ways people talk around and away from discussions of identity and their erotic and emotional attractions (Kanuha 1998), "mask" or degender the sex of their intimate partners and obscure the quality of their social activities (Ritter and Terndrup 2002: 23). Passing occurs in the context of a homophobic, transphobic, unaccepting and often violently oppressive dominant culture (Burstow 1992; Chess et al. 2004). Ritter and Terndrup state that the discrepancy between public and private identities can be painful (2002: 23; see also Lerner 1993).

As a white, university-educated woman in a long-term same-sex relationship, I knew enough to know that there would be things about Nikki's life that I could never directly understand the impact of: the connections among her Aboriginal and trans identities (Roscoe 1998), as well as the impact of sexism, racism, colonization and transphobia (Janoff 2005). Nikki had experiences of victimization that I had not faced — including physical and sexual assault. She was working against addictions to substances I have never tried and trying to make a life for herself in the context of a life-threatening illness she had acquired in her street-involvement. Nikki had cultivated resilience, charm, compassion and humour, which kept her connected to people she trusted and helped ground her in the difficult contextual factors of her life.

So, even though I could not speak directly about what it meant to be Nikki, I could speak on her behalf to the court. As a feminist and an activist/educator in the queer community, I was concerned about potential mistreatment in the disposition of Nikki's case. Nikki and I spoke together about how she would like me to offer information, advocate and raise questions and concerns in the court report that we felt needed to be considered in her case.

Further, I had a personal investment in Nikki's case being heard respectfully. Any queer liberation is my own. At the time, I was beginning to explore how it made sense to me to be a member of such a heterogeneous sexual and gender minority community. Since then, I have actively explored what it means for me to be an ally against all oppressions, including transphobia and related discrimination as it bumps up against gender, sexual and other identities.

Being an ally first and foremost means listening to the experiences of transidentified people as they speak directly about their reality and making sense of one's role in relation to that (Bishop 2002; Hawthorne 2002). During my work with Nikki (over the course of three meetings and telephone contacts with collaterals), I struggled with making sense of how to "do good by her." Fairn herising succinctly points out that, "Institutional pressure to focus one's inquiry to the institutional and disciplinary requirements can run counter to emancipatory knowledges and principles" (2005: 143). I wanted to write Nikki's report in a respectful and helpful way that was true to her and allowed me to fulfill the job I was enlisted to do by the government.

Since then, I have had more time and experience in my professional practice. I have sought out resources and challenge previous learning. I strive to cultivate an anti-oppressive stance that honours people's innate strengths and resilience. In that, I try to suspend the judgement and listen hard for how people's stories are located in their lives. As I did with Nikki, I ask people what they need and how I can use my institutionalized power to assist them.

We know that trans women are stigmatized and experience violence (Feinberg 1998; NAWL 2003). Transgender identity is misunderstood, pathologized and largely written about and researched by people who have no first-hand knowledge of the complexity and diversity of trans issues (Hale 1997). Challenges trans people may face include low self-esteem, emotional stress, depression, anxiety, isolation, homelessness and lack of employment opportunities and role models (Trans Programming at the 519 2006). They may have difficulty accessing housing and medical or family support for fear of reaction or discomfort about disclosing (Feinberg 1998). They may be at risk for experiencing violence, harassment, sexual exploitation, conflict with the law, while also losing a sense of community or access to resources when coming out as trans (Janoff 2005; Trans Programming at the 519 2006).

First-hand accounts in the literature expose their invisibility, or with visibility, the discrimination and oppression trans people are subjected to (Feinberg 1998; Trans Programming at the 519 2006). It is incumbent upon us as non-trans identified persons to accept that trans people can speak more appropriately than we can to their experiences. They know what it is like to be trans, we don't (Hale 1997). That said, all oppressed peoples can use allies to support their struggles for self-determination and liberation.

As discussed, Nikki's location was stigmatized in many ways — challenged to survive as an Aboriginal trans woman and as a sex worker outside the limits of labour law and employment standards (Payne 2002). Nikki needed trans-positive professionals around her with some (albeit limited) power to write and speak for her in a way that the court would understand. In short, Nikki needed all the advocacy she could get. In this sense I became an ally.

Social Work as Resistance

I identify as a queer person (not trans) but as an ally to trans people. Allies need to listen very carefully to avoid appropriating voice (Bishop 2002). To be effective and respectful, allies need to pay attention to how specific people in oppressed groups locate their concerns, interests, values and passion.

The Identifying Allies: A Safe Space Project at the University of Manitoba defines an ally as follows:

> An Ally is an individual who has taken training around homophobia and heterosexism. Allies support and welcome GLBTT people, by being aware of the effects that homophobia and heterosexism can have on people. Allies create change by challenging and providing education around homophobia, heterosexism, stereotypes, and myths about GLBTT people. Allies are aware of GLBTT resources both on campus and off. (Smith and Seymour 2001)

In *Wild Politics*, Hawthorne writes about standpoint theory. This theory emerged from the feminist practice of locating consciousness as arising out of women's direct experiences in their lives — the "recognition of knowledge that exists in social location" (Hawthorne 2002: 50), of course with political implications (Conway 2004). Hawthorne states:

> Reflections on women's position in society was challenged early in its development as feminists discovered that if they took the "objective," dominant view, they could not speak about a host of features of women's lives. These features were impossible to speak about because they were particular, that is, heavily influenced by context and situation. (2002: 50)

hooks recognizes and articulates the connections among different forms of oppression that impact upon women. She speaks about how class, race and sexuality impact one's life and experiences and she attempts to make racism in the women's movement visible. Instead of allowing the concerns of women of colour to stay on the margins, hooks draws attention in such a way as to bring our awareness "from margin to centre" in her aptly titled book on feminist theory (1984). Using this concept to build on Hawthorne's description of standpoint theory, hooks locates cause for political struggle in the actual lived experiences of all kinds of women's lives.

In a similar vein, Bishop writes about both interpersonal and institutional or structural oppression. She makes the links between different forms of intersecting oppressions and identifies the roots of all oppressions as competition and hierarchy, exposing the relationship of power and privilege to oppression (2002, 2005; NAWL 2003). Bishop also speaks about the need for each person fighting oppression to come to an understanding of our own privilege and participation in oppressive structures and to challenge others to consider their positions and interests (see also Dion 2005). To use one's power as an ally is to fight against competition and in solidarity for social justice (2002). There is no hierarchy of oppressions and all oppressions are interrelated (NAWL 2003). Again, hooks was one of the first feminist activists and scholars to make this point when she stated in 1984, "Significantly, struggle to end sexist oppression that focusses on destroying the cultural basis for such domination strengthens other liberation struggles" (40).

I knew that I had the opportunity to present Nikki's life to the court to educate and enlist their awareness of her as a human being beyond the categories of Aboriginal, trans woman, sex worker and drug addict. We know that racism (Commission on Systemic Racism in the Ontario Criminal Justice System 1998; Dunk 1998; James 2003; Ponting 1998), sexism (Burstow 1992; Douglas 1990; Feinberg 1998; Hawthorne 2002; Kitzinger 1993) and homophobia (Banks 2003; Feinberg 1998; Hawthorne 2002; Janoff 2005; Levy 1995) are present in our society and are enacted through structural and institutional means, like law, and also in individual actions in the ways social services, human interaction and legal practices occur (Bishop 2002, 2005; Hawthorne 2002; James 2003; Mullaly 1993, 2002).

My goal as an ally was to share information about Nikki's life with the court and to locate her life experiences within her identities and the limitations of an oppressive social and cultural context.

> Knowledge from the perspective of the marginal reveals the knowledge claims of the powerful not as universal, neutral and objective but as specific, permeated by political interests and informed by particular social locations. (Conway 2004: 62)

I hoped to help the court to see that some of Nikki's "deviant" or law-breaking behaviour existed as a viable option in the context of her life circumstances. Selling sex makes money, and some trans people feel it may be one of very limited options. I also hoped to work with her strengths and show the court that she had had some success in relationships, sobriety and learning new things and that she planned to continue these trends forward. I hoped to help the court see Nikki as a person with possibility — beyond the perceived pathology of gender dysphoria (Hagen 2004; Saleebey 2002).

Strategizing Resistance through the PSR

In a PSR, positive factors can be the presence of housing, education, employment, social and family support, a steady romantic relationship and no previous charges among others.

> The social and legal atmosphere of patriarchal hetero-normativity, which cultivates and institutionally reinforces traditional notions of appropriate gender roles and sexual choices and practices, fuels systemic sex discrimination and the intolerance and stigmatization of all those who do not conform. (NAWL 2003)

What happens for the trans-identified, for example, in the area of employment, is that past work experience or educational transcripts may not be counted (since they were acquired under another identity) or present work may be jeopardized if their coworkers or supervisor are prejudiced. Trans-identified people are at risk for underemployment and may feel they have to take any job just to survive, including sex work. Trans-identified people may be so focused on living through the stressors of each day that they may not have the same encouragement or support to plan ahead or they may face discrimination and harassment in the workplace by fellow colleagues or clients (NAWL 2003; Trans Programming at the 519 2006).

An inconsistent work history is considered a risk factor in a PSR. In the case of Nikki, it was a natural result of her life experiences (family conflict, living in shelters, dropping out of school, experiences of bullying and harassment, etc.) combined with discrimination and what I perceived as a lack of opportunities. No doubt she feared subjecting herself to filling out forms, which impose vulnerability in the moment of placing an "M" or an "F."

In the PSR I acknowledged Nikki's lack of work experience. I also indicated the unpaid work she had done in the community and made sure to speak with one of her supervisors, who was able to comment on her work abilities over time — considered positive indicators of resilience and future success.

I spoke with my supervisor about how to strategically present information. I hoped I could present it so that it would be useful for Nikki and accepted without being off-putting or outside the bounds of a court report — a fine balance. It was also a judgement call on my part in the writing, and on my supervisor's in the signing off, because we knew the way I had approached the report was appropriate, respectful — and unorthodox. For instance, another writer may have used the male pronoun throughout and focused on Nikki's challenges as factors of risk, further stigmatizing her.

Nikki received a community sentence, which included community service, and some uncommon conditions that I had recommended in the PSR. These explicitly included support elements like assistance in gaining a safe work placement opportunity and assistance and advocacy in accessing relevant emotional and physical health services.

Queering Resistance

"Acting on behalf of others, and for oneself, creates change not only in the conditions of our daily lives, but also in our knowledge and understanding of politics" (Hawthorne 2002: 37). We have got to think with our heads and hearts about our purpose at a given point in time. We need to focus on our part in relation to a problem. Fairn herising connects social work research, theory and practice. We cannot remove our own subjectivity from any of that work. The position of researcher or practitioner is implicated with power. To be accountable we need to be attuned to the ways in which we use and enact power or we may have lasting and damaging impacts on marginal communities (2005).

Herising also speaks about social work practice with implications for legal practice(s):

By situating ourselves in history and the contexts of our own multiple locations, we can move toward working through and with differences based on multiple subjectivities. These differences help us uncover the dissimilar and/yet overlapping positions, potentially allowing us to forge solidarity on grounds that reject essentialist categories and demarcate the multiple sites of struggle. (2005:.136)

I could see that Nikki realized agency in her life – she made conscious choices (that were sometime limited), but they were *her* choices, *and she persevered*. Nikki had what was in her hands, in her charge. Our lives were so different, yet had common themes of resilience, resistance, being "Other" and having hopes and dreams of something better. I believe that as people living and working in sites of social change, we get chances each day to see with our eyes open — to see and honour strengths beyond superficial or monolithic judgement. hooks states:

> Living as we did — on the edge — we developed a particular way of seeing reality. We looked both from the outside in and the inside out. We focused our attention on the center as well as the margin. We understood both. This mode of seeing reminded us of the existence of a whole universe, a main body made up of both margin and center. Our survival depended on an ongoing public awareness of the separation between margin and center and an ongoing private acknowledgement that we were a necessary, vital part of that whole…. [this worldview] that sustained us, aided us in our struggle to transcend poverty and despair, [and] strengthened our sense of self and our solidarity. (1984: xvi)

hooks speaks to my heart and says "we need us all." We each have a role to play in enacting our own agency in the liberation of ourselves and others (Bishop 2002, 2005). This endeavour that I speak of is intensely personal, political and immensely significant. I believe that existence of life on the planet depends on it. We are not simply neutrally disconnected as social workers or actors in sites of law. There are dynamic relationships occurring all the time between "service provider" and "client." As a queer woman, I am invested in all liberation, because it has personal meaning for others and myself.

Conway says, "Most of the time and in most places, movements move under the radar, in the interstices of society" (2004: 19). Conway states that she is following the work of Mouffe when she says, "every agent occupies multiple subject positions" (26). Our identities are constructed politically through our everyday actions and practices, and played out as race, class, sexuality and gender have become visible as "powerful axes of social experience, knowledge and politics" (26).

Individual people of all kinds of identities participate every day in ways that contribute to social movements. Movements are grounded in time and place (Conway 2004). Practices of survival, resistance, engagement, organizing, solidarity and some days simple existence contribute to knowledges about "the world as it is and might/should be, and how to change it" (56). Further, the changing politics of social movements question the principles active in dominant discourses (like law and social policy) of universalism, standardization and uniformity. Advocates for transgender rights have been seeking basic human rights protections through policy development and legislative reform (NAWL 2003). The knowledges brought forth by identity-based (women, queer, anti-poverty and ability) activists move us all towards an appreciation for particularity and diversity (Fairn herising 2005). This appreciation assists in balancing both individual and group needs (Rice and Prince 2003) and is necessary for equality (NAWL 2003).

Regnier speaks of how Aboriginal anti-racist pedagogy has developed out of lived struggles against racism and for Aboriginal rights (1995). He relates Canadian Aboriginal experiences to Freire's assertion that "People do not fight because of beautiful ideas that they have in their heads, they fight in order to get a better way of being" (in Regnier 1995: 74). I believe this quote speaks to the relationship between identity, experience, reflection and action, and builds on Freire's concept of "praxis," as described in *The Pedagogy of the Oppressed* (1970). We can act daily, when we get a chance, or make a chance to stand up for others and ourselves. People working in the criminal justice system have a very important role to play in this.

Conclusion

For those of us living in relative positions of privilege, we can decide if and how to step up. We can advocate for alternative views of reality and raise questions in places of power that elicit sensitivity to the realties of people living in a myriad of marginalized positions. We can talk with those that are different from us and listen to what they suggest would be helpful in working with them to support their liberation and resistance. We can do this because it matters for all of us.

Note

Thanks to Rune Breckon, women's studies student and trans activist, for reviewing a first draft and giving me feedback on use of language; Karen Busby, professor, Faculty of Law, University of Manitoba, for assisting me with trans resources; and colleague Gavriela Geller for her support and enthusiasm. Consultations also occurred with Shelly Smith of the Rainbow Resource Centre and Jennifer Davis of Nine Circles.

Chapter 9

In Defiance of Compulsory Mothering

Voluntarily Childfree Women's Resistance

Debra Mollen

Feminists, as Carolyn Morrell cogently argues, have had a capricious relationship with resistance. Perhaps this is because of what resistance commands. Resistance necessitates questioning, action and subversion. It demands a challenging of the status quo and requires effort and impetus. Resistance's antithesis — reception — connotes accession and does not demand such motility. Resistance might be especially pernicious when acted upon by members of disenfranchised groups because of the potential for harm.

This chapter focuses on the lives of nine voluntarily childfree women and how they have resisted the traditional role of women as mothers. Because of the significant social sanctioning of pronatalism, the degree of resistance women need to forge in the face of pressures to become mothers is often substantial. As "woman" and "mother" are still largely conceptualized synonymously, particularly in pronatalist countries, the act of resisting motherhood requires a kind of gender rebellion. In many cases, this rebellion begins in the earliest stages of gender identity development and traverses a lifetime. Legal implications in the face of mounting restrictions in access to contraception and abortion in the United States are also addressed.

Images and Conceptualizations of Childfreedom

Women who choose not to have children violate a gender norm so implicit in our culture that there is a dearth of suitable language to use in the discourse (Lisle 1999). "Childless" more often conjures images of those who cannot — not those who wish not to — have children. Stories of barren women like Rachel in the Bible are replete with shame and guilt, while several childfree characters in Greek mythology are seen as warriors marked by heroism and chastity. Freud equated normal female development with motherhood. He wrote, "Her new relation to her father may start by having as its content a wish to have a penis at her disposal, but it culminates in another wish — to have a baby from him as a gift" (Freud 1949: 77). William Inge, the 1950s-era U.S. playwright, created several leading characters who were childfree wives. They were seen as "lonely, disillusioned, narcissistic, unfulfilled, sexually frustrated (or inadequate), unhappily married, immature, and psychologically maladjusted" (Koprince 2000: 252). As Lisle (1999: 66) lamented, the profile of the childfree woman "has left us with a heritage that is both troubling and inspiring, one composed of expansive archetypes and constrictive stereotypes… in an idealized or demonized form, a saint or a devil but rarely as normal or fulfilled."

Politicians and religious leaders have extolled the virtues of parenthood. Frequently, political enthusiasm for parenting emerges on the heels of periods of great feminist activity and has racist, ethnocentric nuances that translate to backlash for women and ethnic minorities. In 1903, Theodore Roosevelt condemned white women for not procreating, fearful of the influx of immigrants (Griffin 1996). In a 1905 speech to the National Congress of Mothers, Roosevelt analogized women's obligation to have a minimum of six children to men's responsibilities to fight for the country. To abstain from childbirth was a selfish act (Lisle 1999). While such overt pronatalist directives might seem dated, nearly all United States presidential campaigns in the past twenty years have continued to depict the ubiquitous representation of adults who have children (Clausen 2002). The needs and concerns of adults without children continue to be disregarded (Burkett 2000; Clausen 2002).

More recently, a professor of biblical studies lamented about the freedom those who choose not to have children relish: "Such couples forget that true freedom is service to Christ, and that God knows better than we what makes for true happiness" (Van Leeuwen 2003: 24). In California, Reverend Sun Myung Moon unashamedly remarked to a group of 2,000 people that all women should bear children and should a woman choose not to have a child, "I'm sorry to say, you're disqualified as a woman" (Lattin 2001: A28). In other words, a woman's very legitimacy may be called into question should she subvert and refuse to become a mother.

Research Findings on Childfreedom

There is substantial research support for the notion that childfree adults are perceived less favorably than their parenting peers. LaMastro (2001) studied 254 undergraduate students to determine perceptions of childfree people. Participants read short passages about married couples who had no, one, two or six children. They were queried regarding whether they believed the couple had freely chosen their family size and then asked to respond to a series of statements about reasons for the attributions they made. Results indicated that perceptions of childfree adults were more negative than for parents and, regardless of whether their childfreedom was assumed to be voluntary or involuntary, adults without children were perceived as less caring, sensitive and kind than parents.

Mueller and Yoder (1999) studied childfree women and found they were stigmatized as being unhappily married, selfish, too career-involved, not nurturing and irresponsible. Likewise, Park (2002) found that the childfree participants in her study were regarded as being self-centred, cold, materialistic and strange. Two feminist academics (Letherby and Williams 1999) who drew on their own life experiences as childfree women, provided accounts in which they felt challenged, intruded upon with unsolicited advice and comments, and seen as selfish and worthy of pity. Both women found themselves excluded from conversations with colleagues and friends, which tend to focus nearly exclusively on children.

Managing Stigma

Riessman (2000) discussed the implications of stigma among women from South India. She conducted interviews with thirty-one married women without children to gain understanding about how they construct their lives, their reasons for not having children and the social support available to them considering their unconventional lifestyle. Nearly all the participants reported feeling marginalized by others, with those from the lowest socioeconomic backgrounds experiencing the most intense reactions. Those from exceptionally impoverished homes reported feeling dismayed at being called *machi*, a word meaning a farm animal that cannot breed. Those from economically privileged backgrounds managed to avoid such harsh characterization but stated that they still experienced invasive questions about childbearing that many found insulting. Coping with stigma ranged from remaining silent to engaging in resistant thinking and strategic avoidance of people and settings where criticisms were likely to flourish.

Morell (1993) interviewed thirty-four intentionally childfree women between the ages of forty and seventy-eight. While there was considerable diversity among the women's individual autobiographies, the author noted the presence of subversive desires in all the interviews. The women all expressed the wish for something beyond what is normally deemed appropriate for their gender. They wanted self-expression, autonomy, education and economic independence. Challenging the stereotype that women who do not want children are upper-middle-class, Morell (1993) found that almost seventy-five percent of the women she interviewed came from poor or working-class backgrounds and expressed some desire for class mobility and for opportunities and experiences typically not available to them. She concluded by discussing the resistance needed to overcome traditional gender role expectations regarding motherhood.

Byrne (2000: 14) studied childfree single women living in Ireland to determine how they managed the stigma of their relationship status. She wrote: "Groups of people are stigmatized on the basis that they share social or personal characteristics which cause others to exclude them from normal social interaction. The characteristics are regarded as problematic in that they disrupt the basis of expected behavior." Byrne found that the women were regularly asked about their single status, including their childfreedom. She found that the women were frequently discredited in conversations with women who were parents, who insisted that the women could not possibly understand what is involved in childcare. In her study, Byrne found that single women employ various strategies to manage stigma, including refuting the importance of the stigmatized social identity, refusing to adhere to the stereotyped representation of the stigma and becoming comfortable with the identity that they choose.

Gender Identity and Gender Role Resistance

Gender identity refers "not only to an individual's sense of self as a man or woman but also to his or her global sense of masculinity or femininity" (O'Heron and Orlofsky 1990: 134). Choosing not to live within culturally prescribed notions of gender can have an enduring impact on how one is viewed in the world. Resisting traditional gender conceptualizations is often cause for societal rejection and alienation, and can demand resilience and a measured defiance.

Relatedly, Abrams (2003) studied two groups of adolescent girls from distinctive communities in the San Francisco Bay Area to determine what strategies they employed for empowerment and resisting gender-based stereotypes as they formulate their gender identities. The author found that many of the adolescent girls actively resisted gender stereotypes by adopting more masculine forms of behaviour. She wrote that some of the girls "looked toward attributes of the 'masculine' such as physical strength and economic control, to transform the 'feminine' into a more privileged and powerful position" (Abrams 2003: 69).

In her study of fourteen women who self-identified as having been tomboys in childhood, Carr (1998: 549) remarked that, "agency can emerge through resistance to gender socialization or norms." She surmised that the role of volition developed as her participants refused to give in to socially mandated gender roles. Like West and Zimmerman (1987), Carr rejected the notion of either passive acceptance of gender roles or deterministic biological differences, and embraced instead the component of choice in forging identity. In her study of twenty-six adolescent girls from two neighbouring communities, Williams (2002) also found the notion of "trying on gender," of girls experimenting with various roles, including the role of resistance to traditional expectations for females. She found that "resistance is evident as they test boundaries and assert themselves into male-defined territories" (36). Mandel and Shakeshaft (2000: 87) studied middle school youth and found that a small portion of adolescent girls rejected traditional definitions of femininity and that they "were often perceived as unfeminine because they exhibited... confidence, self-assuredness, toughness... independence, and were not focused on their looks."

A Study of Voluntarily Childfree Women's Resistance
Participants and Procedure

Nine voluntarily childfree women, ranging in age from thirty-two to fifty-one, in a Midwest state elected to participate in the study. Five participants self-identified as heterosexual, and of these, four were married and one was single. Two participants identified as lesbian living with their partners, and two participants identified as bisexual living with their partners (one female and one male). Eight of the participants were white with the remaining one of mixed ethnicity (Caucasian, African American and Native American). The participants reported practising a variety of religions, including Judaism, Christianity and Wiccan. Participants' education included high school graduate (n=2), associate's degree (n=1), bachelor's degree (n=1), master's degree (n=2) and doctoral degree (n=3). Personal income ranged from a low of $18,000 to a high of $84,000 annually, with an average of $41,000. All participants were assigned a pseudonym to protect their anonymity.

The investigation examined the responses women received from others in light of their choice not to have children and how they reacted to these responses. Their narratives were collected by three methods: through a semi-structured interview process, semi-structured journal entries and a focus group. Multiple methods of collecting narratives yield richer data as well as increasing validity (Patton 2002).

Interviews took place at the researcher's home, the homes of the participants or the workplaces of participants, depending on the participants' preference. Each interview lasted between sixty and ninety minutes, was audio taped and was transcribed verbatim. Member checks were performed to ensure accuracy and increase validity of the study. Participants received a copy of their transcript and provided commentary and correction.

The focus group occurred after the initial period of analysis had been conducted, so that participants could support or refute emergent themes and categories as well as meet in a supportive environment with other childfree women. The group met in a room with one-way observation capability housed in a university training clinic.

Refusal of Gender Role Conformity in Childhood

The women in the study demonstrated a resistant and even rebellious approach to socially mandated gender roles. For most, this resistance and rebellion initially emerged in childhood and became even more salient as they grew into adulthood. Many of them voiced an early rejection of activities and play experiences, such as playing with dolls, that are largely gender-prescribed. Five of the nine participants were self-described tomboys. For some, this meant a preference for opposite-sex endeavours. For example, Kate remarked,

> *I played with dolls for a while, but I grew frustrated with them, because they wouldn't move the way I wanted them to move, and I remember throwing them and just saying, "these are stupid; I don't want to play with them anymore." I was a tomboy and I ended up being more involved in playing basketball and climbing.*

Likewise, Kelly had no interest in dolls:

> *I didn't want dolls. It wasn't that I wasn't given them. I didn't want them. I just wasn't interested. I used to get guns and holsters for Christmas. I wanted books and I got a microscope and phonograph and that kind of stuff. I just didn't want dolls and especially baby stuff. I didn't want the whole thing.*

Among those women who recollected their early play with dolls were several accounts of realizing they played with them differently than did their peers or sisters. Some, when they looked back at their involvement with dolls, saw early rejections of the maternal role. Clarissa stated:

> *I grew up with "aren't you a good mommy to your dolls?" kind of thing. The first time I remember sort of rejecting the mothering role was when I had a stuffed Snoopy. I got him at about five and I used to carry him around by his neck in the crook of my elbow.*

So consequently after carrying him around everywhere… his neck was about two inches in diameter and he was floppy headed… I used to throw him in the air and swing him around by his ears. People used to say, "don't do that to Snoopy… that's not how you'd be a good mother." And I remember thinking, he's a dog, I'm not his mother.

The accounts about play described in these narratives reflect instances of early resistance to prescribed gender roles. Several of the women expressed preferences for non-stereotyped pursuits, such as books, playing outdoors and games and activities that were often more physically active and exploratory than playing with dolls traditionally allows. Of those who did play with dolls, their narratives indicated either frustration by the dolls' limitations in movement or utility, or they resonated with accounts of doll play that was decidedly not nurturing nor maternal, such as Kate's description of her dolls as "stupid."

Similarly, the women in the investigation engaged in gender role resistance as they refused to be limited by socially derived meanings of what it means to be girls and women. It was apparent from the participants' narratives that the construct of gender — particularly making meaning of one's gender — figured prominently for them. All of the women reflected deeply about the meaning of gender and about their sense of themselves as girls and women. Concurrently, they exhibited an early, sometimes pervasive, refusal to live within the confines of typical gender role socialization. It could well be that this refusal — understood primarily as gender role rebellion — lay the foundation for a lifetime of questioning of these roles, of a skepticism and a healthy resistance to established societal expectations.

Experiencing Stigma

All nine women reported the experience of being pitied, criticized or in other ways stigmatized for being childfree. Stigmatization is, in this case, understood broadly and along a continuum from relatively mild incidents of dismissal to more severe experiences of reprobation. This stigmatization took several forms, which I have classified under five categories. The women (1) were often discounted when it came to discussions focused on children; (2) were sometimes expected to compensate by working extra hours; (3) were considered weird or abnormal and subjected to shock and dismay; (4) experienced pity; (5) experienced discrimination or abuse because of their choice.

Three of the women reported being discredited for not being parents when it came to the discussion of childcare and childrearing. In her interview, Chloe recalled interactions with her friend who has a child,

She says things like, "Oh, you wouldn't understand because you don't want to have a kid." Or, you know, she'll call to tell me that the baby got its first tooth and she's like, "Well, I'm sure you don't care since you don't want to have kids." It's like she's on this superior level now because she had a baby and I can't relate.

Likewise, Kelly reported being silenced by her sister when the conversation turned to her nephew. In her interview she said,

There have been occasions when I've made the mistake of saying something to her about, "Well, I don't understand why [her son] couldn't do that. Or, "Why don't you just have [him] do that?" over a variety of different kinds of things. And her reply is, "You just don't understand, you've never been a mother. You don't understand."

Being dismissed and discredited seemed to result in the women's feeling isolated and exempt from the world of parenting as well as from their friends and relatives.

Three of the women had experienced being expected or asked to work extra hours based on the rationale that they had more time because they were childfree. Jennifer voiced an awareness of an expectation that she work late. She said, "People expect me, because I don't have children, to be the one out of the group that stays late, because I don't have somebody at home that I have to run to." Chloe, who is employed at the university, recalled what happened when she worked in another setting:

One of the jobs I used to work at was an optometry office. There were four other girls that worked there and at one point or another in the five years that I worked there, they all had kids. So it was like, "Oh, Chloe, so-and-so isn't here because she's on maternity leave, so would you care to work late?" or "Do you care to come in on Saturday because we know you don't have kids."

Three of the women reported that their normality has been called into question as women who have chosen not to have children. In her journal, Kelly vividly portrayed her feeling that, "Those of us who may not be so drawn [to motherhood] remain, at best, enigmas to most people, and at worse, mutants." Chloe and Jennifer reported feeling that professionals, friends and relatives speculated about whether they were "normal." Chloe described a pervasive questioning of her normalcy in her interview and in her journal:

If you say you just don't want to [have children], it's like, "What's wrong with you? What did your mom do to you?" People expect you to have kids and if you don't, they either think you can't or you're weird. I told one of my girlfriends that I was in a research study about voluntarily childless women and she said maybe I'd find out what's wrong with me.

The experience of being considered weird or abnormal sometimes contributed to perceptions of being excluded or shunned for the decision to be childfree. Jennifer recalled such an experience. She remembered the conversation in which an acquaintance began, "Well, can you not have children?" I said, "No, we're fine. We just chose not to." She just felt that there was something wrong with us. She has avoided us at parties and stuff.

Jennifer also recalled an experience when she was in counselling to help her process through and better understand her upbringing, specifically her experience of growing up with alcoholic parents. In her interview, Jennifer described her frustration with one therapist who seemed compelled to link her upbringing with her decision not to have children:

[The topic of remaining childfree began with] a general questioning about my own marital status, and, "Well, do you have any children?" kind of in that normal way, and when I said no, she said, "Well, are you going to have children?" and I said, "No," just rather confidently. Then the therapist asked me, you know, about the decision and then really tried to connect it back to adult children of alcoholics. I just felt like she overdid it. It happened rather immediately. I discovered that she really felt like most people wanted to have children and thought it was abnormal that someone didn't.

So, the reactions to participants as being abnormal for remaining childfree came not only from the general public but also from supposedly informed professionals. This questioning of normality was often followed by expressions of shock or disbelief, construed as a subset as described in the following section.

Six of the women in the study reported experiences in which others expressed shock and disbelief after learning of their voluntary childfreedom. Oftentimes the participants' experience of shock and belief seemed to be inextricably related to the questioning of their normality. Chloe recalled a conversation she had had with her husband's cousin, whom she had met only three times:

I answered the phone and the first thing he said to me was, "Are you pregnant yet?" And I said, "No." "Why not?" I said, "Don't want to be." He goes, "Ah! What kind of answer is that?" (because he has two kids of his own).

The taken for granted assumption that any normal person would want to have children was articulated in various ways to these voluntarily childfree women. Naomi reported a similar reaction from her brother's wife:

My sister-in-law that just had the baby, she was really shocked. We were sitting there talking about kids and I said, "I don't want any." She said, "Never?" She said, "It just shocks me, you know. Look at her with [my nieces and nephews]. She would be a good mother. It would be different if she hated kids but she doesn't hate kids." She was trying to say that's why she finds it hard for me not to want to be a mother. I said, "It's just not for me." She's had a change of heart now since she's had the second kid.

Clarissa reported that people are shocked and oftentimes confused about her decision not to have children. In her interview, she said,

There are a couple who think, "Yeah, this is a fairly nice person" [then] they get around to asking if I have kids and I say no, they reach for a reason to try to make it consistent with "This seems like a nice, pleasant person." They can't fathom why someone who appears to be whatever, witty, fill in the blank, wouldn't have kids. People are just flabbergasted by that when they meet me. It's almost as if they're trying to re-categorize me as something other than [what I am, as] cold, unfeeling — I'm none of those things.

Lucy summarized the theme of others' shock and disbelief succinctly when she said, "People still do not know how to react to someone who chooses any sort of alternative way of life no matter what that alternative lifestyle choice may be.

They are always suspicious of someone different from the norm."

Six of the women experienced pity as a common response from people who learned of their childfreedom, even when they were clearly informed about the volition in regards to their childfree status. Expressions of pity described by participants ranged from outright shame and disappointment to more subtle expressions of sorrow and encouragement to reconsider their decision. Chloe said, "People initially think, 'Oh, how awful for you that you don't want to have a child.'" During her interview, Kate recalled the reluctance of others to freely accept her decision and their subsequent encouragement that she re-think her choice:

> *And my neighbour actually — who had the two kids — used to come over and say, "Why don't you… why aren't you a mom?" I said, "I don't want to be a mom." She was another one who said, "Oh, you'd be great at it." I've had neighbours and coworkers who have said things like that. It's been more questioning: "You'd have been a good mom. Why aren't you a mom?"*

Both Jennifer and Naomi reported responses from others who assumed they were childfree only because they had not yet met the right man. Jennifer remembered reactions she received when she had been single and an active member of her church. She said, "It was more just kind of like, 'Oh well, when you meet the right person.' It was all just very patronizing." Likewise, Naomi's sister-in-law, who had initially expressed shock at learning of Naomi's decision not to have children, attributed her choice to not having yet met a suitable partner. Naomi said, "She said, 'I can understand now because you're not married and haven't met the right guy.'" The clear assumption was that Naomi would change her mind once she met the "right guy."

Three women recalled experiences of discrimination — two participants observed or heard of such incidents and the other directly experienced one — in response to being childfree. One woman experienced abuse. Clarissa, who currently works as a university professor, recalled what she observed when she worked for a Fortune 500 company. Her account reflected the dual suspicions against women who are both single and childfree. Furthermore, the coalescing of a single, childfree woman with increasing age suggests a multifaceted discrimination against women who do not conform to societal standards:

> *If you were unmarried and a staff accountant, young, in your twenties, that's cool. But toward the end of your twenties, you better start looking for somebody [to marry]. If you got promoted through the ranks 'til you were in your mid-thirties and you made manager, that's where the speculation really started to grow. God forbid you be single, thirty-five, and childless. The idea that sacrificing a child and a relationship for a career — there was a sense of distrust. It was almost like if you would do that, I can't trust you. For the women it was as if in order to be viewed as a trustworthy coworker, you better not make it look like your career is the most important thing in your life because people will believe that you will steamroll over them to get what you want.*

Lucy, who herself wanted a tubal ligation but did not actively seek the procedure due to the expense, wrote in her journal about the discrimination involved in women seeking permanent sterilization:

> *Doctors are apparently reluctant to perform the surgery on young women for fear that she will change her mind. If the woman is married, [some doctors] will actually refuse [to perform the procedure] if the husband does not give his permission! I know a woman this happened to. She had to travel to another state to get her procedure.*

Jennifer described what happened when she and her husband asked their physician to perform a vasectomy. She found the practice of refusing to grant a simple medical procedure blatantly discriminatory. In her interview she said,

> *Well, one doctor, the physician we had been going to, just said, "No, it's not my policy… I won't do it until a man is at least thirty-eight and has either had children or there's some real specific reason that they don't want to have children." So then we found somebody else and he was just kind of like, "I don't really feel very comfortable about this and I'd really like you to think about it more." And I just said, "Forget it," and we went to another guy and he was fine with it.*

These examples can be construed as the subtle and usually unexamined ways that organizations and people with power — namely the corporate world and physicians — exert their influence over individuals and couples who do not have, nor want, children. In both cases, the discrimination is tied to the woman-as-mother (and person-as-parent) phenomenon, with those refusing to adhere to societal mandates the target of unfair treatment. Limiting the options of women who do not want children and who do not act, in Clarissa's words, "feminine enough" is understood as an example of discrimination.

One woman in the study reported having been abused in relation to the issue of children in her first marriage. Lucy discussed how her husband had been cajoling her to reconsider her decision not to have children. During her interview she recalled what happened between her husband and her:

> *We were in the course of foreplay, were getting ready to have intercourse. We had been involved together for three years, had been married for about a year and [my husband] was big time, "I want children, I want children," very much pushing on the subject. We're getting ready to have intercourse and I'm like, "Excuse me, haven't we forgotten something here?" We used condoms as birth control and you really don't think after you're in a relationship with someone for three years you need to discuss every time whether or not you are going to use a condom. He was on top of me and just said, "No, I'm tired of waiting. I want a baby and I want a baby now."*

In Lucy's story, her husband's demand for a child is interpreted as a desire to manipulate and control her. Such domination over women around the issue of reproduction symbolizes the greater societal patriarchy in which women's choices are routinely restricted, their personal power oftentimes usurped by men.

All nine women reported experiencing some degree of stigmatization due to their childfreedom. These experiences ranged from subtle but persistent questions from family members, co-workers and strangers to more blatant expressions of shock, dismay, pity and sympathy. In some cases, women reported having their sanity questioned, were discriminated against or observed such discrimination, or experienced sexual assault in an intimate relationship around the issue of children.

Saying No, Resisting the Mandate, and Getting Angry

In seven of the women's narratives, there were discernible examples of anger and frustration in response to societal and familial pressures to conform to proscribed gender roles. Some of the women struggled in their ability to say no and get angry, traditionally domains not largely acceptable for women. Some gave sarcastic responses to questions about their decision not to have children. Eventually most claimed to have developed an assertive voice to answer their doubters. This sense of assertiveness was incorporated into their sense of identity. Lois stated emphatically in her interview,

> *My responses have run the gamut. I did go through a period of time where I decided I was so sick of these questions [about my childfreedom] that I was going to answer every one of them sarcastically, and so I did. It was just to let them know it was a totally inappropriate question as far as I was concerned.*

One of Chloe's tactics was to lie and tell those who asked her that she was unable — not unwilling — to have children. She noticed that people had contempt and scorn when she said she did not want to have children but that "they feel sorry for you when you say you can't." Coming to some resolve, Chloe continued, "I'm not ashamed of it and I'm not embarrassed of it. I'm just to the point now where if you don't like what I have to say or the way I am, just don't be around me." Clarissa has taken a similar no-nonsense response. In her interview, she said,

> *For those times I have said to women who have children, "I don't want them," I get a very defensive, "Well, what do you have against kids?" There's a real defensiveness that enters into that. I don't have anything against other people's kids. I don't want them.*

Kate, too, arrived at some degree of peace in her quest to say no: "I had to do a lot of therapy to realize that I can say no, or that I could do what I want to do, and not [only] make other people happy in life." Jennifer recalled her experience of saying no to her therapist, who thought it was abnormal not to want children:

> *So I ended up asking her more about her views on having children and then after I discovered that she really felt like most people wanted to have children and thought it was abnormal that someone didn't, I said well we can't continue this relationship because I think it is normal.*

Three of the women experienced a good deal of anger over being told what to do, being unfairly treated or being emotionally and/or physically coerced. They sometimes took calculated steps toward achieving some resolution and seemed empowered by their anger as it compelled them to make change. In response to the physician who had refused the couple's request for a vasectomy, Jennifer said:

> *I was just shocked. I wrote a long letter to him and said, "I find this appalling and you cannot refuse people who want a medical procedure that seems safe," and I really had a fit with him. I also told everybody that I knew that this guy picks and chooses what kind of medical procedures he wants to practise, and that's not fair. I was really angered by the whole thing because I was just like, "How dare you impose your values on us!"*

Lucy, whose husband had attacked her and had refused to use birth control in an effort to get her pregnant, physically defended herself in response to the assault:

> *And I finally managed to get him off of me by kicking and screaming. I was trying to move all my weight toward his side of the bed where he had a gun hanging in a holster on the bedpost. But he finally got off and got out and I said, "Look, that was a terrorist tactic. The time to discuss these things is at the dinner table and not when someone is pinned underneath you with her legs spread." That was the one that really kind of nailed it for me.*

Naomi reported having an instinct to fight back when she sensed she was being manipulated, controlled or constrained. She talked about how she felt about some of the men she has dated:

> *It seems the ones that I tend to date that are my age, they tell me what to do, boss me around. The one that I did date, we dated for probably ten years and we just fought constantly for the same reasons: do this, don't do this. I dated one guy for six or seven months. He asked me to quit one of my jobs because he could never see me. But like I said, I'm not going to be told what to do.*

The Emerging Resilience: Feeling Strong in the Face of Stigma

In recent years, scholars have proposed definitions of resilience and studied the conditions under which it is most likely to flourish. Masten (2001: 228) defined resilience as "good outcomes in spite of serious threats to adaptation or development." In a study that discovered favorable coping skills among some women who had had abortions, resilience was encapsulated as the notion that "a person with a... positive view of him- or herself, a sense of control over his or her own life, and an optimistic outlook on the future — all resources that should contribute to more positive appraisals of... stressful life events" (Major, Richards, Cooper, Cozzarelli and Zubek, 1998: 737). Todd and Worell (2000: 119) studied resilience among low-income employed African American women and likened resilience to "a positive sense of well-being… the manifestation of competence or effective functioning [in] the presence of serious stress or adversity."

The women in the study wrestled in their quest to have a positive sense of who they were in a culture that has often stigmatized and chastised them for their choice to remain childfree. Four of them implicitly questioned their normalcy and yielded to the notion that, having made an unorthodox choice, they are different. At times the notion of "different" seemed to be equated with abnormal or deviant. Chloe said, "When I got into my twenties and everyone was saying, 'You've got to get married and have a kid,' I was like, 'Is there something wrong with me?'" Similarly, Naomi stated, "It's like I'm the different one." In the focus group, Lois stated that she sees herself as different as well: "I've just always been a little different than my friends and way different than society. It's just been across the board in my life." Kelly recalled questioning her sense of normalcy as well:

I used to wonder what is wrong with me because there are plenty of women that say, "Oh, a baby!" You know, a woman is walking with a baby and says, "Do you want to hold it?" No, I really don't.

In spite of those who questioned their normalcy, all nine women in the study expressed some sense of feeling strong, capable and empowered. This sense of resilience arose in the interviews, journals and focus group. During her interview, Nicole said,

What I expect of myself is I try to build up and grow as a human being. I see myself as a woman who has chosen to live a certain way, who's also a very strong woman but is also real sensitive and caring and who likes herself. Kind of has a temper on occasion but that's okay.

Jennifer voiced a sense of pride regarding her decision. In her interview, she said, "In some ways, I feel more like an empowered woman because I've resisted the social pressure to do this [have children]. So it makes me proud to be a woman and have made this choice." Naomi saw herself as very capable and self-sufficient:

I have the tendency to be very strong, very independent, very own-willed. I never settled and I think a lot of girls settled. I'm more independent than most women I know. I don't care a lot what other people think. I learned how to take care of myself.

Both Kate and Lois who identified as lesbians spoke about how being comfortable with their sexual orientation aided in their comfort with their decision not to have children. They had had ample experience with navigating a culture that has often stigmatized their lifestyle, and they had developed resilience in the face of the stigma that proved useful in other areas of their lives. In her interview, Lois said,

My coming out as a lesbian was a huge, huge factor for me in my comfort level about not having children. I immersed myself in the lesbian culture… I was one of those people who got to know it and help shape it. Through all those years that I was in a place where I would have really been questioning whether this is a good thing or not and having angst over it and stuff, I was in the midst of this incredibly lively culture that was giving birth to itself. We were all about being amazing, powerful, unique, creative women.

Mounting Threats against Choice

Although abortion was made legal in the United States in 1973, prompt steps were taken to challenge and dismantle this law almost the moment it passed (Baird-Windle and Bader 2001). In the past fifteen years alone, tremendous strides have been accomplished by anti-choice politicians and private groups who collectively have increased the number of states with mandatory waiting periods, enacted restrictive teen parental notification and consent laws, restricted abortion for poor women and enforced mandatory counselling, which often includes lectures on and photos of fetal development (Benshoof 2002; Hontz 1998; Makin-Byrd 2002; Page 2006). When abortion restrictions are imposed, the choice about whether to become mothers is endangered. Women who do not want to become mothers but whose access to safe abortion is compromised must seek illegal abortions, thereby putting their health in jeopardy, or may face compulsory motherhood when abortion is not available as an option. Indeed, as legal restrictions continue to mount against abortion rights, women who self-abort may themselves be criminally prosecuted (Page 2006). Women in Portugal (Cancio 2005), Peru, Chile, the Dominican Republic, El Salvador and in nearly every African country face even harsher conditions for controlling and directing their own reproductive destinies (Senanayake and Newman 2002).

The right to choose whether or not to become a mother, once heralded and championed in the United States and elsewhere, has become, in many instances, both plausibly and legally prohibited. Those who have made the unorthodox choice to refuse the societal, religious, familial, and national pressures to mother now face greater restrictions, moral condemnation, and legal castigation which threaten the right to choose.

Conclusion

Being resolute in the face of stigmatization, particularly for women and people of colour, commands a sense of resilience and rebellion, a willingness to question societal mandates and to live with authenticity and purpose. Laws and policies that threaten, restrict or eliminate access to abortion signify that those women who wish not to have children quite literally live outside the law. Childfree women living in pronatalist societies can and do live outside the bounds of acceptability for their gender, and they do so with conviction.

Chapter 10

Playing Games With the Law

Legal Advocacy and Resistance

Karen Rosenberg

When I began working as a legal advocate for Safe Haven, a domestic violence agency in Seattle, Washington, in 1996, I frequently heard stories of the 1970s: the cramped two bedroom apartment that served as the shelter when Safe Haven first opened in 1976, the dedication of the feminist volunteers, the women who went out at night in bullet proof vests and plucked (hopefully willing) women from their abusive homes. The tireless women who planned rallies, ran consciousness raising groups, unclogged toilets, cooked stews and played with children — all in the same day. None of this specialization of work duties, or intake forms, or procedure manuals, or worries about funders ("Money? What money? We had nothing to lose") that characterizes our current work. I did not know what to make of these stories, knowing that without my colleagues, salary and job security I could not devote my time to helping abused women navigate the legal system. There was always the sense that the work in the 1970s was the real deal and that though we talked about resistance now, though our mission statement was about changing society, though we talked about working ourselves out of our jobs, we had somehow missed the boat.

I'm talking, of course, about the paradoxes of institutionalization in feminist organizations: in this case, the success of the battered women's movement allowed shelters like Safe Haven to move from cramped, cheap apartments to large, rambling houses (though in our case, a house like a never-quite-well patient, always in need of care and attention). As the battered women's movement created discourse around wife abuse, bringing it, as the cliché goes, "from behind closed doors," it accomplished the monumental task of casting battering as a public problem, one worthy of public attention, public funds and public scrutiny. As the battered women's movement shifted from a grassroots effort to a more mainstream concern, profound changes occurred. These changes, which have been documented extensively and eloquently (Schechter 1982, Schneider 2000), included a shift from a gendered language of "wife abuse" to (in the case of.the United States) the gender neutral "domestic violence," from codified policies of legal inaction to zealous legal intervention, and from a feminist structural analysis linking wife battering with sexist social structures to mental health and legal discourses emphasizing individual deviance. The impacts of institutionalization on feminist movement organizations in general and battered women's organizations in particular have been widely studied (Ferree and Martin 1995; Profitt 2000; Walker 1990). This literature traces the ways in which initial movement agendas shift, and seeks to evaluate how resistive impulses play out in organizations that have institutionalized.

As I grapple to understand the resistive impact of my work as a legal advocate for an institutionalized feminist organization in the late 1990s, I walk on well-travelled terrain. I explore this landscape asking several questions: in what ways did my work contribute to a larger, meaningful resistance effort? In what ways did my work fall short? How can we think about the resistive potential of institutionalized domestic violence programs in the United States? How can feminists work to increase this potential? These questions are not new. Neither, however, have they been (nor can they be) fully answered. These are questions that those of us committed to social change must ask continually, as the ground beneath and between us changes and shifts.

I divide my analysis into three sections. In the first section, I introduce Ewick and Silbey's (1998) theory on legal stories to situate my work with women and the law. In the second section, I discuss one of the most troubling and complicated issues I dealt with in this work: women who considered the "underground" as their only option to stay safe. In the final section, I evaluate my work within the larger context of feminist resistive and transformative social action.

"Think of It Like a Game"

There was a lot of wiggle room in my role as legal advocate, which I found profoundly distressing when I first began the job and which I now realize helped clear space for more transgressive work. My written job description ranged from the reassuringly specific — accompany women to court, answer the crisis line, give referrals — to the utopian — change the systems that oppress battered women and children. I was not an attorney, and I knew I could not give legal advice, both because it was illegal and because our philosophy was to empower women to make their own choices. There was also a strong emphasis on cultivating relationships with legal aid attorneys, police officers and prosecutors (defence attorneys were left out of this equation when I first began the work; however, increased attention to the issue of "victim defendants," victims arrested on domestic violence charges, has led to increased communication with defence). In fact, these "systems folks" provided much of my training. The legal advocate role was a flexible insider-outsider position that at times aligned with criminal legal institutions and at times critiqued them.

In trying to make sense of the work that I did, I have found the typology for classifying legal stories developed by Ewick and Silbey in *The Common Place of Law* (1998) particularly useful. Drawing from over 400 interviews with people from diverse backgrounds, Ewick and Silbey sought to understand how people think about the law in their everyday lives. They conclude that people tell three general stories about their relationship to the law, which Ewick and Silbey classify as *before* the law, *with* the law and *against* the law. In the *before* the law story, people talk about the law as removed from everyday life, and as objective, remote and fair. They approach the law as supplicants, prepared to defer to the law and seeing themselves as powerless to change it.

People who tell stories of being *with* the law view the law as a game. In this narrative, people conceive of themselves as players who have power to strategize and play the game to their advantage. They don't emphasize the fairness or unfairness of the law as a whole. "These stories" Ewick and Silbey write, "describe a world of competitive struggles; they seem less concerned about law's power than about the power of self or others to successfully deploy and engage with the law" (48).

Finally, the *against* the law story begins from the premise that the law is inherently unfair, with ordinary people at a disadvantage. Individualized resistive strategies — such as being deliberately vague or withholding information — are key ways of acting from the *against* the law narrative.

For good and for ill, the narrative of being *with* the law is the one I inhabited most often as a legal advocate. This narrative enabled me to provide direct assistance to women without alienating either my agency or the legal actors with whom I cultivated relationships. And though this narrative is not one that will ultimately foment radical change, it provides important tools for individual women to empower themselves. It provides a method for women to engage with the law in a "strategically essentialist" (Spivak 1990) manner, consciously taking on the flattening labels of the law as part of a larger resistance effort.

Many women I talked with narrated themselves as being *before* the law. They made comments such as "the judge probably knows best" and "I don't want to bother these people with my problems." These women treated me as an authority figure, asking me to tell them what to do. I remember early conversations with women where it felt like we were playing hot potato with decision-making power — they asked me for advice, and I refused to give it. It was only after I realized that we needed to talk directly about our understandings of the law that I broke out of these conversational cul-de-sacs. Women who saw themselves as being *before* the law believed that legal professionals knew best. They viewed the law as right and sane; they saw their role as following the law's rules — if only they could figure out what they were.

In these encounters, I realized it was important for me to acknowledge my authority as a legal advocate and speak from my professional experience. This helped women understand that I wasn't willfully withholding information. From this perspective I explained my view that the law offered no clear answers. Legal maneuvers often produced unanticipated consequences. There were no right or wrong moves, only factors to consider. For example, women often asked me if I thought it was a good idea for them to get protective orders. "Can they really protect me or not?" women asked. I sought to move the conversation towards their experience and expertise. "How has your husband reacted to court papers in the past? Does he follow rules? What does your gut tell you?" Placing women's own experiences and opinions on par with my legal information often elicited a dual reaction: on the one hand, as one woman told me, "after all these years, it's nice to know that what I think really matters." On the other hand, women found it profoundly distressing to realize that the "expert" at the domestic violence agency could provide no simple answers.

I worked with women who considered themselves *before* the law to imagine themselves *with* the law. Just as Silbey and Ewick show in their study, I used metaphors of games and players to talk about the law. One of my most common discursive interventions was to recast the terms of engagement. I noticed that women were profoundly affected not only by legal outcomes, but by how legal actors treated them. I accompanied many women to court who got the legal remedy they sought (e.g., a favourable custody ruling or a civil protection order) but who left the courthouse feeling that the endeavour had been a failure because of offhand comments legal actors made. A judge's careless "both parties need to control their anger," or "that information isn't relevant," or "maybe it's a cultural thing," often left women frustrated, angry, and regretting their choice to make a legal claim.

In response to these encounters, I talked with women about coming up with a legal and emotional strategy for dealing with court hearings. I offered women a somewhat schizophrenic approach to the law — play the legal game with a carefully constructed "game self," while carefully leaving the "true self" outside of the legal realm. This construction is flawed in many ways: social life and the law are mutually constitutive and cannot be separated; we don't possess a fixed "true self," and if we did, we certainly don't have the means to excise it from power relations. Nevertheless, as a strategy this construction gave women discursive tools to recast their struggles with their batterers and with legal institutions. In this reconstruction, I sought to recast judges from wise authority figures to fallible players. We would then strategize about how they could play their part in the game. This included talking through every aspect of presentation, from dress to demeanour to storytelling.

Storytelling was a particularly complicated area in my work with survivors of violence. One of the most truly inspiring aspects of my work was simply sitting and listening to women as they began to tell new stories about themselves, ones that acknowledged the devastating impact of the abuse and began to see beyond it. I remember one woman whose new story began simply, "he told me I was stupid every day. After a while, I believed him. But I got up this morning and I realized that he was wrong." One of the most deeply resistive practices that happens within the contemporary domestic violence agency is the recasting of stories, with women able to explore new narratives in supportive, confidential spaces. Women can (though they don't always) make connections between their own experiences and larger structural oppression and inequalities. These new stories can help them imagine new futures, aspirations, careers and relationships.

However, if women interact with the legal system during this time, either by their own choosing or not, they are often compelled to craft truncated, victim-heavy stories about themselves. They must also focus on the physical manifestations of abuse, even if what they would most like to denounce doesn't involve punches or kicks. For example, the Washington State Civil Protection

Order application asks women to write about "the most recent incident of abuse" and the "history of abuse," both relying on the statutory definition of domestic violence that only recognizes physical violence, threats of physical violence and stalking. Here is where the game metaphors became relevant again: I would explain the rules of engagement — what the law said, what the judges looked for, what outcomes were possible, what factors we simply could not control — and asked if they wanted to play (deciding whether to apply for protection orders was one gig where women had the luxury of choice; when they were served with papers the stakes of not playing rose astronomically). Even when they did not have control over whether or not they were in the legal game, these strategies gave women a more resistive space from which to act.

Parallel to the legal storytelling, women had the opportunity to embark on storytelling on their own terms. This most often took the form of extensive journal writing and sometimes involved painting, drawing, collage and other arts. I attempted to bifurcate my role as legal advocate, helping women navigate the legal terrain on the one hand and encouraging the telling of their story on their own terms on the other hand. All of these efforts fall fairly squarely within the *with* the law narrative, and I argue that this narrative gives women powerful tools with which to approach the legal system. What about the *against* the law story?

Many battered women I worked with narrated themselves in and out of *against* the law narratives. In fact, as Ewick and Silbey make clear, there is not only overlap between these three narratives, but individuals talk from within different frames at different times. My social location as a legal advocate limited my ability to observe this particular narrative. While some women shared their strategies for working *against* the law, others viewed my role with as being more closely aligned with the systems they sought to resist. And, perhaps more significantly, my own strong faith in the *with* the law narrative made it more difficult for me to hear stories in the *against* the law frame.

The Underground and Disappearing Acts

There were certain situations, however, where I was painfully aware of the limitations of the *with* the law approach. One of the most deeply disturbing issues I dealt with at Safe Haven was the issue of going "underground," essentially disappearing in an attempt to escape the homicidal violence of the abuser. Battered women who go underground, who seek to disappear in an effort to save their lives and the lives of their children, are engaging in a fierce, difficult, never finished act of resistance. They must resist not only the abuse of their partners but the arm of the law that — especially in their absence — can take on the voice and demands of their batterer.

I was introduced to this issue three days after I started my legal advocate job. I got a call from Margie, who told me that she had been underground for several years and needed help finding resources in our area. We made a date for her to come to the office the following afternoon.

Margie told me her story before I had a sense of my role and before I had developed lenses through which to view situations of abuse, such as the *with* the law narrative I have been discussing. My ignorance of my own position enabled me to hear Margie's stories without the self-protective strictures of known job duties and limitations, which came to shape my interactions with women over the next several years.

Margie was a slight white woman with long dark hair she wore in a braid. She quickly figured out that she knew far more about the legal system than I did. Nevertheless, she decided to share her story and her insights with me. She explained that though her husband Gary had always been controlling and violent, she never thought of him as murderous. Then, one evening shortly after their son Tommy turned three, her husband took them to the woods with their dog, an eight-year-old chocolate lab. He forced them to watch as he shot and killed the dog. Still holding the gun, he forced Margie to bury the dog's still warm body. "If you get out of line, this is what will happen to you," he said. The following week, when her husband was at work, Margie packed a small suitcase and got a neighbour to take her to the bus station. She went to her sister's house in a town several hours away. However, when her husband called her sister and threatened her, she decided to move to a shelter so as not to put her sister's family at risk as well.

Margie, who had worked as a teacher before her marriage, tried to make a new life for herself and her son in four separate places. But each time she tried to put down roots, her husband would appear. Once he took Tommy for a week, once he beat her up in an alley outside of her apartment.

"I knew if he kept finding me like this that he would kill me, or kill Tommy, which would amount to the same thing." She realized that he kept finding her through work records, and through her family's phone records. "So I decided to disappear — to go underground." For Margie, this meant using a false name and never giving out her social security number. She stopped contacting her family and friends. She taught her son a new name and how to keep secrets. She couldn't find work as a teacher because she couldn't give potential employers references or a resume. She couldn't go on public assistance because that also required a social security number. She couldn't enroll Tommy or herself in school.

Meanwhile, when he realized he could no longer find her, Gary called the police and then filed for custody. He accused Margie of kidnapping Tommy. Since she did not file a response with the court, the court awarded Gary full custody. Margie learned this when she called her sister from a pay phone the previous Christmas.

Margie survived by seeking out a string of bureaucrats, service providers and business people who were willing to bend or break the rules for her. Her skill as a teacher, with her patience and her ability to break down complicated issues, was evident. Staying underground was a full time job, and she was always on the lookout. "I'm tired," she said. "But I'm safe, and my boy is safe."

That first day we brainstormed about getting library cards for her and

Tommy. It was a small thing, and one that she could have done herself. She said that any opportunity to break out of the intense isolation of hiding was welcome to her. Small tasks that I could do helped mitigate my own feelings of powerlessness. The projects we worked on together over the next few years varied in scope — helping her find housing, get into a technical school, find medical care. I never had a number for her, and I never knew when I'd hear from her next. And then, after a few years, she stopped calling.

Over the six years I worked for Safe Haven, I talked with hundreds of women in Margie's situation — women who felt their lives and the lives of their children were at stake and that the law could not provide sufficient protection. Many of these encounters were short phone conversations made from undisclosed locations throughout the United States and Canada. Many of them were in the confidential shelter, where women used their twenty-eight-day stay to plan their next moves.

Through my conversations with women, I came to understand that the underground functions primarily as an anti-place, a place that resists location, both temporal and spatial, and that remains fluid and unpredictable. It is profoundly isolating. Women talked about the underground in rich and diverse ways, describing both the freedom and "almost dead" feeling they experienced moving through the world. For many women, the reality of living underground revealed itself in quotidian details: refusing the simple comfort of an accustomed haircut, eyeing the mailbox with suspicion, forbidding fingers from dialing familiar numbers. At the same time, many women compared their plight to other collective struggles, such as the U.S. anti-slavery Underground Railroad or efforts to escape the Holocaust.

Ironically, the very existence of legal remedies designed to protect victims of domestic violence often worked against women in the greatest danger. In my work with bureaucrats and lawmakers, the prevailing attitude was that existing legal remedies were sufficient to keep women safe. They pointed to protections available to battered women and argued that women had the best chances of staying safe if they availed themselves of these resources. Within this understanding of the law as adequate, women who refused to cooperate with legal agencies were often cast as hysterical or trying to hide for ulterior motives (such as to support a life of crime or to deny fathers their parental rights). Interlocking oppressions, especially racism and xenophobia, contributed to a dangerous gap between the rhetoric of legal protection and the reality of intense vulnerability. The existing web of legal remedies, therefore, sometimes became the justification for discounting women who went underground.

I was particularly struck by the ways that existing legal remedies combined with stereotypic notions of the "good victim" to punish women on the margins, no matter how expertly they attempted to play the law game. Scholars and activists have written about the construction of the "battered everywoman," a classically good, passive, "deserving" victim who merits society's sympathy and resources (Loeske 1992; Kanuha 1996; Richie 2000). Though this construction did important work in casting battering as an issue worthy of public attention, it left women who did not fit an image of the "good victim" out in the cold.

In my work with women attempting to go underground to escape lethal abuse, I saw how women dealing with multiple oppressions were particularly disadvantaged. Women who had committed crimes had few places to turn, even if their abusers forced them into illegal activities. Richie discusses this phenomenon in terms of "gender entrapment" in her study of Black women convicted of crimes (Richie 1996). My work helping women to play the law game was frustratingly limited in these cases. However, I sought to make some impact by bringing stories of marginalized women to local policy discussions. For example, as I mentioned earlier, our community collaborated to examine the issue of "victim defendants," survivors of violence who were charged with domestic violence crimes (Crager, Cousin and Hardy 2003). This project allowed advocates such as myself to bring stories of marginalized women to the fore. Overall, however, I felt frustrated by my lack of power to provide meaningful assistance for women with whom the *with* the law frame offered limited or no help. This frustration eventually helped push me out of this job and into a doctoral program in women's studies, where I hoped I could learn better tools for resistance.

Learning new ways to theorize power has helped me to make sense of the potential and limits of my legal advocacy work. I have found Westlund's (1999) theorization of battered women and power particularly thought provoking. Drawing on Foucault's work in *Discipline and Punish*, Westlund argues that battering is a pre-modern form of power: "Some of the most overt and pervasive methods of maintaining power and control over women remain distinctly 'pre-modern' in nature, to use Foucault's term. I am speaking, in particular, of the techniques of domestic and sexual violence, techniques that are intensely corporal and brutal and that are wielded in a personal and sporadic, rather than an impersonal and meticulous, manner" (1046). At the same time, battered women are subjected to the disciplinary forces of modern forms of power. Battered women "experience pre-modern and modern forms of power side by side: not only do they have to deal with the instigation of terror by an all-powerful 'sovereign,' but they are also often compelled to turn for help to modern institutions such as medicine and psychiatry, police, courts and so on" (1046). These modern forms of power emphasize regulation, discipline and surveillance techniques instead of overt displays of physical power. Dealing with these two types of power is a complex and contradictory project. At times modern power exercised through the legal system succeeds in controlling the pre-modern violence of batterers. However, at other times, disciplining discourses of court neutrality, acting in the best interests of children and pathologizing battered women leave women who follow the rules profoundly vulnerable to abusers' violence. Women who go underground clearly illustrate the rock-and-hard-place difficulties in negotiating these two forms of power simultaneously.

Modern forms of power have changed drastically over the last several decades. It is worth remembering that the legal response to domestic violence is only a few decades old. In the 1970s, the criminal justice system's response-of-no-response permeated every aspect of the legal system (Schechter 1982; Fineman and Mykitiuk 1994). In contrast, the state is now deeply involved in identifying, treating and punishing domestic violence. For example, in the civil justice system, judges rely on an array of evaluations, tests and reports to determine if domestic violence claims are "credible" and how these claims affect a woman's ability to parent. The civil justice system intersects with medical and mental health institutions in their efforts to study and evaluate battered women. "These institutions often revictimize battered women by pathologizing their condition and treating them as mentally unhealthy individuals who are incapable of forming legitimate appraisals of their situations and exercising rational agency over their lives" (Westlund 1999: 1046). These distinctly modern forms of control hold significant power over battered women.

Computer technology and the Internet have also significantly altered the power relations battered women must negotiate. Whereas abuser-initiated cyberstalking has convinced many women that they need to go underground, information technology has made it nearly impossible to do so. Even during the six years I worked with Safe Haven I saw a marked difference in women's abilities to successfully disappear.

Lee Quinby (1999) argues that current articulations of technoculture are gendered, reinforce systems of domination and function "through patriarchal systems of kinship" (1083). Indeed in my work I observed how the Internet can help abusers maintain patriarchal systems of kinship, as the following case of "custodial interference" illustrates. I worked with a woman who had fled her home after her husband sexually abused their two-year-old daughter. The husband found his wife through a complicated series of maneuverings that involved breaking into her email account and stealing phone records of her parents. He then filed custody papers. The court awarded him custody, and the mother refused to comply with the order. She fled our shelter and moved to a different part of the state. The father then got a writ of habeas corpus (literally "seize the body"), and law enforcement worked with the husband to find the woman. It was the surveillance technology available to law enforcement that eventually led to the woman's capture. The daughter was forced to live with her father. Unable to imagine leaving her daughter alone with her father, the woman decided to return home, thus fulfilling her husband's stated wish that "they just become a regular family again."

In spite of the critique of the regulatory power of modern institutions, Westlund remains optimistic about the potential of domestic violence agencies to help battered women resist abuse. "Foucault's unmasking of the sinister side of disciplinary practices should lead not to denial of the usefulness of the law and the 'helping professions' for battered women generally but, rather, to recognition of the need to become both more proficient at diagnosing the ways these institutions do fail women and better able to imagine forms of local resistance and transformation" (1046). The stories of women who go underground certainly provide a detailed rendering of the ways that legal institutions fail battered women and children. They also suggest modes of resistance and transformation.

The Law and Its Alternatives

Women going underground were expert not only in keeping themselves and their children safe, but also at discussing and describing the deep injustices that pushed them into hiding. They were keenly aware of the limits of their resistance while hiding — although they were evading the power of their abusers and (at times) the law, they felt anything but free. However, for many women I worked with, their journey underground was temporary, and they found ways to re-emerge and work for justice for other women in similar situations.

Several women who had gone underground began to tell their stories in public — at community events, volunteer trainings, religious gatherings and the like. Their stories clearly demonstrated not only their strength and tenacity, but also the failure of society to offer real protection. Their stories ask us to radically re-imagine our approach to domestic violence. Longtime battered women's activist and scholar Ellen Pence poses the question, "why do we expect battered women to give up everything and move into a shelter? Why don't we send the abusers to a big house, give them a curfew, make them sign up on chore charts and scrub the toilets and cook meals, like we require of battered women?" Though I don't think that finding new ways of corralling and controlling abusive men will ultimately lead to peaceful homes, the idea of helping battered women shoulder the responsibility for their safety is crucial.

As I evaluate my legal advocacy work and the impact of legal advocacy work within institutionalized battered women's programs more generally, I find another observation of Westlund's helpful: "An outright rejection of the modern institutions to which a battered woman can turn would be absurdly self-defeating, since the very possibility of resistance to domestic violence depends, for a significant number of women, on the existence of the relatively safe spaces that these institutions offer. The deeper question we might pose here is: What theoretical sense can we make of this apparent fact?" (1049). I draw three conclusions from this statement. First, working from the *with* the law frame is a crucial intervention, since it enables battered women and their advocates to make material and discursive gains, albeit within a flawed system. Second, since institutionalization poses real challenges to resistive work, the practices of battered women's programs must be continually evaluated. Rejecting dichotomous assessments of institutionalization as either good or bad for feminist activism, feminist sociologists Ferree and Martin ask us to consider the "important, and largely unasked, question about feminist organizations that survived... what [does] their institutionalization mean for feminism?... Did they abandon their feminist goals, practices and agendas?" (Ferree and Martin 1995: 6). Safe Haven had good mechanisms for self-evaluation and critique, including monthly meetings, monthly diversity trainings and bi-annual retreats, and this gave staff and volunteers time to discuss issues of feminism, battered women's organizing and the tensions of institutionalization. This self-reflexivity has allowed Safe Haven to evaluate its work within a larger social frame, even as it faces institutionalization-related constraints.

Third, established legal advocacy and crisis intervention services may help to open up space for more radical thinking and organizing outside of the main-stream domestic violence agency. Increasingly, scholars and activists are looking beyond individual legal remedies to alternatives that seek to minimize and/or eliminate the role of the law (Ptacek 2005; Stark 2004). I have found the work of Incite! particularly inspiring in this area. Incite! self-identifies as "a national activist organization of radical feminists of color advancing a movement to end violence against women of color and their communities" (Incite! 2006). At the national level, Incite! brings together grassroots organizers, academics and self-identified allies to share ideas, resources and strategies. They explicitly link violence against women activism with anti-prison work, thus fundamentally challenging current reliance on the legal system. In Seattle, Incite!-affiliated organizations are helping reshape the way mainstream agencies such as Safe Haven think through reliance on the legal system, work with women who have used violence and question gender binaries (e.g., woman equals victim and man equals perpetrator). These new ways of thinking through key issues improve the practice within mainstream agencies.

Meanwhile, as activists debate understandings and approaches to the law, women in abusive relationships continue to resist in ways both visible and hidden. They make calculated choices of how and when to participate in legal actions. They decide how to present themselves in different situations and which stories to tell about their experiences of abuse and survival. They work individually for their own safety and collectively, informing our resistance efforts and our agendas for change.

Chapter 11

Resistance and Recovery

Three Women's Testimonies

Jean Toner

I remember posing a question in clinical supervision some years ago aimed at understanding a client's behaviour, which was deemed "deviant" yet seemed to be empowering for that person. My clinical supervisor, an expert on trauma, replied that he never failed to be amazed at the incredible creativity with which traumatized people meet and respond to their traumatizing situations. I have not forgotten his words, and they did indeed answer my inquiry. The meaning of the resistant behaviour was its statement of non-defeat and non-surrender to an oppressive and cruel situation. The fact that the behaviour may be characterized as "deviant" made the agency inherent in the behaviour invisible and rendered it pathological. I began to understand the import of acts of "everyday resistance" (Wade 1997) that provide protection from the violence of racism, sexism and other status oppressions.

Since that time I have treated many women deemed sick or suffering from a disorder because of their drug using behaviour. I have wondered if the vilification of women who use drugs, particularly women of colour, has more to do with a war on women (Boyd 2004) than on any reasonable assessment of women's behaviours. I have wondered if women who use drugs have been ghettoized into a socially constructed definition of pathology structured to silence or trivialize any genuine outcry against the violence of poverty, discrimination and functional disenfranchisement. I have wondered if substance abuse is a response to oppressions and their effects, and if the real disease is a disease of power carried and spread by a patriarchal political economy. Such questions came into high relief most poignantly when prompted by court-mandated referrals of women from sociocultural groups that have historically experienced social, economic and/or physical confinement by the law, policy or customary practice.

As women brought these questions forward, I began to see them as a pre-articulated way of knowing. I was reminded of Bepko's characterization of addiction as a "a microcosmic process that reflects and is perhaps a metaphor for imbalances in power in the larger social arena" (1991: 1). If the purpose and intent of the behaviour is resistance to status oppressions and supporting labelling, then in fact women may be demonstrating agency by their behavioural choices. More specific to this study and viewed through a lens of resistance, substance abusing behavioural choices serve to challenge and subvert legal and policy practices intended to force the assimilation of indigenous peoples into the majority culture. If one defines resistance as employment of strategies that ensure physical and cultural survival, ensure identity formation and preservation, and foster joining with others to assure the continuity of the physical and psycho-cultural self, then the stories that follow show how substance abuse is one strategy among several that women use to resist efforts to compromise or destroy their identity and cultural connections.

This analysis does not in any way disregard the potential and actual enormous risk to health and life posed by substance abusing behaviours. It simply recognizes that such choices, viewed through a lens of agency and resistance, provide a different conceptualization of both the intent and impact of women's choice to engage in such behaviour. Viewing women's substance abusing behaviours through a lens of resistance and persistence provides illumination of structures of power that have constructed a definition of women who use substances. It has implication for the conceptualization of treatment as more productively founded upon a genuine empowerment process, rather than an individualized, medicalized regimen.

Theorizing Social Construction of Addiction

The stories that follow are drawn from a larger qualitative study that explored women's substance abusing behaviours as a resistance to status oppressions of race, class and gender. To fully appreciate the stories that follow, one must understand two things. One must understand the context of laws and policies that affected Native American people of the United States in general, and the women in this study specifically. One must also understand the context for women created by the nature and function of the United States' dominant political economy and culture, which has constructed female substance abuse as deviant, and which engages a medicalized ideology of individualism to facilitate control of these often unruly, often poor women. I briefly discuss the construction of women and addiction, then briefly highlight selected policies and laws of the United States that are a part of centuries of genocidal policies targeted at the original inhabitants of North America.

Feminist scholars have been critiquing socio-legal responses to women's addiction behaviours for several years. Following the emergence of crack cocaine as a perceived epidemic, feminist scholars were quick to challenge the legal and media construction of women (usually women of colour) who used crack cocaine. They critiqued the misguided, damaging social policy spawned by the "drug scare" (Boyd 1999, 2004; Campbell 2000; Gomez 1997; Humphries 1999; Maher 1997; Roberts 1991; Young 1994). Laws were enacted aimed at punishing these women, such as mandatory minimum sentences for possession of even the smallest amount of crack cocaine. In a wave of state intrusion into the affairs of pregnant and parenting women, certain groups of women (poor, of colour) were targeted for surveillance because of their "at-risk" status and were disproportionately drug tested in hospitals in the United States (Humphries 1999). In a clear abuse of states' interpretation of *parens patriae*, women were often separated from their children if they tested positive for an illegal drug. In some states, such as Florida and South Carolina, women were prosecuted for "delivery of a controlled substance" to their unborn babies (Roberts 1991). In the decade of the peak crack cocaine frenzy, 70 percent of the women so treated were poor women of colour (Boyd 2004).

In ongoing cooperation between medicine and legal structures, courts have engaged in the mandating of treatment for women deemed "at-risk." Such labelling of women, in what amounts to racial and class profiling, enables intervention in women's lives without their consent and provides justification for increased levels of surveillance and control of their lives. In an interesting double-speak, much of what contributes to an "at-risk" profile involves the very structures of oppression, such as poverty and discrimination, that create conditions that foster a substance abusing gesture of response in women (Campbell 2000).

Women whose stories appear in this chapter, through good fortune, fate, guidance or resistance avoided the criminalizing of their substance abusing behaviour. Had they not been so fortunate, they would have found themselves mandated to a system and delivery of treatment services that has evolved in response to the development of gender-sensitive models and protocols (Beckman 1994; Brown et al. 2002; Burman 1994; CASA 1996; Covington 1999; Finkelstein et al. 2004; Hiebert-Murphy and Woytkiw 2000; McNeece and DiNitto 1998; Moses, Huntington and D'Ambrosia 2004; Pieri 2002; Rasmussen 2000; SAMHSA 2002). A review of the literature shows that what is defined as gender-sensitive is founded upon depoliticized notions of a medical model of addiction or a psycho-social assessment that recognizes oppressive conditions but seeks to ameliorate those conditions rather than deconstruct and overturn them (Campbell 2000; Keane 2002). Had they been mandated to treatment, they would have found a profession that recognizes etiological differences between men and women, both biological and psychosocial, that have been accepted by the consensus in addiction science (Angrove and Fothergill 2003; S. Brown 2002; Covington 1999; Hernandez-Avila, Bruce and Kranzler 2004; Jang, Livesley and Vernon 1997; Lillehoj, Trudeau, Spoth and Wickrama 2004; Mulia 2000; Ostlund, Spak and Sundh 2004; Prescott 2002; Sohrabji 2002). They would have found that such depoliticized notions of causation continue to label women as deviant or disordered and continue to stigmatize, even as claims are made of explanation and empowerment. Such a construction undermines efforts by women to envision and act collectively for change. It does not take into account the effects of degrading and dehumanizing systems of social welfare that reinforce and perpetuate inequitable and unequal economic stratification and other barriers to care (Mulia 2003; Segal 2001).

To understand the women's stories that follow one must have an understanding of laws and policies that constituted acts of genocide of Native American peoples. Of particular relevance to women in this study are the policies of removal of children from their homes and placement in boarding schools that began in the late nineteenth century and continued as an official policy of the United States government into the 1930s. Laws that prohibited spiritual practices indigenous to their cultures and the introduction of alcohol by white traders were blatantly self-serving acts of bio-terrorism. Such policies have been the practice of Euro-Americans since first contact in the fifteenth century (Stannard 1992), along with legal sanctioning of land theft. As an additional tool of enforcing subjugating law, primary jurisdiction over behaviours deemed criminal has been maintained, with limited exception, by the federal government of the United States and has continued to be a contested issue in the complexities of sovereignty (Ross 1998).

Prior to first contact with Europeans, use of alcohol was nearly non-existent in the Americas. Euro-Americans discovered that use of alcohol greatly facilitated the exploitation of indigenous peoples and enabled the ultimate theft and control of lands across the continent. It became common practice for white traders to encourage drunkenness among Aboriginal peoples to enable unfair trading practices. By the latter part of the nineteenth century, as practices of enclosure confined indigenous peoples to reservations, their possession or consumption of alcohol was eventually outlawed. This was not in response to health concerns. It simply created a new category of criminality with which to control indigenous peoples (Boyd 2004).

In an effort at genocide through assimilation, spiritual practices were prohibited and children were stolen from the reservations and placed in government boarding schools, where their indigenous ways could be disciplined out of them, often through violence. Children's use of their native language was prohibited, their traditional dress was destroyed and replaced by militaristic uniforms, and their hair was cut in final insult to their culture. The true aim of this policy was the dismantling of indigenous culture and the destruction of tribal bonds (Morris 2000). Some languages and ceremonies have been lost forever, and some people have lost any record of their tribal membership. However, resistance from Native peoples has enabled survival of lifeways and thoughtways. Examples of resistance are presented by the women in this chapter. Depending upon their personal histories, these women found ways to appear complicit with the majority culture, while at the same time refusing to suspend use of their original language, or they found ways to challenge dominant power structures in a public way rather than stay silent while their heritage or integrity were questioned. They found ways to bring other women along in their journeys to sobriety in ways consistent with their cultures, and they uncovered counterstories to replace the dominant culture version of history.

Methodology

Two studies provided a framework for my inquiry into women's resistance to labelling and framing. Profitt (2000) focused on the process women formerly battered by men went through as they experienced a *conscientization*, or consciousness-raising leading to social praxis. The concept of substance abuse as a resistance to status oppression drew from work by Friedman and Alicea (2001) with women heroin addicts in two methadone clinics. They say: "We found that women's relationship with heroin could be better understood by looking beyond popular deviance models to a theoretical framework of resistance centering on gender, class, and racial inequality" (2). They contend that the causes and meanings of oppositional behaviour have little to do with deviance and learned helplessness, but a great deal to do with moral and political indignation (25).

This chapter, taken from a larger study, focuses on reactive resistance through substance abuse and more strategic practices of resistance that have enabled persistence and thriving of three Native American women. The larger study was conducted through a series of focus groups and individual indepth interviews with women with two or more years of sobriety. Questions explored how women experienced their earlier lives and drug using years from the perspective of their gender, class and race or ethnicity. The three focus groups, recruited from Twelve Step Recovery programs, were ethnic-specific, with one group comprised of Latinas, one group of Native American women and one of white women. The choice of ethnicities was representative of the general population in the area of the United States southwest, where the study was conducted. A total of fifteen women participated. Standard protocols for protection of human subjects and for collection of data were followed. Analysis of data was performed according to grounded theory methodology (Strauss 1987). It is essential to note that as a feminist researcher, I was and am attuned to the pervasive influence of my positionality as a white, middle-class social worker and social work educator, as well as the influence of many years of mainstream mental health and substance abuse treatment provision. I acknowledge that my interpretation of the data is shaped by my history, my place in space and time, and the assumptions born of my white privilege.

Theoretical Framework

Turiel, in his work on moral psychology, indicted popular psychological adjustment theories: "Many explanations of social and moral development are, indeed, tied mainly to social adjustment insofar as they focus on compliance and internalization of societal norms. If tension in society is needed for social change, and if resistance is a part of everyday life, then those theories have serious shortcomings" (Turiel 2003: 117). In keeping with Turiel's analysis and in writing about the "everyday" ways people resist violence and other forms of abuse, Wade offers the following definition of "everyday resistance":

> I propose here that any mental or behavioral act through which a person attempts to expose, withstand, repel, stop, prevent, abstain from, strive against, impede, refuse to comply with, or oppose any form of violence or oppression (including any type of disrespect), or the conditions that make such acts possible, may be understood as resistance. (1997: 25)

Resistant responses and "shared critique of domination" were expressed in certain themes in Native American women's stories of resistance, which included, but were not limited to, an array of behaviours: 1) substance abusing behaviours themselves, 2) talking back, 3) passing on knowing and 4) creating or experiencing a counterstory. They also engaged in strategies involving apparent complicity with dominant power structures that, in truth, were disguised "performances" of resistance (Scott 1990). These behaviours and strategies were embedded in the "everyday-ness" of their lives, enabling what Dorothy Smith describes as "inquiry that begins with the issues and problems of people's lives and develops inquiry from the standpoint of their experience in and of the actualities of their everyday living" (Smith 2002: 18). Stories told by women reveal and uncover trans-local structures of power, their resistance and complicity, and the tension in between.

I have highlighted certain parts of the stories of Native American women in the study that reflect resistance to status oppressions, both in active addiction and recovery. Their stories are embedded in the context of genocidal policies of the United States government that spanned centuries. The women's stories demonstrate how substance abuse was often a reactive resistance to oppression, with other, more strategic, resistances allowing the persistence that is evident in their words.

A'sdzaan's Story of Resisting
Identity Annihilation and AA Racism

A'sdzaan, a Native American woman in her thirties, named the injustice, as well as trauma, of racism in her story of forced learning in the boarding school for Native American children:

> I know that it was a struggle to learn English. I was an older girl being in the beginner reading group. I was in the remedial reading group. I knew that I was an older girl — like a bigger girl and the kids were little. So just knowing that was another — one more thing to be ashamed of. And then because it was a boarding school it was not a very gentle way to learn how to read. It was like you were put on the spot. Why don't you know — this is Jane and Dick. And why can't you say it — pronounce it like that. And, you know, the little children looking at me — this big girl. And, you know, it was another pain to step into and walk through and be afraid of and have angst about. And I think that was one of the reasons I kept telling myself I will learn to read. I am going to learn how to read. And I did. (March 2005, Arizona)

A'sdzaan's story reflects her determination, agency and persistence in succeeding in the face of overwhelming psychological injury and social humiliation. In Wade's schema she "withstood the injustice and strived against it."

A'sdzaan's story reflects one of the most powerful and structurally violent forms of oppression, the destruction of language. Worldview is contained in language. When "relations of the ruling" perpetrate language destruction, they effectively dismantle a culture. Morris (2000) says that the function of boarding schools extended from the direct "destruction of cultural identity" to the expectation that students would return to their homes, "where they could pass on this new reality to their family and friends" (201). A'sdzaan's resistance was to more than a humiliating and psychologically violent boarding school experience. Her resistance was to the destruction of her personhood as expressed in her culture. It is important to recognize how multi-layered A'sdzaan's resistance was. Learning the dominant language and reading skills, while appearing complicit, enabled her to live in both worlds of white dominant culture and her Native culture, and negotiate the sometimes treacherous waters of biculturalism, allowing for the preservation of her traditional culture. Scott (1990) finds that complicity by exploited people and groups is not adequate evidence for the existence of false consciousness in the mind of the dominated. He argues for the efficacy of "hidden transcripts" that interpret apparently complicit behaviour quite differently than the norm. In the presence of dominating social structures, where it is not safe to openly challenge the power structure, disguised "performances" of agreement, as in A'sdzaan's learning to read, carries a meaning that is preservative of an inner reality and a critique of dominant power arrangements.

A'sdzaan's experience with addiction functioned as a resistance to the spirit-killing and culture-destroying practices of the dominant culture. She talks about her experience with alcohol in the context of the double life she led:

> *I led a double life... I was student council. I was academic. I was Vocational and Industrial Club of America. I was in National Honor Society... but as soon as, like school let out, like on the weekends, then I was like off on a spree. Just full force drinking. And then I would come back on Monday [to the boarding school] like nothing had happened.*

A'sdzaan could not find peace or security within the structures of oppression in her life; however, she found ways to feel excitement and vitality via drinking and drugging. She later refers to the "medicinal" qualities of alcohol in response and resistance to the incomparable stress of living with feet in two worlds.

A'sdzaan found great comfort in the counterstory provided by her grand-mother, who had raised her on the reservation until she was removed to attend boarding school. She says of her grandmother:

> *My grandmother is 102... she is not formally educated, but I think she is very traditional and very strong. And I think she did her very, very best... the way she tried to teach me to be strong... prayer was her biggest strength. She would pray for everything... there are so many prayers. She always had a medicine person involved in her life.*

A'sdzaan talks about how much pain it brought her grandmother to see her drinking, but expressed profound gratitude that her grandmother never pushed her away. "She would always welcome me." Ultimately A'sdzaan re-introduced and integrated the traditional ways into her life, gaining the identity and the spiritual strength that were legacies from her grandmother.

A recurrent strategy of resistance that subverted master narrative constriction was the practice of "passing on" knowing from one woman to another, primarily through oral methods. The strategy was executed in different ways with different women. A'sdzaan talks about how she subverts the Christian, white, male discourse that underlies the program of Alcoholics Anonymous and, according to A'sdzaan's analysis, alienates women (and men) who have a different worldview and spirituality:

> *Don't you change your being. Whenever I hear people share at the meetings the Jesus Christ savior and this and stuff… I always share even if I have shared already… I always have to share one more time and say, you know what? I have been sober however many years and I have never had Jesus Christ the Lord as my higher power ever. I haven't read the Bible. You don't… if you are new here, please come back. That is another reason they don't come back… because they hear that.*

A'sdzaan comes into AA recovery with an experience set of a woman of colour, a Native woman whose culture has been marginalized through silencing and the talking over, sometimes outlawing, of her spirituality. But, in the interest of creating safety and affirmation within Alcoholics Anonymous for other women of colour and different worldviews, she has spoken up. In doing so, she is passing on her recovery wisdom, which could be lost to silence, to other women who come from a non-dominant culture. She developed strategies of coping with the structural oppression that enabled other women of colour to continue with a recovery program that was life-saving for them.

Kaybe's Story of Resisting Alienation, Loss and Racism

Women in this study were astute in recognizing injustice and calling attention to it and to the interlocking nature of multiple oppressions. An example of substance abuse itself serving as a resistance to status oppressions is illustrated in Kaybe's story. She found that substance abuse helped her to resist the loneliness that came with the sense of separateness and the isolation of racism. She experienced a new-found sense of belonging with the initiation of substance abusing behaviours:

> *I felt like I never fit in because of that [race]. I felt like I did not fit in anywhere in any kind of group of people. When I used and I got that effect from alcohol or whatever it was I was doing, I didn't have to think about that part. I could just shut that off. This was like one of the first things that was like… that I liked. Was that I could turn that off. Then after I shut that off, I was able to open up and talk to whomever I wanted to talk to. (April 2005, Arizona)*

Her involvement with alcohol and other drugs enabled her to resist loneliness through "repelling" and "withstanding" (Wade 1997). The dominant culture is founded upon "in-group, out-group" mentality that structures power to remain with the in-group through constructing non-white races as "other" (Maher and Tetreault 1998). She identified how alcohol actually enabled a shift in self concept that compelled an alternate narrative to the racism she experienced growing up:

I think what I found out was that the people I was using with, they were impressed that I was Native. A lot of people were. And I think that also changed a lot of what my foster parents taught me about it being a bad thing. I started to see it in different ways... I really did think it was a bad thing, but then there were these people I was partying with and they were just impressed to hell that I was and I just thought, "wow." I never thought that before. It made me feel really good.

In terms of "hierarchies of oppression" (Krestan 2000), Kaybe's space of intersecting zones of race, class and gender oppressions became occupied, through the use and sharing of substances, by a more accepting set of persons who affirmed her self, rather than diminished her. These behaviours underpinned a counter-narrative to the narrative of racism she learned in foster homes. She learned that with her new "partying" associations she could find acceptance and begin reversing the effects of years of racism and self-disregard. While substance abuse is undeniably harmful to the person abusing substances, the positive effects named in Kaybe's story demonstrate a powerful resistance to equally deleterious effects of intersecting oppressions.

Kaybe told a story from her perspective of the American Holocaust (Stannard 1992) and intergenerational trauma (Duran 1995; Segal 2001; Walters, Simoni and Evans-Campbell 2002). The fracturing of the cultures of indigenous peoples left unspeakable grief and trauma and a justified mistrust of the government that sanctioned, and continues to sanction, such abuse. She told the story of her aunt's participation in the capture and occupation of Alcatraz during the 1970s. When asked about other experiences of activism, she issued this warning:

I think people have to be really careful because the government doesn't like that kind of stuff and a lot of people got eliminated because of that kind of stuff. And that is the message I got from my aunt.

Kaybe issued that warning from oral history and in the context of generations of attempted genocide of her people, as well as persistent attempts by the dominant power structures to dilute and destroy her culture and traditional way of life. Such a warning is not without basis in history. Neither is the resistance that Kaybe goes on to state:

The other message that I got from it was that the government can't take away your identity and nobody really can.

Kaybe identifies a core of self that has resisted efforts by the dominant culture's socio-political structures and resultant federal policies to erase her Native identity. She has prevailed with an assaulted, but intact identity, and clearly named the forces that threatened her.

Kaybe also tells of the strength of a counterstory that she found when she reunited with her relatives on the reservation:

I didn't go back home until I was in my twenties... And I think what I learned from my grandfather was that, you know, something to do with kindness and something to do with... I think love. See, he lived to be 107, or a little past that... I learned a lot from him... I had to get a cultural grounding... I didn't have that kind of connection with [foster parents]. I had that with my relatives. So I had to go back and find them.

In spite of the racism Kaybe experienced growing up in foster care, she resisted permanently internalizing it. The counterstory of her heritage as a strategy of resistance to racism was not available to her in her early years, but her internal knowledge of the strength of her heritage became a guide leading her back home when she became an adult.

Kaybe's refusal to be denied her personhood and to resist conditions that denigrated her self and Native identity was strongly evidenced in recovery. The same persistence and identity underpinned her challenge to a racist supervisor in a substance abuse treatment centre:

I think where I work at there are a lot of double standards. On one hand, I am told one thing, but then they go and do something else, the opposite of what they say. To me, I dealt with that. I just told my boss I am not taking any of that shit. You know? I have come a long way from where I came from to be treated like that. Working with the people that I work with now, I don't need to be treated that way. Put down and all that stuff. I just have to make sure that I talk with her one to one because nobody else there will.

Kaybe refuses to be humiliated and in the process contributes to the improved position of her co-workers as well. This is suggestive of Campbell's and Burstow's view that the antidote to addiction and presumed powerlessness is empowerment (Burstow 2003; Campbell 2000). Kaybe's traits of resiliency and critical analysis were present from her early years of using into her recovery years.

DeeDee's Story of Resisting Identity Loss and Absence of Protection from Abuse

DeeDee, a Native American woman in her forties, was raised by her white mother and step-father. She learned that her step-father was not her biological father when she was fifteen and applying for a driver's licence. She needed to produce her birth certificate, and it was then that she learned the identity of her father, a Native American man she had never heard of, much less met. She reports that all of a sudden it made sense why her skin was darker than most of her friends. She talked about the lack of protection she received from legal resources when attempting to find safe harbour from her step-father's abuse:

There was someone who tried to intervene for me when I was in high school. I lived with her and her two daughters. I had told her about my step-father molesting me and she was trying to get help. She had applied for foster care and everything. And my mom threatened me... I remember I rode my bike to the police station and I asked them... can she actually do that? And they go, "yes, unless something else happened." Why didn't they just say, "what happened that you need to get out of the house?" (March 2005, Arizona)

Protections were not present for DeeDee, either from the violence of being stripped of her true identity or the physical and sexual violence experienced at the hand of her step-father. In a legal reality similar to the predicament of a stalked or battered woman, if an event has not actually happened, the law is not designed to protect a child from the predictable execution of threats. DeeDee knew there was no help from the authorities presumably mandated to protect vulnerable persons. Yet, on some level, she found ways to resist, through alcohol and other drugs as a protector, then later in recovery through a reconnection with and reclaiming of her heritage. She tells this story of learning about how her father's identity was lost to her:

My father was stolen from the reservation. And there were so many Natives stolen from that reservation. Hundreds, thousands across Indian Country. And the families, the women, the mothers, they weren't even reporting it anymore because nobody was doing anything about it. So there is no way to trace my family.

Again, the authorities mandated to protect were either not protecting or were actually being complicit in the stealing of Native children from the reservations. While DeeDee acknowledged that the grief cannot be taken away, she found ways to resist the cultural violence by reconnecting with other Native peoples and joining with Native ways of recovery that resonated within her psyche, her soul.

DeeDee's story reflects the resistance strategies of emotionally numbing substance abuse and of reconnection with her heritage, which she carried into recovery from drug abuse. In recovery, she employed the particular strategy of "talking back." She tells a story of talking back in her position at a university. She challenged a new educational policy that disadvantaged off-campus students, most of whom were people of colour. She tells of the meeting with her supervisor and subsequent actions:

So I went to her office and tried to talk to her and just tried to ask her if she realized the effect of her policy. And she went on saying how she was advocating a higher standard... that they needed to be held to a higher standard... anyway, it didn't go well. And then I just read this article that she published in [names an education journal]. It was like a personal introspective piece... in it she said, "I recall being called a racist by a newly Native woman... she had just married a Native man." And she goes on to talk about the meeting we had and how I was just wanting the Indians given the degree and not held to a higher standard. I wrote a letter to her and I sent a copy to the Dean... "I question your scholarly research"... she didn't research to see if I was Native or not.

In talking back, DeeDee not only advocates for off-campus students of colour, but risks personal and professional exposure to "paybacks." Her story demonstrates a subtle, but powerful, ongoing legacy of colonialism that pits non-dominant people against each other and ultimately is a disguised service to the white patriarchy. A "divide and conquer" strategy can keep the spotlight of clarity trained away from the ongoing structural racism. Such distraction maintains the status quo, which is one way power reproduces itself. Some may argue that the academic's position embraces a privileging of dominant culture measures of achievement, potentially to the exclusion of other ways of knowing (Hartman 1992). DeeDee resisted what some may argue was her director's colonized position, and she resisted the legacy of excluding people of colour from accessing mainstream education. Her "talking back" in this situation required no small amount of courage and insight.

Summary Statements about the Women's Stories

In viewing the functioning of and effects of substance abuse on women's lives, it would be a mistake to conflate complicity with powerlessness. Women in this study are surely not powerless. The effectiveness of their strategies of resistance is testimony to their creativity in resisting control and discipline. Women in this study demonstrated effective strategies in claiming their worth and their place, while simultaneously challenging oppressive statements or practices. Whether their resistance was to racist foster care or racism in Alcoholics Anonymous, their strategies went around oppressive structures through counterstory, passing on knowing and practising disguises of complicity. Their strategies challenged oppressive structures through talking back and reclaiming and celebrating their previously stolen heritage.

The women in this study all experienced profound trauma. Edkins (2003) identifies the political dimension of trauma when she refers to the altered view of self engendered by trauma. Rather than be silenced or, in the words of Edkins, accept "victimhood [that] offers sympathy and pity in return for the surrender of any political voice" (9), these women chose activism. They have not succumbed to the potential destructiveness of a legacy of childhood abuse or psycho-cultural annihilation. They have named the injury or the offending oppressive structure, extended their analysis to a broader span of society and engaged in social action that goes to the heart of healing and change. In a Frierian sense, these women have become "actors in praxis," theorizing about their experience, extending it to others and taking action.

Some may say, and a case could be made for the argument, that I am simply reframing stories and meanings that have already been told. I would argue that it is language, including reframing, that creates the parameters of knowledge. Reframing, then, can be an intensely political act. Reframing can create the workspace for epistemic exploration, discovery and un-covery. The women in this chapter, and many other women, have and continue to strive daily to usher in a little more justice and little more care. I am reminded of DeeDee's words when asked why she chose to participate in the study. She said simply, "our voices must be heard." These women are not victims. They are resisters.

Section Five

Literary/Historical Forms of Resistance

The final section provides examples of literary criticism as historical forms of women's resistance. Using examples of breast giving and infanticide (Lynn Makau) and political activism and writing (Janice Matsumura) as resistance, these final chapters describe historical and symbolic forms of resistance by women who resisted slavery and political imprisonment. Using breast giving as an example of resistance for slave women who do not own themselves or the product of their selves, Lynn Makau elucidates the empowering symbolism of the black woman's rebellion against the most severe forms of enslavement – rape and sexual harassment – by white men and women. The colonization of the non-propertied, non-entitled, non-personed female body and soul and culture makes Sethe in Toni Morrison's *Beloved*, chattel. Since Sethe's children are also chattel and not hers to own or to keep, the giving and denying of breast milk, and committing infanticide in order to save her children from the inevitable horrible future, become forms of resistance available to enslaved women. The choice to abort, to kill and to deny food, love, shelter and safety are forms of subversion available to women who have no options open to them. In this way Sethe's breast giving is political activity and resistance to slavery.

Challenging the universal ideology of the right to sexual abuse and exploit enslaved and outcaste women, Morrison positions Sethe as a symbol of all women who find themselves challenging oppressive practices. While infanticide and denial of breast giving may seem to be extreme measures, they can also be read as rational acts when women are given no other option. Situated among the other forms of resistance discussed in this volume this chapter does not seem out of place. It provides a symbolic example of a woman's resistant struggle in one of the most unendurable examples of violence imaginable.

In a second example using literary analysis as cultural innovation, Janice Matsumura explores the life of Nakamoto Takako, whose writings as a political prisoner provide a powerful example of resistance through writing and recollection. Nakamoto Takako was a strong figure in Japan as a writer, rule-breaker and a woman who sought to subvert her masculinist culture. As a political prisoner who was alleged to have supported the Japanese leftist movement, Nakamoto Takako was tortured, labelled as mentally ill, imprisoned in a psychiatric institution and forced to commit ideological conversion. Nakamoto Takako's imprisonment and nervous breakdown as a result of torture and confinement is documented in her writing. She endeavours to challenge the label of mental illness so often applied to political dissidents, by labelling herself insane and playing along with psychiatrists in order to be designated "sane" and released.

Her story provides insight into the sexist role of women as "housekeepers" for men within the Japanese leftist movement, thus diminishing their role as true comrades. Nakamoto Takako endured shunning from her family and party members upon release yet she rejected the criminal label and label of insanity applied to her. After she healed and regained her health she continued to write about her experience with the hope that her writings would encourage other female political prisoners to engage in resistance through recollection. As the old saying goes, writing is the best revenge.

Chapter 12

Milk Enough for All

Breast-giving, Fugitivity and the Limits of Resistance

Lynn Makau

The most dramatic scene of self-determination in Toni Morrison's novel *Beloved* is the protagonist's murder of her own child. This shocking act prevents the return of Sethe and her other children to bondage, yet it is not the only case in which Sethe does what she feels is best for her family in opposition to their enslavement. Before she is pressed into murderous action by schoolteacher's appearance in her mother-in-law's yard, Sethe exhibits her "motherlove" by reuniting her family following a harrowing escape from bondage, during which she gives birth to her fourth child. Her success in bringing her children "their milk" despite seemingly insuperable obstacles confirms Sethe's maternal identity and defies her overseer's attempts to rob her of the right to mother as she sees fit. Because this confirmation precedes the eventuality of Beloved's infanticide, however, it can only be read as a partial triumph; yet by claiming her children and her breastmilk as her own, Sethe asserts her autonomy and rejects the system that enslaves her, becoming a fugitive even before she escapes Sweet Home. I propose that Sethe's "breast-giving" — my term for actively determining the recipients of her milk — must be viewed on a spectrum of defiant maternal slave behaviour. This nonviolent means of resistance catapults Sethe into a state of "fugitivity" and thus warrants greater scrutiny.

My analysis of breast-giving in *Beloved* has multiple goals: to expand the concept of fugitivity; to elucidate the affects of antebellum property law on enslaved mothers' resistance; and to contribute to existing discourse on Sethe's motherlove. I also intend for this chapter's definition of fugitive acts to provoke recognition of Sethe's agency and to demonstrate the exigency of crafting new analyses of literary breastfeeding, specifically in relation to female subjectivity.

My interpretation of breast-giving challenges not only conventional notions of property but the assumption that breastfeeding is a benign activity. Though often naturalized in the service of maternal allegory as a metaphor of selflessness, the breastfeeding bond between mother and child can perform political duty as well, making visible, for instance, the denial of motherlove by the slave system. In *Beloved*, where otherwise disempowered women have the ability to breastfeed and may do so outside the boundaries of institutional control, breastfeeding becomes a threat to traditional power structures. After her breastmilk is "stolen" within this power structure, Sethe resolves henceforth to determine who will receive it. Her commitment challenges the ownership by slaveholding society of her body and what it produces. Though this act alone fails to secure Sethe's freedom, it precipitates her growing self-determination.

Morrison's fiction often engages issues of power, gender, violence and racism that infuse the dynamic process of claiming autonomy. By keeping these intersecting issues in mind while studying breast-giving in *Beloved* we may better understand the economic nuances of race-based slavery and breastfeeding, and their potential challenge of one another. I find Samira Kawash's concept of fugitivity a particularly useful tool to understanding this relationship. Defined in brief as a figure "outside" the modern liberal dialectic of property/person that distinguishes subjects from what may be owned, the fugitive refuses her status as chattel by recognizing and claiming her subjectivity. Fugitivity in its various forms shapes my reading of Sethe's resistant maternal behaviour as it outlines the bold and highly risky choice an enslaved woman makes in using her lactation for her own purposes rather than having that purpose determined by her owner or overseer. Naming breast-giving a fugitive act, moreover, illustrates the self-determining social and philosophical categories that Kawash so illuminatingly describes.

In her article "Fugitive Properties," which addresses property rights, subjectivity and slave narratives, Kawash expounds the modern liberal tenet that property and the subject "are indissociable" (1999: 277). Nineteenth-century political philosophies based political and economic subjectivity on one's ability to be propertied, a restrictive criterion for disenfranchised subjects typically denied property ownership, such as women and slaves. Kawash argues that by regarding people as chattel, the American institution of slavery collapsed the discrete categories of "property" and "person," making it possible for the two to be one and the same in the interest of "true," e.g., propertied, subjects. The legal machinations used to deny enslaved people's obvious personhood and to maintain the illusion of human/property required effort and revealed each category to be "neither natural nor neutral." Any recognition in slaves of their subjectivity or "property-in-person" that could elicit their right to self-ownership and lead to their resistance had to be vigilantly prevented (Kawash 1999: 277–78). Ultimately this system failed due in part to ambiguous laws that simultaneously imposed "certain obligations on the owners for the care and welfare of the slave," thus acknowledging slaves' personhood, while also according slaveholders the "right to [all] the slave's labor and product," thereby treating slaves as property (277). This legal ambiguity reveals the constructed nature of liberal ideology and the awkward division of people and property in a slave state, which likewise failed to account for bonded laborers, who recognized their humanity without or despite the sanctioned denial of their right to property ownership. This self-recognition produced what Kawash calls "a third figure outside this order: the fugitive."

The paradoxical legal dialectic of property/person echoes the curiously self-reflexive vernacular slave term for escape from bondage, "to steal oneself." As simultaneously object and agent of this action, the former slave assumes a middle category of fugitivity, straddling property and personhood by simultaneously embodying elements of both. Although the fugitive figure "counter[s] the logic of master and slave," Kawash stresses the limits of fugitivity to effect legal recognition of one's autonomy. "Fugitivity" or stealing oneself, she writes, does not "transform slavery under the law into freedom under the law. It is only by remaining outside the law that the fugitive escapes the status of (human) property" (279). She presents, for example, Harriet Jacobs's "loophole of retreat," in which Jacobs hid for seven years to evade discovery and her return to slavery. Kawash concedes that the crawlspace above Jacob's grandmother's home enabled Jacobs' fugitive status. However, this retreat did not in fact constitute her "triumph[ant]" emancipation or produce Jacobs' subjectivity; rather she hovered in the liminal space between property and person, remaining, in effect, a nonentity for nearly a decade while in hiding (287). I propose that Sethe enters this liminal space apart from yet not entirely outside the law once she gives primacy to her maternal identity over her status as property.

Sethe's breast-giving and related resistant behaviour allow her the brief opportunity to transgress the boundaries separating autonomous subjects and human chattel by entering a state of fugitivity. Once she actually escapes from Sweet Home her fugitive identity becomes explicit and recognizable as well as punishable by the law, but she challenges the conventions of slavery's cultural economy prior to this point by choosing to give her breastmilk to her children rather than allowing anyone to take or otherwise determine its use. Sethe's choice to *give* away her milk rather than have it appropriated as a commodity like all other slave-produced goods can be read within the parameters of modern liberal theory as indicative of her economic agency. It is a means of asserting her autonomy since only persons and not property may engage in exchange relations. However, just as renting out one's labour on Sabbath days does not liberate the enslaved labourer, breast-giving alone while in bondage cannot, and does not, free Sethe. Only the combination of this activity and her refusal to have her milk ever again stolen finally ensures her fugitive status.

I append breast-giving to the oddly transitive relationship between the slave who steals herself and the body that she steals both to emphasize its requirement of agency on the enslaved woman's part and to illuminate how this action affects legal human property ownership. Like escape, breast-giving doesn't transform the law but rather exposes its inability to contain enslaved people's natural propensity toward freedom. Breast-givers like Sethe view their milk as an extension of their maternal bodies, there to sustain their biological children, not their owners, overseers, slaveholders or their children. By refusing to allow her breastmilk to be appropriated, Sethe exposes the fallacy of treating humans as property. Though she does not explicitly acknowledge breast-giving as a contest of her enslavement, the act nonetheless reveals her humanity as a feeling, thinking, active person rather than endlessly usable property.

Breast-giving as a profound demonstration of inalienable motherlove seems threatening to institutional hierarchies that distinguish property from persons. Those who do it therefore risk retaliation for their failure to conform to their proscribed status and attendant restrictions. Sethe's relative freedom to interact with and care for her own children at Sweet Home before schoolteacher's arrival likely instigates his cruel method of asserting power over her. The violent theft of her breastmilk by his nephews — two "mossy-teethed white boys" — is meant to fix Sethe's status as property. That this act instead serves as the final catalyst of her fugitive flight seems radically opposed to its intended result.

Samira Kawash confirms that retaining or controlling the fugitive body necessitates violence, which draws attention to the limits of what this figure can accomplish as well as the risks to which it is exposed. Locating the breast-giving fugitive's power in her breasts proves additionally perilous given the vulnerability of the subjugated (female) body. Writing about breastfeeding in *Beloved*, Michele Mock observes that Sethe's "breasts signify a power that can be too easily snatched away" (1996: 121). The rape of Sethe's milk confirms Mock's claim. Andrea O'Reilly asserts that Sethe's "'stolen milk' metaphorically signifies the [right to provide] motherlove that is denied to her as a slave woman" (2004: 130). This violence done against Sethe directly contributes to her eventual murder of her own child. The multiple infanticides committed by real women of this period who were prevented by their enslavement from performing their maternal obligations suggests that attempts to foreclose motherlove can prove fatal, if not to the mother then to her children.

Schoolteacher's pseudo-scientific experiments on all the Sweet Home slaves codifies his dehumanization of them and sustains their unspeakable violation. His instruction to his nephews to list Sethe's "human" versus "animal" characteristics directly precedes their violent treatment of her "like an animal," as Sethe notes, "or worse." He officiates their rape with his notebook in hand, "watching and writing it up" (Morrison 1987: 70). Such bestial characterization of their human property by some slaveholders helped to justify their abuse and makes plausible the nephews' violation of Sethe. Their theft of her milk echoes a contemporary saying from the Indian region of Uttar Pradesh documented by anthropologist Leela Dube that asserts an "untouchable woman may be milked like a she-goat" at any time (1996: 36). These similar ideologies, used to warrant sexual abuse and exploitation of enslaved and outcaste women, indicate the immense difficulty of avoiding such violations, which may be socially sanctioned if not institutionally protected. What is "permissible" in this context, therefore, is highly relative, dependent on each woman's particular circumstances and opportunities for agency. Morrison's novel imagines one response to the powerful, seemingly inviolate connection between schoolteacher's lessons, his nephews' actions and Sethe's victimization. Sethe's refusal to ever have her milk stolen again engenders her fugitivity since she must flee Sweet Home to ensure her conviction.

Sethe's recount of the events leading to her flight from the plantation exemplifies the importance of her maternal identity to making her escape. "I had milk," she tells Paul D, "I was pregnant with Denver but I had milk for my baby girl. I hadn't stopped nursing her when I sent her on ahead with Howard and Buglar" (Morrison 1987: 16). She continues:

Anybody could smell me long before he saw me. And when he saw me he'd see the drops of it on the front of my dress. Nothing I could do about that. All I knew was I had to get my milk to my baby girl. Nobody was going to nurse her like me. Nobody was going to get it to her fast enough, or take it away when she had enough and didn't know it. Nobody knew that she couldn't pass her air if you held her up on your shoulder, only if she was lying on my knees. Nobody knew that but me and nobody had her milk but me. (16)

Sethe's repetition of what "nobody" but she knew emphasizes her unique maternal awareness of her child's needs. But although this knowledge inspires her journey toward freedom, the rape of her milk immediately following this inspiration reinforces Sethe's determination to reach her children and prevent them from suffering a similar dehumanizing fate.

Sethe tells Paul D that before she could escape, "those boys came in there and took my milk. That's what they came in there for. Held me down and took it" (16). When they discover that Sethe disclosed their violation to the slaveholding mistress, one of the boys whips Sethe until her back opens up. Stunned by this second violation, Paul D asks Sethe,

"They used cowhide on you?"
"And they took my milk."
"They beat you and you was [nine months] pregnant?"
"And they took my milk!" (17)

His incredulous response to learning that Sethe was whipped counters her repeated indignation that her milk was stolen; for Sethe, this violation exceeds all others.

These combined incidents form Sethe's resolve to escape to protect her children, particularly her daughters, once she realizes her ability to do so while enslaved is untenable. As slaves, Sethe's children are legally not hers, but rather the slaveholder's property. Thus, by escaping the plantation to bring them "their milk," Sethe commits multiple fugitive acts: "stealing" her children, herself and the peculiar property (breastmilk) that fuels them both. Sethe later expresses her determination to Beloved, declaring, "only me had your milk, and God do what He would, I was going to get it to you" (198). Her commitment involves more than making sure that her children are properly fed; her delivery of their milk symbolizes a maternal bond only achievable through escape. Sethe steals herself so that she may behave as an unrestricted mother.

Sethe's commitment to unrestricted motherlove ensures her fugitivity and her tragic demise. The costs of her resistance are dear and evoke key features of fugitivity: its imperfect success as a means of liberation and the violence of restoring order that it necessitates. Sethe's indomitable commitment to bringing her children "their milk" evidences fugitive self-determination that sets into motion the violent consequences of claiming the use of her body and the substance it creates. Breast-giving and infanticide may be thought of as poles marking either end of a spectrum of motherlove available to the maternal fugitive. Sethe moves inexorably from one end to the other and is ultimately forced to commit violence against those she loves most. Yet even by enacting their murder, Sethe paradoxically maintains her commitment to providing for and protecting her children at all costs.

Although her infanticide has elicited greater critical attention, I suggest that it is equally important to analyze Sethe's breast-giving, which presents another extreme example of her motherlove. The related acts of breast-giving and infanticide, though obviously distinct if not inverse in outcome, both demonstrate maternal autonomy and two powerful means of expressing enslaved women's resistance of their victimization. Sethe, moreover, is not the only enslaved character in *Beloved* to use either method to express or protect her maternity. Ella, the friend of Stamp Paid who leads the procession of thirty women to Sethe's door, "delivered, but would not nurse, a hairy white thing, fathered by 'the lowest yet'" (258–59). This infant represents years of rape Ella experienced while sequestered in the home of a white father and son during which she "had been beaten every way but down" (258). Her refusal to nurse the product of this horror constitutes an oblique but effective infanticide that tacitly rejects Ella's abuse.

Similarly, Nan tells Sethe that her mother disposed of the products of her rape by white men on the crew of the slave ship and those from "more whites" following the Middle Passage. All these she "threw away. Without names, she threw them" 62). Conceived by choice with the one man her mother "put her arms around," Sethe is distinct from this group and consequently saved. In contrast, Baby Suggs loses all of her children, produced by six different fathers, some of whom she, too, had no choice but to mate with. Rather than "throwing them away," Baby Suggs expresses her autonomy by withholding her affection: "she could not love" the one child produced "by the man who promised not to [impregnate her] but did... and the rest she would not" (23). Baby Suggs' awareness that children can and will be forced upon her only to be sold away curtails her motherlove for them.

Despite these intriguing precedents, most scholars locate Sethe's claim of autonomy at the point of her infanticide rather than highlight her breast-giving or other acts of motherlove, though in fact, all these acts are linked by their economic similarity. Like the "theft" of her children and herself, Sethe's decision to kill her family and commit suicide forces a reckoning of her value to the slave system. When schoolteacher arrives in Ohio intent on reclaiming his stolen property, upon witnessing the chilling tableau of Sethe and her apparently slain children, he concludes that there is "nothing" here for him to collect. His assessment describes the non-entity Sethe becomes as a fugitive and secures when she answers the violence of potential re-enslavement with a radical violence of her own. Ironically, Sethe's murderous behaviour toward her children renders her worthless to a system that wishes to suppress her natural maternal rights, perversely freeing her in the moment when she acts most like a mother and least like a slave. In rejecting the "thingness" or property status of slave identity, she becomes, like Jacobs in her hiding place, neither a subject nor a thing, and loses her reason for living in the process.

Sethe's dedication to breast-giving prior to this point therefore seems both a more strategic rejection of enslavement and a more preferable one than death. She succeeds in liberating her children from Sweet Home, birthing her last child, Denver, along the way, and reuniting with Baby Suggs for a lunar month of respite in Ohio, where she plays with her children, learns the alphabet and becomes part of the free black community. These four weeks are comprised of "Days of healing, ease and real-talk," during which Sethe learns "how it felt to wake up at dawn and *decide* what to do with the day" (95). Here Morrison juxtaposes freedom and the arbitrary, brutal restraints of slavery and emphasizes the effort and time necessary to transition from property to personhood. "Bit by bit" Sethe "claimed herself," realizing that "Freeing yourself was one thing; claiming ownership of that freed self was another" (95). Her realization underscores the struggle of the fugitive to mentally free herself from her formerly bonded status.

Once familiar, albeit briefly, with a life of freedom, Sethe views the possibility of re-enslavement with renewed resistance. Unwilling to be further violated or to have her children taken from her, she gives what is in her power to effect, e.g., death, with the same determination with which she gave her children life and breastmilk. This irrevocable act exemplifies her commitment to remain united with her family despite all institutional attempts to impede her. Her prior dedication to enabling her children's escape and following them with "their milk" prepares Sethe to follow through with their protection by putting them "out of harm's way," her euphemism for what she does in the storehouse. Recalling the spectrum concept of motherlove as inclusive of breast-giving along with infanticide, Sethe's commission of these related activities seems more consistent than not. Motherlove permits her to focus on the single goal of protecting her children, which she enacts first through escape and nurturing, then via death, the one place in which she can ensure their safety from schoolteacher. Even in post-mortem shock Sethe attempts to fulfill her maternal obligations through breast-giving. Baby Suggs retrieves Sethe's dead child from her only by reminding the traumatized mother, "'It's time to nurse your youngest'"; Morrison blurs the line between death and breastfeeding by having Denver suckle "her mother's milk right along with the blood of her sister" (152).

Despite these powerful testaments to Sethe's motherlove, her tenacious dedication to providing her children with "milk enough" comes at too great a price. Although she succeeds in preventing her children's enslavement by Southern whites, her infanticide of Beloved instigates the family's captivity by the murdered baby's ghost. Rather than losing her offspring to slaveholders, Sethe ultimately comes close to losing herself to the all-consuming motherlove on which Beloved feeds. Trapped with the guilt of having ended her child's life too soon, Sethe gives all that she has and more to appease her hungry spectre. The nearly fatal result of Sethe's desire to placate her insatiable daughter illustrates the danger of linking her survival to the fulfillment of her children's needs — a necessarily debilitating economy with a child who can never have milk enough. While Sethe's attachment to her children may attempt to make up for a truncated relationship with her own mother, Beloved represents a composite of the "Sixty Million and more" that died during the Middle Passage, to whom Morrison dedicates her novel; she can never be reciprocated for her loss. Sethe's attempts to "feed" her, therefore, will always be inadequate. This failure perhaps even more poignantly than Beloved's murder indicates the far-reaching devastation American slavery wrought on maternal bonds.

Breastfeeding one's own children in *Beloved* represents unmitigated maternal care, a privilege that accompanies autonomous subject status typically withheld from slaves. Sethe's determination to breast-give thus constitutes a dangerous opposition of social and legal boundaries and makes her a fugitive of the law. She nevertheless claims her right to express motherlove due to her self-identification as a person, not property, and despite the risks to which doing so expose her. Fleeing to a place where she can freely mother her children allows Sethe's brief experience of emancipation, but her safety there proves illusory. Samira Kawash explains that "[Harriet] Jacobs as fugitive cannot be reduced to property, but neither can she be availed of the securities of person[hood]" (1999: 286). Likewise, Baby Suggs' home in Ohio provides Sethe with only a liminal retreat in which she retains her fugitive status. Nevertheless, through her breast-giving, escape and ultimately murder, Sethe refutes her status as a bestial possession and the possibility that slaveholding society might not permit her to mother her biological children. By having her protagonist claim maternal rights despite her enslavement, Morrison exposes aporias in both rational liberal philosophy and antebellum slave law, and highlights the paradox of treating people as property. Moreover, by having Sethe claim her personhood through breast-giving, Morrison creatively expands the precedent of resistance offered by Margaret Garner's historical infanticide, on which the novel is based.

I have shown that while neither breast-giving nor escape ensure Sethe's liberation nor wholly avert the threat of re-enslavement, it is useful to trace how these expressions of motherlove precede her eventual act of murder. Exploring this path with an eye on both the limits of fugitivity as well as its opportunities improves our understanding of the stakes of Sethe's behaviour and what ultimately brings her to commit infanticide.

Chapter 13

Insane but Not an Ideological Convert

Nakamoto Takako's Claim to
Political Dissidence in Prewar Japan

Janice Matsumura

As an historian of Japanese women, Vera Mackie reminds us: "Feminist historians do not simply reveal a pre-existing reality. We construct our own narratives of resistance and liberation" (Mackie 1997: 169). However, some cases of resistance are open to dispute, especially in the period before 1945, when official persecution forced supporters of Japanese leftist movements to commit *tenkō* (ideological conversion) and publicly repudiate their political beliefs. As the case of the short story writer Nakamoto Takako (1903–1991) illustrates, it is at times the subject and not just the researcher who must establish or defend a reputation of uncompromised defiance of authority. Although known both in Japan and abroad mostly for her fictional work, a few pieces of which have been translated into foreign languages (Tanaka 1987: 135–44; Gluck 1963: 159–73), in her autobiography, Nakamoto emphasizes her career as a leftist political dissident during the late 1920s and beginning of the 1930s.

In her study of twentieth-century Japanese women writers, Yukiko Tanaka observes that "it is generally believed that [Nakamoto] Takako recanted her communist beliefs under police pressure, probably at the time of her last arrest" (Tanaka 1987: 132–33). Having become a member of the postwar Japan Communist Party, which was re-established and acquired legal status immediately after the end of the Asia-Pacific War (1931–1945), Nakamoto would have been compelled to refute such accusations and defend her standing within the Party. The result was her autobiography, which was first published in 1950 and then again in 1973 under a new title and with additional information.

James A. Scott has demonstrated that resistance is not limited to direct confrontation with authority in the form of governments or elite groups and may manifest itself in various forms, including dissimulation and disparagement (Scott 1985). In her autobiography, Nakamoto expresses resistance through recollection and attempts to assert her autonomy in defining herself. In providing an account of her struggle against the prewar state, which resulted in her torture by the police and incarceration in a mental hospital, she refutes the accusations of ideological conversion put forward by one-time allies and subverts by reinterpreting positively the labels applied to her by representatives of the prewar state.

Established in 1868 and lasting until 1945, the Japanese prewar state attempted to determine and closely regulate the social and political values of the people. According to official propaganda, the state was similar to a patriarchal family in which the emperor exercised absolute but supposedly benevolent authority over his subjects, who, in turn, expressed their devotion to this ruler by being law-abiding and productive members of society. In promoting the fiction of equality under the rule of the emperor, this family-state ideology dismissed the existence of class conflict and thus stood in the way of political movements addressing disparities in wealth and privileges among the people. Schools as well as government controls on the mass media ensured the dissemination of state-sanctioned ideas. Thought control police (*tokkō*) and laws, most notably the *Peace Preservation Law* of 1925 (*Chian iji hō*), targeted not just members but anyone who might appear supportive of organizations, most notably the Japan Communist Party, opposed to the national polity and the private property system.

In the 1930s, police and justice officials seeking to undermine the potential appeal of such organizations adopted a policy of coercing dissidents into publicly refuting their outlawed beliefs. Sociologist Kazuko Tsurumi has observed that coercion could be blatant or subtle: "Arrest, torture, court trial, imprisonment and death belong to the former; job discrimination, praise or denunciation through mass communication media, and social pressure of various kinds belong to the latter" (Tsurumi 1970: 37). This policy of *tenkō* or ideological conversion was successful, resulting in the destruction of all organizations that officials defined as leftist, and scholars have focused on the personality (Tsurumi 1970: 29) and socialization of individuals in accounting for the high number of converts (*tenkōsha*) (Shunsuke 1991).

Nakamoto presents herself in her autobiography as one of the few non-converts (*hi-tenkōsha*), pointing to the court's pronouncement of her as ideologically unreformed. Contrasting herself with Communist Party members who renounced communism as an ideal as well as a movement and who, in her opinion, became true ideological converts, Nakamoto provides material for testing explanations as to why certain persons were better able to withstand government pressure to abandon outlawed ideas.

Nakamoto's Life Narrative: Defending a Dissident Identity

As her goal in writing her memoirs was to defend her reputation as a prewar dissident, Nakamoto discusses her family relationships and her literary career only to demonstrate her independent spirit and her enduring commitment to political ideals. She observes how she rejected the feudalistic attitudes in her hometown of Yamaguchi and defied her ex-military officer father by running away to Tokyo to become a writer. She eventually achieved critical attention in 1929. Yet rather than remain focused on producing more stories, she moved from a rather upscale part of the city to the working-class neighbourhood of Kameido in order to overcome what she believed was her petty bourgeois mentality (Nakamoto 1973: 77, 8, 124).

Nakamoto claims that, with the rise of proletarian literature, writers were moving beyond a bourgeois literary preoccupation of liberating the self and dedicating themselves to the liberation of the oppressed classes. Her goal was to become a supporter of labour unions, but she realized that she was ignorant of theories of class struggle and had little knowledge of actual conditions among workers. To learn more, she rented a house beside the labour activist and women's historian Orimoto [Tatewaki] Sadayo (1904–1990), who was running a night school for female factory workers. According to Nakamoto, just moving to the area aroused the suspicions of the military police, one of whom paid her a visit almost immediately after she had relocated. Undeterred by this police inquiry into her activities, Nakamoto participated in educational and work-related activities for female labourers. Eventually a member of Zenkyō [*Nihon rōdō kumiai zenkoku kyōgikai*], a Japan Communist Party-controlled union, asked her to help in *Zenkyō's* recruitment of women employed in the area's textile mills. Agreeing to the request, she devoted her afternoons to signing up members and her evenings to union meetings and the production of handbills. Such a life, she observes, required that she minimized her expenses and subsisted on the cheapest and most meagre amounts of food (Nakamoto 1973: 8–11, 17, 27, 30).

From about the middle of January 1930, she learned that the Tokyo Metropolitan Police were questioning female workers recruited by Zenkyō. Nakamoto realized that she could soon be arrested, but ignored the warning of workers who urged her to go into hiding. She claims that she could not withdraw from the struggle as it was gathering more worker support; rather pompously, she describes herself as a general who could not abandon his troops in battle. At the beginning of February, just prior to the Tōyō Muslin Strike, which erupted into street fighting by female strikers, she was apprehended by officers of the Metropolitan Police Board's Labour Division who detained her for thirty-one days. The police were infamous for abusing suspects, and Nakamoto states that, incensed by her refusal to divulge information about her activities, her interrogating officers slapped her until they had exhausted themselves. At the end of March, she was released from custody and soon approached by members of the Japan Communist Party, who requested her assistance (Nakamoto 1973: 31–32, 34, 36–40). The Party had adopted the practice of calling upon women supportive of the movement to act as housekeepers and help male activists maintain the appearance of being law-abiding, family men (Mackie 1997: 15364; Makise 1976). Nakamoto's account of her experience and that of other women called upon to assist the Party in this manner reveal that the practice was open to abuse. Housekeepers often had to find jobs to support the male activists and, in passing themselves off as wives, had to cook, clean and even sleep with these men. Nakamoto recalls that, despite her desire to return to writing, she felt compelled to assist the cause of the working classes and eventually ended up living with two high-ranking Party members, Iwao Iesada (1904–1940) and then Tanaka Kiyoharu [Seigen] (1906–?). Neither of these men treated her as a comrade or an equal. She was not permitted to participate in meetings held in her home and was never invited to formally join the Party, a situation that resulted in her concealing her romantic relationship with Iwao Iesada. According to Nakamoto, the Party leadership had become concerned that communists were acquiring a reputation for promiscuity and implemented a strict policy of forbidding members to marry non-members. She states that she could not understand why anyone would object to two single people becoming a couple, but, when pressed by the aforementioned Tanaka Kiyoharu to confess to her relationship with Iwao, she realized that she would have to sacrifice her feelings both for Iwao's sake and that of the Party. The Party was plagued with rivalries among members, and news of the affair, she feared, could trigger an internal split as well as diminish Iwao's standing within the movement (Nakamoto 1973: 40–50).

Nakamoto worked as a housekeeper for only a few months. In July 1930, during a mass arrest of communists, the Metropolitan Police Board's thought control police apprehended and charged her with supporting the Party. Sickly at the time of her arrest, Nakamoto learned that she was exhausted, not just because she had to perform so many tasks to support and care for Iwao and Tanaka, but also because she was pregnant. In August, after being repeatedly tortured and sexually assaulted by police interrogators, she was forced to undergo an abortion. Conditions in jails and prisons in pre-1945 Japan were notoriously harsh and unsanitary, resulting in the death of more than a few inmates. Describing herself as mentally as well as physically wrecked by her experience in jail, Nakamoto recalls that at the beginning of January 1931 she started to hallucinate. Her trial was consequently postponed, and the next month the police transferred her to Matsuzawa Hospital, the foremost psychiatric facility in the country. Eight months later, in October 1931, she was discharged and placed under probation (Nakamoto 1973: 53, 56–66, 72–78, 88, 90–91, 103–105, 107, 110).

Nakamoto states that at that time she believed that her personal salvation, the preservation of her mental health, depended on her mastering revolutionary theory and practice, becoming a Party member and marrying Iwao. While she was recuperating in a hospital following her abortion in August 1930, Nakamoto had a visit from a thought control officer who informed her that Iwao was a member of the Japanese "pariah" caste, the *burakumin*. She states that the officer's disclosure about Iwao's "pariah" origins did not diminish but instead intensified her love, as she began to see Iwao as representative of the oppressed classes that she sought to help. Upon her release from Matsuzawa, she immediately visited Iwao in prison and proposed marriage. Iwao agreed, but insisted on two conditions — that the Party approve of the union and that Nakamoto rid herself of her bourgeois mentality by labouring in a factory. She herself had hoped to take on such work, but as a communist sympathizer who had previously been arrested for promoting seditious ideas among workers, officials would have opposed her employment in a factory. She thus had to violate her probation and, in early 1932, she went into hiding and found employment in a factory on the outskirts of Tokyo. Although her experience as a manual labourer lasted a few months, cut short by her self-acknowledged inability to endure the physical demands of her job, she found some means to support herself and elude the police until the spring of 1933. Re-arrested for violating her parole, Nakamoto had also to await trial on charges of supporting the Japan Communist Party, charges stemming from her arrest in 1930, because the courts had postponed the proceedings due to her mental breakdown. While she was in detention, the police encouraged her to commit *tenkō* and showed her a newspaper article about two famous imprisoned Party leaders, Sano Manabu (1892–1953) and Nabeyama Sadachika (1901–1979), who had publicly declared their rejection of Marxist ideology. In her written recollections, Nakamoto insists that she could never abandon a life of resistance. As all things must struggle to survive, she notes, to abandon resistance is to abandon life (Nakamoto 1973: 115–16, 65–66, 122, 127–46, 156, 169, 171, 174, 178).

As proof of her refusal to capitulate completely to the authorities, Nakamoto drew attention to her defiant protest during her November 1933 trial. Requesting an opportunity to speak on her own behalf, she declared that she had been a victim of police torture and called for the abolition of the *Peace Preservation Law*. Because she was charged as a Communist Party sympathizer, she was not tried alongside actual Party members — which would have guaranteed a larger audience to witness her condemnation of the police and her repudiation of her ideological conversion. However, she observes that it was important for her just to be able to expose these crimes perpetrated by the police, to make it clear that any statement that she had made had been given under duress and to have the court record her statements. Infuriating the judge and prosecutor, both of whom declared that "the defendant shows no evidence of repentance or ideological conversion" (*hikoku wa tenkō mo kaishun mo shiteru mono de wa nai*), Nakamoto was equally infuriated by her own attorney, who tried to appeal to the mercy of the court by noting that she had suffered from mental illness. Nakamoto points out that, at the time, the courts often sentenced ordinary Party members to three years in prison and granted those who committed *tenkō* a stay of execution and a term of probation. She was thus surprised when the judge imposed upon her a prison sentence of four years. The authorities commuted her sentence to three years in celebration of the birth of Crown Prince Akihito in December 1933 (Nakamoto 1999: 166), but before she was finally released, she was confronted by Iwao Iesada's abandonment of communism. In a letter to her, Iwao declared that he had been informed that Nakamoto had renounced communism and that his newfound respect for religion had helped him recognize the deficiencies of Marxist ideology. At the close of her autobiography, Nakamoto announces that while her feelings for Iwao ended with his *tenkō*, she remained devoted to the country's oppressed classes, whom she believed Iwao had represented (Nakamoto 1973: 186–96, 208, 228–32, 65–66, 236; 1999: 202, 204).

Nakamoto's Discussion of the Party:
Individual as Opposed to Group Resistance

The contents of the two versions of her autobiography are almost identical, but the in the 1973 edition, Nakamoto provides more information about individuals, even giving the names of the police officers who had tortured her (Nakamoto

1973: 59). Perhaps the latter additions may be attributed to Nakamoto's greater confidence in her status as a dissident and her receding fears about censorship. Following Japan's defeat in the Asia-Pacific War, the country was under the control of American Occupation officials, who, by the time Nakamoto first published her autobiography, had adopted a more openly anti-communist position. After her release from prison in the late 1930s, Nakamoto had married the leftist writer Kurahara Korehito (1902–1999), and her 1950 autobiography appeared around the time that Kurahara lost his civil service job due to his membership in the Japan Communist Party (Shiota 1979: 224; Tanaka 1987: 133). Even after the Occupation ended in 1952, Nakamoto remained cautious about her publications. Fearing that her short story about a Japanese mistress of an American soldier would come under fire for being critical of the United States, she permitted its translation in 1953 only on condition that the author remained anonymous (Gluck 1963: 247). However, by 1973, when she published another version of her autobiography, Nakamoto may have been less concerned about censorship and more confident of her activist reputation. As she noted in the afterword to this work, after 1955 she participated in anti-nuclear demonstrations and during the 1960s was active in protests against the U.S.-Japan Security Treaty, which leftists condemned as a tool of American imperialism (Nakamoto 1973: 241). Armed with this reputation for dissidence, Nakamoto was less hesitant about criticizing the conduct of former comrades, including her former lover, Iwao Iesada.

Unlike other female leftists, such as prewar Japan Communist Party member Fukunaga Misao (1907–1991), who was a severe critic of the chauvinism and andocentricism of her male comrades (Loftus 2004: 229–69), Nakamoto lacks a robust sense of feminist consciousness. Historians such as Murakami Nobuhiko have observed a discrepancy between the political ideals and private lives of many male communists, who were unable to abandon the gender values of the very society they sought to overthrow. Murakami has also taken the Party to task for its use of so-called housekeepers and for calling upon female members to use their feminine charm to solicit funds from left-leaning individuals (Murakami 1978: 133, 153, 159–60). Although Nakamoto never addresses the issue of the Party's exploitation of women or makes a clear-cut attack of the practice of housekeepers, she does solicit the reader's sympathy and indignation by recounting episodes of sexist treatment. In her autobiography, she recounts how Iwao ordered her to get him a glass of water and violently berated her for thinking that he might prefer some sugared water (Nakamoto 1973: 47); 1999: 31). However, Nakamoto levels her most direct criticism at Tanaka Kiyoharu, whose views and attitudes she depicts as representative of the Party leadership of the time. Recalling in her autobiography how top members of the Communist labour union, Zenkyō, questioned her moral character, she claims that the police had informed her that Tanaka had also described her as a loose woman who had damaged the reputation of the Party and who would henceforth be shunned by all of its members. Nakamoto never explores the possibility that Tanaka might have been trying to protect her from police interrogators by downplaying her role and cutting her off from future association with the Party. Instead, she attempts to refute these aspersions by attacking the qualifications of Tanaka and others like him to judge her. Tanaka announced his ideological conversion while in prison and became a right-wing businessman after the war, and Nakamoto dismisses him as a traitor to the Party and the working class. While depicting Tanaka as a pompous, self-centred hypocrite, she draws attention to her own sacrifices of her writing career, family and health in the service of the Party (Nakamoto 1973: 30, 42–3, 51, 29–30, 67–69).

Nevertheless, Nakamoto admits that she deserved some censure. She berates herself for getting pregnant, observing that she had let the Party down by giving the authorities an opportunity to use her as an example of leftist immorality. Moreover, she reveals that while in prison she failed to join jailed communists at the beginning of November 1930 in singing the Party anthem, "Red Flag" (Akahata) as an act of protest. In her own defence, Nakamoto explains that another inmate informed her only at the last moment that some kind of protest was about to occur and that, still not fully recovered from her abortion and her torture, she was both too weak and surprised to sing. Nakamoto states that, even though she was not a Party member, the jailed members failed to take this and her clearly debilitated physical state into consideration and ostracized her as a revolutionary deserter. She contests this charge of being a deserter by revealing how she, in contrast to Party inmates, continued to resist the prison authorities and was able to resist pressures to commit *tenkō* (Nakamoto 1973: 68, 72-8, 85-6).

Nakamoto states that when she was rearrested in 1933 she was in better health both physically and mentally than she had been in 1930 and thus more capable of opposing her jailors. She had been caught talking to an inmate in the cell next to her and, as punishment for protesting the removal of this inmate to another area, she was forced to wear handcuffs and denied reading material. According to Nakamoto, the majority of her fellow inmates in 1933 were members of the Party or other political prisoners and both the food and facilities for inmates had greatly improved since her incarceration in 1930–31. However, Nakamoto claims that among these inmates she was now the only one willing to defy the prison authorities. She attributes this collapse of resistance to the 1933 *tenkō* of captured communist leaders Sano Manabu and Nabeyama Sadachika. Their public repudiation of the tactics and even purpose of the Party demoralized their followers and fuelled the authorities' efforts to encourage *tenkō*. Nakamoto explains that she may not have been as susceptible to the arguments of Sano and Nabeyama as many communists because, unlike Party members, she was less familiar with theories of revolutionary action, which were open to debate, and had reinforced her commitment to the working classes by actually living with them. Having become bored with life as a housekeeper for communists, before her arrest in 1930, she had already decided to go back to her work with female factory employees, whom she credited with teaching her about the hardships and aspirations of the working class. The Party's need for secrecy and her busy schedule restricted her contacts and access to information, and Nakamoto observes in her autobiography that participation in the Party's activities actually made her feel cut off from society and the world around her (Nakamoto 1973: 170, 176, 182, 138, 52, 45; 1999: 60).

Nakamoto's description of Party members, her suggestion that many of them were too dependent on theory for their loyalty to the revolutionary cause and thus vulnerable to the pressures exerted by others fits with the arguments of Kazuko Tsurumi and Patricia Steinhoff regarding ideological converts. In a later publication of her 1969 study of *tenkō*, Steinhoff acknowledges the deficiencies of a functionalist approach to the study of society, which neglects the issue of conflict and places too much emphasis on how institutions and practices contribute to social harmony. However, she finds that concepts of social integration associated with functionalism are still useful for understanding the phenomenon of ideological conversion among prewar Japanese communists insofar as many converts maintained a residual allegiance to the existing society — feelings of nationalism and the institution of the family — that their captors could exploit (1991: vi–vvii). Kazuko Tsurumi appears to support this notion of residual allegiance in discussing the *tenkō* of communist leaders Sano Manabu and Nabeyama Sadachika, who not only abandoned communism but became advocates of the state's emperor-centred ideology. As Sano and Nabeyama attended elementary school where values such as filial piety and loyalty to the emperor were inculcated in students, Tsurumi concludes that "their shift from communism back to Emperor worship should therefore be called ideological reconversion" (1970: 52).

Steinhoff contends that the political dissidents' hyperactive life of evading the police, numerous clandestine meetings and constant reading meant that many of them had no time or opportunity to prepare themselves psychologically for imprisonment. When faced with the possibility of death or injury while in custody and routinely isolated from captured comrades who could provide a sense of solidarity, they became vulnerable to the threats of police, procurators and especially the emotional entreaties of relatives recruited by the authorities to encourage *tenkō* (Steinhoff 1991: 106–109). With regard to the non-converts (*hi-tenkōsha*), Steinhoff can only suggest that strength of personality or the ability to function independently and outside of a group was a notable feature of those who could sustain their resistance. *Hi-tenkōsha*, such as Tokuda Kyichi (1894–1953) who would reconstitute the Japan Communist Party and become its secretary general after the war, did not view jail as divorced from the society outside, the society that he rejected and had to triumph over. Tokuda and, by her own account, Nakamoto were able to maintain their revolutionary identity through small acts of defiance, such as talking back to jailors (Steinhoff 1991: 184, 111, 119, 195, 185, 189).

Nakamoto's depiction of herself conforms to Steinhoff's profile of the *hi-tenkōsha*, who is able to withstand pressures from the police and family members. Regarding her arrest in July 1930, Nakamoto recalls that during one interrogation session the police informed her that her father had written to them and asked that they help to make her into a "true Japanese," who could appreciate the benevolence of the emperor. Learning of the extent to which she had disappointed her parents, Nakamoto asserts, caused her more anguish than the torture that she had suffered at the hands of her captors and weakened her psychologically (Nakamoto 1973: 67). Both Nakamoto and the psychiatrist called in by her jailors to examine her suggest that a letter that she received from her father, who was reportedly unrestrained in expressing his anger, may have triggered her mental breakdown (Nakamoto 1973: 87–88; Kikuchi 1934: 167–68). In recounting her stay in Matsuzawa Mental Hospital, Nakamoto also recalls that she seemed to recovering but suffered a relapse after receiving yet again a letter from her father (Nakamoto 1973: 102–103). However, Kazuko Tsurumi notes that some individuals, such as the proletarian writer Kobayashi Takiji (1903–1933) who was beaten to death by the police for reputedly refusing to capitulate to their demands, could respond to coercion and pressures to convert by becoming more rather than less committed to their beliefs (Tsurumi 1970: 42–46). In the case of Nakamoto, she had often opposed her parents — by becoming a writer, by aspiring to marry Iwao despite his *burakumin* origins and later by violating her parole. Each act of defying parental authority may have had a snowball effect, adding to Nakamoto's ability to resist the demands of her family, who, by the time of her trial in 1933, were pressing her to commit *tenkō* and acknowledge her ideological conversion in court (Nakamoto 1973: 173–74, 197–98).

Moreover, whereas the potential converts whom Steinhoff had studied viewed jail as "a meaningless void, or death itself," Nakamoto asserts that life in jail was less hellish than in Matsuzawa Mental Hospital, which she describes as "life's graveyard" (*jinsei no hakaba*) (Steinhoff 1991: 84; Nakamoto 1973: 91). More thoroughly cut off from allies and subjected to potentially life-threatening forms of isolation for resisting her institutionalization, Nakamoto's stay at Matsuzawa in 1931 no doubt helped her to contend with conditions in jail after the police arrested her once again in 1933.

Nakamoto's Discussion of Institutionalization: Training in Resisting Authority

Labelling theories as applied to the mentally ill tend to present the subject as passive, as eventually persuaded to accept or play a role assigned to them by so-called experts (Scheff 1975). A question remains as to the degree to which individuals accept such labels because they have reinterpreted and infused the labels with personally positive or self-affirming meaning. In her autobiography, Nakamoto adopts the label of insane as something acquired in her struggle to remain a non-convert and as proof of her enduring commitment to revolutionary ideals. In other words, she states that she did indeed go insane, but insists that even in this state of mental disorder, characterized by what she admits were hallucinations, she found her thoughts were focused on her political concerns or goals. She assigned significance to whatever she saw, and, watching from a hospital window the construction of a building, she imagined that this was symbolic of the emergence of a new and better Japan (Nakamoto 1973: 89, 99, 96–97).

In recounting the supportive responses of others to her breakdown, Nakamoto justifies and even further valorizes her episode of insanity. Nakamoto feared that she had lost all credibility in literary circles because her fellow writers would simply reject her as a lunatic. However, after her discharge, she was surprised to learn that the famous novelist Chōjō [Miyamoto] Yuriko (1899–1951) had collected donations from various female authors to help Nakamoto resume her writing career. The harshest rebuke that she received came from her ex-lover, Iwao Iesada. When she visited him in prison in 1931 and told him that she had been institutionalized, he dismissed her breakdown as nothing more than petty bourgeois weakness under pressure. In contrast, when Nakamoto visited Iwao's mother and made her disclosure about staying at Matsuzawa, the latter attempted to reassure Nakamoto by telling her that her breakdown was a delayed reaction to her abortion. Finally, soon after her sentencing in 1933, Nakamoto received a congratulatory letter from a writer friend who declared that it was clear, judging from what he had read in newspapers about her actions in court, that she had recovered her sanity. Nakamoto recalls being much encouraged by this letter, the message of which was that resistance was the most mentally healthy action that one could take against an insanely oppressive state and society (Nakamoto 1973: 111–12, 116, 120, 198–99).

While adopting for herself the label of insane, Nakamoto nevertheless condemns the treatment that she received at Matsuzawa. Convinced that the psychiatrists were only perfunctorily examining her, she insulted one young doctor by telling him that he needed to study psychoanalysis and had to be dragged away by nurses when she confronted the head of the hospital during his rounds and informed him that patients were not being effectively treated. She explains that the doctors had the patients living like hippopotamuses, forcing them to stay in tubs of hot water even to take meals and allowing them out only to go to sleep. Nakamoto discloses how she once expressed her opposition to this treatment by getting out of the bath and defecating in front of the nurses, who responded by holding her down and twisting her arms until she agreed to apologize to them (Nakamoto 1973: 104–105, 99–100).

Nakamoto asserts that the relationship between patients and the staff was so adversarial that she suspected that the nurses were in league with the thought control police. As a result, she would occasionally sneak into their quarters and search through their closets. Nakamoto explains that, unable to sleep and thus control her emotions, she sometimes grabbed her dishes during a meal and pitched them down the hall. As punishment, the nurses sedated her, stripped her and locked her overnight in a room. Nakamoto had heard from other patients that before her arrival the police had transferred two female Party members to the hospital and that the nurses had punished one of them, Itō Chiyoko, in the same fashion. Nakamoto reports that such rooms could become bitterly cold at night and that Itō was unable to endure the ordeal, developing a fatal case of pneumonia. Public indifference to the fate of the insane, Nakamoto asserts, allowed such deaths to go uninvestigated. According to Nakamoto, she was locked away in such a manner two or three times and not wanting to share the same fate as Itō, she struggled to prevent herself from falling asleep for fear of freezing to death (Nakamoto 1973: 99–101, 103–104).

With regard to her recovery, Nakamoto suspects that this was promoted less by psychiatric therapy than by treatments to improve her physical health. Nakamoto had been admitted to Matsuzawa in early 1931, and she observes that, by June of that year, after receiving weekly injections of calcium and vitamin B as well as sedatives to help her sleep at night, she felt emotionally calmer. As she became more mentally composed, she came to the conclusion that her acts of defiance were only delaying her discharge from the hospital and that she would have to adopt a passive, obedient guise if she wished to return to society and resume her mission of assisting the working classes. She thus strove to build up her strength and win the confidence of the hospital personnel, taking care of her appearance, busying herself with sewing and asking the doctors for books on medicine and science. By September, the hospital authorities appear to have notified the police and justice officials of her progress because Nakamoto recalls that around that time she received a visit from the public procurator, who had her compose a written statement of *tenkō* prior to her release. Nakamoto does not deny that she signed such a statement of conversion, insisting that she only paid lip service to the authorities' demands in order to regain her freedom and resume her political activities. Although she would later become disillusioned with the prewar Japan Communist Party, at the time of her discharge from Matsuzawa, Nakamoto was still confident of its ability to effect change and had resolved to "place herself once again under its flag" (*futatabi tō no hata no shita ni*) (Nakamoto 1973: 105–106, 109–10).

Conclusion

It is because she signed a statement of *tenkō*, which she nevertheless repudiated in court, and became less politically active following her release from prison that Nakamoto acquired a reputation for conversion. Consequently, one could suspect that the narrow focus of her autobiography, which omits any mention of her life following her release from prison around 1936, is rather disingenuous and intended to avoid accusations that she had capitulated to the authorities and abandoned her political ideals. However, even in the 1950 version of her auto-biography, Nakamoto states that by the time of her final arrest in 1933 she had decided that she would no longer be involved directly in Party activities, which she found had achieved nothing concrete for the working classes (Nakamoto 1999: 147–49). Moreover, in the afterword to the 1973 version, she observes that she had not done enough to oppose Japan's war of aggression and even participated in efforts to comfort wounded soldiers, but argues that such failings do not oblige her to accept the insults of individuals, presumably former Party members, whom she considers traitors and converts (Nakamoto 1973: 239). According to Nakamoto, defiance of authority in the person of parents, police, judicial officers and doctors characterized her early life, and her depiction of herself conforms to Steinhoff's profile of the *hi-tenkōsha*. Nakamoto enjoyed a good degree of emotional independence from her family as well as from her political allies, declining an invitation in 1931 to join the Japanese Proletariat Writers' Union because she wished to pursue her own activities (Nakamoto 1973: 114–15). Moreover, scholars of autobiography, personal narrative or oral history note that any statement, even a biased comment or outright distortion, is revealing of the subject (Smith and Watson 2001: 12; Ochiai 1999: 235), and even if one were to contest Nakamoto's claims to prewar dissidence as exaggerated, she certainly expresses in her autobiography resistance through recollection. Rejecting the accusations of loose woman and ideological backslider, she directs attention to the prewar court's pronouncement of her as an unreformed and unrepentant thought criminal and accepts as self-affirming rather than shameful the label of insane. While selecting from among the identities applied to her by others, she attempts to be the final arbiter in defining herself.

References

Abrams, Laura S. 2003. "Contextual Variations in Young Women's Gender Identity Negotiations." *Psychology of Women Quarterly* 27: 64–74.

Ackelsberg, Martha A. 1991. *Free Women of Spain: Anarchism and the Struggle for the Emancipation of Women.* Indianapolis: Indiana University Press.

Alcoff, L. 1991. "The Problem of Speaking for Others." *Cultural Critique* 20.

Allen, Paula Gunn. 1992. "Who Is Your Mother? Red Roots of White Racism." *The Sacred Hoop: Recovering the Feminine in American Indian Traditions.* Boston: Beacon.

Altink, Sietske. 1995. *Stolen Lives: Trading Women into Sex and Slavery.* London: Scarlet Press.

Anderson, I. 1999. "Characterological and Behavioral Blame in Conversations about Female and Male Rape." *Journal of Language and Social Psychology* 18: 377–94.

Anderson, I., and G. Beattie. 1995. "Gender Differences in Attributional Reasoning about Rape During Actual Conversation." *Issues in Criminological and Legal Psychology*: 3–12.

Andrews, D.A., and James Bonta. 1994. *The Psychology of Criminal Conduct.* Cincinnati: Anderson.

Angrove, R., and A. Fothergill. 2003. "Women and Alcohol: Misrepresented and Misunderstood." *Journal of Psychiatric and Mental Health Nursing* 10: 213–19.

Anthias, Floya, and Nira Yuval-Davis. 1989. *Women-Nation-State.* London: Macmillan.

Antropos, Peggy. 2004. *The Global Women's Movement: Origins, Issues and Strategies.* London: Zed Books.

Aptekar, L. 1994. *Environmental Disasters in Global Perspective.* Toronto: G.K. Hall; New York: MacMillan.

Athey, Jean. 2006. Personal communication. February 15.

Atkinson, Ti Grace. 1973. "Lesbianism and Feminism." In P. Birkby, B. Harris, J. Johnston, E. Newton and J. O'Wyatt (eds.), *Amazon Expedition: A Lesbian-Feminist Anthology.* Washington, NJ: Times Change Press.

_____. 1974. *Amazon Odyssey.* New York: Links Books.

Avakian, Arlene Voski. 1981. "Women's Studies and Racism." *New England Journal of Black Studies* 31–36.

Ayres, Jeffrey M. 2004. "Framing Collective Action Against Neoliberalism: The Case of the 'Anti-Globalization' Movement." *Journal of World-Systems Research* 10, 1: 11–34.

_____. 2005. "From 'Anti-Globalization' to the Global Justice Movement: Framing Collective Action against Neoliberalism." In B. Podobnik and T. Reifer (eds.), Transforming Globalization. Leiden, Netherlands: Brill.

Baird-Windle, Patricia, and Eleanor J. Bader. 2001. *Targets of Hatred: Anti-abortion Terrorism.* New York: Palgrave.

Bala, N. 2000. "A Differential Legal Approach to the Effects of Spousal Abuse on Children: A Canadian Context." In R.A. Geffner, P.G. Jaffe, and M. Sudermann (eds.), *Children Exposed to Domestic Violence: Current Issues in Research, Intervention, Prevention, and Policy Development.* New York: Haworth Press.

Bala, N.M.C., Lorne D. Bertrand, Joanne J. Paetsch, Bartha Maria Knoppers, Joseph P. Hornick, Jean-François Noel, Lorraine Boudreau, and Susan W. Miklas. 1998. *Spousal Violence in Custody and Access Disputes: Recommendations for Reform.* Ottawa: Status of Women Canada. #98-5-001.

Banks, Christopher. 2003. *The Cost of Homophobia: Literature Review on the Human Impact of Homophobia In Canada.* Saskatoon: Gay & Lesbian Health Services of Saskatoon.

Bannerji, Himani. 2000. *The Dark Side of a Nation: Essays on Multiculturalism, Nationalism and Gender*. Toronto: Canadian Scholars' Press.

Barry, Kathleen. 1994. *Female Sexual Slavery*. New York: New York University Press.

Bass, Jonathan. 2000. *Stay the Hand of Vengeance: The Politics of War Crime Tribunals*. Princeton and Oxford: Princeton University Press.

Bavelas, J.B., and L. Coates. 2001. "Is it Sex or Assault? Erotic vs. Violent Language in Sexual Assault Trial Judgments." *Journal of Social Distress and Homelessness* 10, 29–40.

Beadle, Gert. 1986. "The Nature of Crones." In Marilyn J. Bell (ed.), *Women as Elders: The Feminist Politics of Aging*. New York: Harrington Park Press.

Becker, David. 2000. *Ohne Hass keine Versöhnung*. Freiburg: Kore.

Beckman, L.J. 1994. "Treatment Needs of Women with Alcohol Problems." *Alcohol Health and Research World* 18(3): 206–11.

Bell, Laurie (ed.). 1987. *Good Girls/Bad Girls: Sex Trade Workers and Feminists Face to Face*. Toronto: Women's Press.

Bell, Marilyn J. (ed.). 1986. "Introduction." In Marilyn J. Bell (ed.), *Women As Elders: The Feminist Politics of Aging*. New York: Harrington Park Press.

Bell, Shannon. 1994. *Reading, Writing and Rewriting the Prostitute Body*. Indianapolis: Indiana University Press.

Benshoof, Janet. 2002. "The Dismantling of Choice." *NCJW Journal* 25: 12.

Bepko, C. 1991. *Feminism and Addiction*. New York: Haworth Press.

Berns, N. 2001. "Degendering the Problem and Gendering the Blame: Political Discourse on Women and Violence." *Gender and Society* 15: 262–81.

Best, J. 1987. "Rhetoric in Claims-Making." *Social Problems* 34.

Bhopal, Kalwat. 2002. "Teaching Women's Studies: The Effects of 'Race' and Gender." *Journal of Further and Higher Education* 26(2): 6–16.

Birch, Simon. 2001. "Where Middle Age is All the Rage." *SAGA* (Britain), September.

Birkbeck, C. 1983. "'Victimology Is what Victimologists Do' but What Should They Do?" *Victimology* 8: 270–75.

Bishop, Anne. 2002. *Becoming an Ally, Breaking the Cycle of Oppression in People*. Second edition. Halifax: Fernwood Publishing.

_____. 2005. *Beyond Token Change: Breaking the Cycle of Oppression in Institutions*. Halifax: Fernwood Publishing.

Blais, Denise M. 2003. "(Avoid) Kicking Sacred Cows." In D. Keahey and D. Schnitzer (eds.), *The Madwoman in the Academy: 43 Women Boldly Take on the Ivory Tower*. Calgary, AB: University of Calgary Press.

Blom, Ida, K. Hagemann and C. Hall (eds.). 1999. *Gendered Nations. Nationalism and Gender Order in the Long Nineteenth Century*. Oxford, New York: Berg.

Bogoeva, Julija. 2002. *Srebenica*. Frankfurt: Suhrkamp.

Bohner, Gerd. 2001. "Writing about Rape: Use of the Passive Voice and other Distancing Text Features as an Expression of Perceived Responsibility of the Victim." *British Journal of Social Psychology* 40: 515–29.

Böltken, Andrea. 1995. *Female leaders im, Führerstaat'* (Führerinnen im Führerstaat'). Pfaffenweiler: Centaurus.

Bonisteel, M., and L. Green. 2005. "Implications of the Shrinking Space for Feminist Anti-violence Advocacy." Paper presented at the Canadian Social Welfare Policy Conference "Forging Social Futures" in Fredericton, NB.

Bonta, James. 1996. "Risk-Needs Assessment and Treatment." In A.T. Harland (ed.), *Choosing Correctional Options that Work*. California: Sage.

References

Bornstein, Kate. 1994. *Gender Outlaw: On Men, Women, and the Rest of Us*. New York: Routledge.

Bouclin, S. 2004. "Exploited Employees or Exploited Entrepreneurs? A Look at Erotic Dancers." *Canadian Woman Studies/les cahiers de la femme* 24: 3.

Boyd, S.B. 2004. "Backlash Against Feminist: Canadian Custody and Access Reform Debates of the Late Twentieth Century." *Canadian Journal of Women and the Law* 16: (2): 255–90.

Boyd, S.C. 1999. *Mothers and Illicit Drugs*. Toronto: University of Toronto Press.

_____. 2004. *From Witches to Crack Moms: Women, Drug Law, and Policy*. Durham, NC: Carolina Academic Press.

Boyd, Susan. 1997. *Challenging the Public/Private Divide. Feminism, Law and Public Policy*. Toronto: University of Toronto Press.

_____. 2003. *Child Custody, Law, and Women's Work*. Toronto: Oxford University Press.

Boyd, Susan, and Helen Rhoades. 2006. Law and Families: The International Library of Essays on Law and Society. Aldershot: Ashgate.

Boyd, Susan, Margot Young, Gwen Brodsky, and Shelagh Day (eds.). 2007. *Poverty: Rights, Social Citizenship and Governance*. Vancouver: University of British Columbia Press.

Brockman, Joan. 2001. *Gender in the Legal Profession: Fitting or Breaking the Mould*. Vancouver: University of British Columbia Press.

Brown, L.M. 1991. "Telling a Girl's Life: Self-Authorization as a Form Of Resistance." In A.G. Rogers, C. Gilligan, and D.L. Tolman (eds.), *Reframing Resistance: Women, Girls, and Psychotherapy*. New York: Haworth Press.

Brown, S. 2002. "Women and Addiction: Expanding Theoretical Points of View." In Shulamith Lala Ashenberg Straussner and Stephanie Brown (ed.), *Handbook of Addiction Treatment for Women: Theory and Practice*. San Francisco: Jossey-Bass.

Brown, V.B., Lisa A. Melchior, Nancy White-O'Brien, and G.J. Huba. 2002. "Effects of Women-sensitive, Long-term Residential Treatment on Psychological Functioning of Diverse Populations of Women." *Journal of Substance Abuse Treatment* 23: 133–44.

Brownmiller, S. 1975. *Against Our Will: Men, Women and Rape*. New York: Bantam.

Broz, Svetlana. 2004. *Good People in an Evil Time*. New York: Other Press.

Bruckert, Chris. 2002. *Taking it Off, Putting it On: Women in the Strip Trade*. Toronto: Women's Press.

Bruckert, Chris, and Colette Parent. 2004. *Erotic Service/Erotic Dance Establishments: Two Types of Marginalized Labour*. Ottawa: Law Commission of Canada.

Buechler, S.M. 1995. "New Social Movement Theories." *The Sociological Quarterly* 36(3): 441–64.

Burkett, Elinor. 2000. *The Baby Boon: How Family-Friendly American Cheats the Childless*. New York: Free Press.

Burman, S. 1994. "The Disease Concept of Alcoholism: Its Impact on Women's Treatment." *Journal of Substance Abuse Treatment*,11(2): 121–26.

Burns, John. 1992. "Raging Grannies." *Canadian Theatre Review 72*.

Burstow, B. 1992. *Radical Feminist Therapy*. Newbury Park: Sage.

_____. 2003. "Toward a Radical Understanding of Trauma and Trauma Work." *Violence Against Women* 9, 11.

Burt, M.R. 1983. "A Conceptual Framework for Victimological Research." *Victimology* 8: 261–69.

_____. 1991. "Rape Myths and Acquaintance Rape." In A. Parrot and L. Bechhofer (eds.), *Acquaintance Rape: The Hidden Crime*. New York: Wiley.

Butler, Judith. 1990. "Performative Acts and Gender Constitution: An Essay in

Phenomenology and Feminist Theory." In S. Case (ed.), *Performing Feminisms: Feminist Critical Theory and Theatre*. Baltimore: Johns Hopkins University Press.

Butler, Sandra, and Barbara Rosenblum. 1991. *Cancer in Two Voices*. San Francisco: Spinsters.

Byrne, Anne. 2000. "Singular Identities: Managing Stigma, Resisting Voices." *Women's Studies Review* 7: 13–24.

Byrne, Dara. 1999. "'Yonder They Do Not Love Your Flesh.' Community in Toni Morrison's *Beloved*: The Limitations of Citizenship and Property in the American Public Sphere." *Canadian Review of American Studies* 29 (2): 25–59.

Campbell, N.D. 2000. *Using Women: Gender, Drug Policy, and Social Justice*. New York: Routledge.

Canadian Center for Justice Statistics. 2005. *Family Violence in Canada: A Statistical Profile* 2005. 85-224-XIE. Available at <http://www.statcan.ca/bsolc/english/bsolc?catno=85-224-X> accessed October 2008.

Cancio, Fernanda. 2005. "When Abortion Is a Crime: The Reality that Rhetoric Ignores." *Conscience* 25, 28.

Carr, C. Lynn. 1998. "Tomboy Resistance and Conformity: Agency in Social Psychological Gender Theory." *Gender and Society* 12: 528–53.

CASA (The National Center on Addiction and Substance Abuse). 1996. *Substance Abuse and the American Woman*. New York: Columbia University.

CWWV (Center for Women War Victims). 2003. *Women Recollecting Memories: Centre for Women War Victims Ten Years Later*. Zagreb.

Chahal, Taina. 2003. "Lucy in the Sky with Diamonds." In D. Keahey and D. Schnitzer (eds.), *The Madwoman in the Academy: 43 Women Boldly Take on the Ivory Tower*. Calgary: University of Calgary Press.

Chandler, C. 1999. "Feminist as Collaborators and Prostitutes as Autobiographers."*Hastings Women's Law Journal* 1, 10.

Chapkis, Wendy. 1997. *Live Sex Acts: Women Performing Erotic Labour*. New York: Routledge.

Chess, S., A. Kafer, J. Quizar, and M. U. Richardson. 2004. "Calling All Restroom Revolutionaries!" In Mattilda, aka M. B. Sycamore (ed.) *That's Revolting! Queer Strategies for Resisting Assimilation*. New York: Soft Skull Press.

Chilly Collective (eds.). 1995. *Breaking Anonymity: The Chilly Climate for Women Faculty*. Waterloo, ON: Wilfrid Laurier University Press.

Chovil, N. 1991/92. "Discourse-Oriented Facial Displays in Conversation." *Research on Language and Social Interaction* 25: 163–94.

Chunn, Dorothy E., Susan B. Boyd and Hester Lessard (eds.). 2007. *Reaction and Resistance: Feminism, Law and Social Change*. Vancouver: University of British Columbia Press.

Cixous, H. 1983. "The Laugh of the Medusa." In R. Warhol and D. Herndel (eds.), *Feminisms: An Anthology of Literary Theory and Criticism*. New Brunswick, NJ: Rutgers.

Clark, L.M.G., and D. Lewis. 1976. *Rape: The Price of Coercive Sexuality*. Toronto: Women's Press.

Clausen, Christopher. 2002. "Childfree in Toyland." *American Scholar* 71: 111–21.

Coates, Linda. 1997. "Causal Attributions in Sexual Assault Trial Judgements." *Journal of Language and Social Psychology* 16: 278–96.

_____. 2000a. "Language and Violence: A Discourse Model of Violence." Duncan, BC: Women's Resistance Group.

_____. 2000b. "The Treatment of Consent in Sexual Assault Cases." International Conference on Language and Social Psychology (ICLASP). Cardiff, Wales: UK.

_____. 2000c. "Twice a Volunteer: Mutualizing Violence." Duncan, BC: Women's Resistance Group.

_____. 2004. "The Mystification of Consent: An Analysis of Sexual Assault Trial Judgments." University of Lethbridge.

Coates, Linda, J.B. Bavelas, and J. Gibson. 1994. "Anomalous Language in sexual Assault Trial Judgements." *Discourse and Society* 5: 191–205.

Coates, Linda, Nathan Hoyt, Melissa Tatlock, and Krista West. 2005. "Mutualizing Violence: Concealment and Blame in Canadian Sexualized Violence Trial Judgments." University of Lethbridge.

Coates, Linda, Nick Todd, and Allan Wade. 2003. "Shifting Terms: An Interactional and Discursive View of Violence and Resistance." *Canadian Review of Social Policy* 52: 116–22.

Coates, Linda, and Allan Wade. 2004. "Telling It Like It Isn't: Obscuring Perpetrator Responsibility for Violence." *Discourse and Society* 15: 499–526.

_____. 2007. "Language and Violence: An Analysis of the Four Discursive Operations." *Journal of Family Violence* 22, 7 (October): 511–522.

Comack, Elizabeth. 1993. *Women in Trouble. Connecting Women's Law Violations to Their Histories of Abuse.* Halifax, NS: Fernwood.

_____ (ed.). 1999. *Locating Law: Race, Class and Gender Connections.* Halifax, NS: Fernwood.

Commission on Systemic Racism in the Ontario Criminal Justice System. 1998. "Racism in Justice: Perceptions." In V. Satzewich (ed.), *Racism & Social Inequality in Canada: Concepts, Controversies & Strategies of Resistance.* Toronto: Thompson Educational Publishing.

Conway, Janet. M. 2004. *Identity, Place, Knowledge — Social Movements Contesting Globalization.* Halifax, NS: Fernwood.

Cooke, A. 1987. "Stripping: Who Calls the Tune?" In L. Bell (ed.), *Good Girls/Bad Girls: Sex Trade Workers and Feminists Face to Face.* Toronto: Women's Press.

Copper, Baba. 1988. *Over the Hill: Reflections On Ageism Between Women. Freedom,* California: Crossing Press.

Cornwell, A. 1983. *Black Lesbian in White America.* Tallahassee, FL: Naiad Press.

Cosić, Bora. 2006. "Dead Man Walking. Slobodan Milosevic is Dead but his Sinister Legacy is Still Looming." *Neue Zuricher Zeitung* 60 (March 13).

Cottin, Lou. 1979. *Elders In Rebellion: A Guide to Senior Activism.* Garden City, NY: Anchor Press/Doubleday.

Covington, S. 1999. *Helping Women Recover: A Program for Treating Substance Abuse.* Special Edition for Use in the Criminal Justice System, Facilitator's Guide. San Francisco, CA: Jossey-Bass Publishers.

Crager, Meg , Merril Cousin, and Tara Hardy. 2003. "Victim-Defendants: An Emerging Challenge in Responding to Domestic Violence in Seattle and the King County Region." Seattle: King County Coalition Against Domestic Violence. Available at <http://www.kccadv.org/Reports/victimdefendantfinalreport1.pdf> accessed October 2008.

Crawford, Maria, and Rosemary Gartner. 1992. *Woman Killing: Intimate Femicide in Ontario 1974–1990.* Toronto: The Women We Honour Action Committee.

Crowder, Dianne Griffins. 1998. "Lesbians and the (Re/De)Construction of the Female Body." In D. Atkins (ed.), *Looking Queer – Body Image and Identity in Lesbian, Bisexual, Gay, and Transgender Communities.* New York: Harrington Park Press.

Daly, Mary. 1978. *Gyn/Ecology: The Metaethics of Radical Feminism.* Boston: Beacon Press.

Danet, B. 1980. "'Baby' or 'fetus'? Language and the Construction of Reality in a Manslaughter Trial." *Semiotica* 32: 187–219.

Davis, K. 1986. "The Process of Problem (Re)Formulation in Psychotherapy." *Sociology of Health and Illness* 8: 44–74.

Dawson, T. Brettel (ed.). 2002. *Women, Law and Social Change: Core Readings and Current Issues.* Third edition. North York, ON: Captus Press.

de Beauvoir, Simone. 1964. *The Second Sex.* Translated and edited by H.M. Parshley. New York: Knopf.

De Vos, George, and Hiroshi Wagatsuma (eds.). 1972. *Japan's Invisible Race: Caste in Culture and Personality.* Berkeley: University of California Press.

Delacoste, Fredrique, and Priscilla Alexander (eds.). 1987. *Sex Work: Writings by Women in the Sex Industry.* San Francisco: Cleis Press.

DeLancey, Dayle B. 1990. "Motherlove Is a Killer: Sula, Beloved, and the Deadly Trinity of Motherlove." *SAGE* vii (2): 15–17.

Demir, J.S. (United Nations High Commission for Refugees). 2003. "The Trafficking of Women For Sexual Exploitation: A Gender-Based and Well-Founded Fear of Persecution?" UNHCR Working Paper No. 80 (March). Available at <http://www.unhcr.org/research/RESEARCH/3e71f84c4.pdf> accessed October 2008.

Denfeld, Rene. 1995. *The New Victorians: A Young Woman's Challenge to the Old Feminist Order.* Sydney: Allen & Unwin. [originally published: New York: Warner Books, 1994].

Department of Justice. 2000. *Pre-Sentence Report Writing Workshop Manual.* Winnipeg: Province of Manitoba.

DERA (Dancers' Equal Rights Association). 2002. "Current Issues Concerning Exotic Dancers." Unpublished Document. Ottawa.

_____. 2003. Mission Statement.

Dion, Susan. 2005. "Aboriginal People and Stories of Canadian History, Investigating Barriers to Transforming Relationships." In C.E. James (ed.), *Possibilities and Limitations, Multicultural Policies and Programs in Canada.* Halifax, NS: Fernwood Publishing.

Domestic Abuse Intervention Project. "The Power and Control Wheel." Available at <http://www.duluth-model.org/documents/PhyVio.pdf> accessed October 2008.

Donnan, Mary Ellen. 2003. "Slow Advances: The Academy's Response to Sexual Assault." In D. Keahey and D. Schnitzer (eds.), *The Madwoman in the Academy: 43 Women Boldly take on the Ivory Tower.* Calgary, AB: University of Calgary Press.

Douglas, Carole Anne. 1990. *Love and Politics: Radical Feminist and Lesbian Theories.* San Francisco: Ism Press.

Doyle, Doran. 1998. May 14. Personal communication. Victoria, B.C.

Drakulic, Slavenka. 1995. *Marble Skin: A Novel.* New York: Perennial.

_____. 2005. *They Would Never Hurt a Fly: War Criminals on Trial in the Hague.* London: Penguin.

Dube, Leela. 1996. "Caste and Women." In M.N. Srinivas (ed.), *Caste: Its Twentieth Century Avatar.* New Delhi: Viking.

Dunk, Thomas. 1998. "Racism, Ethnic Prejudice, Whiteness and the Working Class." In V. Satzewich (ed.), *Racism & Social Inequality in Canada: Concepts, Controversies & Strategies of Resistance.* Toronto: Thompson Educational Publishing.

Duran, E., and B. Duran. 1995. *Native American Postcolonial Psychology.* Albany, NY: State University of New York Press.

Eberts, Mary. n.d. *Sexual Assault and the Common Law: A New Perspective.* Toronto: Tory, Tory, DesLauriers and Binnington.

References

Edkins, J. 2003. *Trauma and the Memory of Politics*. Cambridge, UK: Cambridge University Press.

Egan, D. 2003. "I'll be your Fantasy Girl, if you'll be my Moneyman: Mapping Desire, Fantasy and Power in Two Exotic Dance Clubs." *Journal for the Psychoanalysis of Cultural and Society* 8, 1.

Ehrlich, Susan. 1998. "The Discursive Reconstruction of Sexual Consent." *Discourse and Society* 9: 149–71.

———. 2001. *Representing Rape: Language and Sexual Consent*. London and New York: Routledge.

Eistenstein, Zillah. 1997. "Feminism of the North and West for Export: Transnational Capital and the Racializing of Gender." In Jodi Dean (ed.), *Feminism and the New Democracy: Resisting the Political*. London: Sage.

Eley, Geoff. 1999. "Culture, Nation and Gender." In Ida Blom (ed.), *Gendered Nations: Nationalisms and Gender Order in the Long Nineteenth Century*. Oxford and New York: Berg.

Elias, Robert. 1993. *Victims Still: The Political Manipulation of Crime Victims*. London, New Delhi, Newbury Park: Sage Publications.

Enloe, Cynthia. 2004. *The Curious Feminist*. Berkeley, Los Angeles, London: University of California Press.

Estrich, Susan. 1987. *Real Rape: How the Legal System Victimizes Women Who Say No*. Cambridge, MA: Harvard University Press.

Evasuk, Stasia. 1990. "Never Underestimate Granny Power." *The Toronto Star*, April 2.

Ewick, Patricia, and Susan S. Silbey. 1998. *The Common Place of Law: Stories from Everyday Life*. Chicago: University of Chicago Press.

EDA (Exotic Dancers Alliance). 2001. *The Naked Truth*. Winter (1). Toronto

Feinberg, Leslie. 1998. *Trans Liberation Beyond Pink or Blue*. Boston: Beacon Press.

Fenlon, Brodie. 2000. "Raging Grannies Take a Swipe at Squeegee Law." *London Free Press*, February 13.

Ferguson, Rob. 1995. "Harris Stalling on Election Promise to Ban Lap Dancing, Critics Say." *The Montreal Gazette* August 2: A5.

Ferree, Myra Marx, and Patricia Yancey Martin. 1995. *Feminist Organizations: Harvest of the New Women's Movement*. Philadelphia: Temple University Press.

Fineman, Martha, and Roxanne Mykitiuk (eds.). 1994. *The Public Nature of Private Violence: The Discovery of Domestic Abuse*. New York: Routledge.

Fineman, Martha Albertson, and N.S. Thomadsen (eds.). 1991. *At the Boundaries of Law: Feminism and Legal Theory*. New York, London: Routlege.

Finkelstein, Norma, Nancy VandeMark, Roger Fallot, Vivian Brown, Sharon Cadiz, and Jennifer Heckman. 2004. *Enhancing Substance Abuse Recovery Through Integrated Trauma Treatment*. National Trauma Consortium for the Center for Substance Abuse Treatment (CSAT). Available at <http://www.nationaltraumaconsortium.org/documents/IntegratedTrauma.pdf> accessed October 2008.

Finn, G., and A. Miles (eds.). 1982. *Feminism in Canada: From Pressure to Politics*. Montreal: Black Rose Books.

Fodden, Simon R. 1999. *Canadian Family Law* Toronto: Irwin Law.

Ford, Janet, and Ruth Sinclair. 1987. *Sixty Years On: Women Talk About Old Age*. London: Women's Press.

Foucault, Michel. 1976. *Histoire de la sexualité*. Paris: Gallimard.

———. 1977. *Discipline and Punish: The Birth of the Prison*. New York: Pantheon Books.

Frank, Katharine. 2002. *G-Strings and Sympathy: Strip Club Regulars and Male Desire*. London:

Duke University Press.

Freeman, Marilyn. 2000. "Rights of Custody and Access under the Hague child Abduction Convention: 'A Questionable Result?'" *California Western International Law Journal* 31, 1.

Freire, Paolo. 1970 and 2000. *Pedagogy of the Oppressed*. New York: Continuum.

Freud, Sigmund. 1949. *An Outline of Psychoanalysis*. New York: W.W. Norton.

Friedan, Betty. 1963. *The Feminine Mystique*. New York: Norton.

Friedman, J., and Marixsa Alicea. 2001. *Surviving Heroin: Interviews With Women in Methadone Clinics*. Gainsville, FL: University Press of Florida.

Fulton, Keith Louise. 2003. "The Possibility of Professing Changes." In D. Keahey and D. Schnitzer (eds.), *The Madwoman in the Academy: 43 Women Boldly take on the Ivory Tower*. Calgary, AB: University of Calgary Press.

Gelles, Richard, and Murray Strauss. 1990. *Physical Violence in American Families*. New Jersey: Transaction Publishers.

Giddings, Paula. 1985. *When and Where I Enter: A History of Black Women's Movement*. New York: Bantam.

Gilbert, Neil. 1991. "The Phantom Epidemic of Sexual Assault." *The Public Interest* 103: 54–65.

_____. 1992. "Realities and Mythologies of Rape." *Society* (May-June): 4–10.

_____. 1993. "Examining the Facts: Advocacy Research Overstates the Incidence of Date and Acquaintance Rape." In Richard Gelles and Donileen Loseke (eds.), *Current Controversies in Family Violence*. Newbury Park, California: Sage Publications.

Gillespie, Marcia. 1994. "The Posse Rides Again." Editorial. *Ms. Magazine* May/June.

Gluck, Jay (ed.). 1963. *Ukiyo: Stories of 'The Floating World' of Postwar Japan*. New York: Grosset and Dunlap.

Gödl, Doris. 1998. "Women's Contributions to the Political Policies of National Socialism." In Günter Bischof (ed.), *Women in Austria: Contemporary Austrian Studies*. New Brunswick: Transaction Publishers.

_____. 2007. "Challenging the Past: Serbian and Croatian Aggressor/Victim Narratives." In Tadeusz Krauze (ed.), *International Journal of Sociology*. New York: M.E. Sharpe.

Goldberg, Katherine. 1987. "Only Municipal Bylaws can Prevent Lapdancing." *Toronto Star* July 4: A4

Gomez, L.E. 1997. *Misconcieving Mothers: Legislators, Prosecutors, and the Politics of Prenatal Drug Exposure*. Philadelphia, PA: Temple University Press.

Gould, Stephan. 1996. *The Mismeasure of Man*. New York: W.W. Norton.

Granny Grapevine. 1995. Summer. Saltspring Island Raging Grannies, B.C.

_____. 1996. Summer. Edmonton Raging Grannies, Alberta.

_____. 2001. Spring. Kingston Raging Grannies, Ontario.

Greenberg, Jeremy. 1999. "These Grannies are Raging." *Excalibur*, October.

Greer, Germaine. 1971. *The Female Eunuch*. New York: McGraw-Hill.

Greif, Geoffrey, and Rebecca L. Hegar. 1993. *When Parents Kidnap: The Families Behind the Headlines*. New York: Free Press.

Griffin, Katherine. 1996. "Childless by Choice: Can I Live a Rich, Balanced Life without Joining the Parenthood Procession?" *Health* 10: 98–104.

Gunn, Rita, and Rick Linden. 1997. "The Impact of Law Reform on the Processing of Sexual Assault Cases." *Canadian Review of Sociology & Anthropology* 34: 155–75.

Hadrill, Joan. 2001. "Grannies March, Rage in Song." Reprinted in *Grapevine*, Spring.

Hagan, John, and F. Kay. 1995. *Gender in Practice: A Study of Lawyer's Lives*. New York: Oxford University Press.

References

Hagen, D. 2004. "Growing Up Outside the Gender Construct." In J. McNinch and M. Cronin (eds.), *"I Could Not Speak My Heart" Education and Social Justice for Gay and Lesbian Youth*. Regina, University of Regina.

Hale, J. 1997. "Suggested Rules for Non-Transsexuals Writing about Transsexuals, Transsexuality, Transsexualism, or Trans…" Available at <http://sandystone.com/hale.rules.html> accessed March 15, 2006.

Hampton, A.S.C. 2008. "I Don't Think Canadians Are Going to Sit Still and Let it Happen": The New Brunswick Ad Hoc Committee on the Constitution and Citizens' Response to the Meech Lake Accord. Master's thesis, University of New Brunswick. (January).

Hartman, A. 1992. "In Search of Subjugated Knowledge." *Social Work* 137: 483–84.

Harvey, David. 2005. *A Brief History of Neoliberalism*. Oxford: Oxford University Press.

Harvey, Joan. 2002. Personal communication. March 18. Toronto, Ontario.

Hawthorne, Susan. 2002. *Wild Politics*. North Melbourne: Spinifex.

Hayner, Priscilla. 2002. *Unspeakable Truths. Facing the Challenge of Truth Commissions.* New York, London: Routledge.

Heald, S. 1997. "Events Without Witness: Living/Teaching Difference within the Paternalist University." *Curriculum Studies* 5,1.

Hendly, Nate. 1999. "Live Girl Productions." *The Eye* July 1.

Henley, N.M., M. Miller, and J. Beazley. 1995. "Syntax, Semantics, and Sexual Violence: Agency and the Passive Voice." *Journal of Language and Social Psychology* 14: 60–84.

Herising, Fairn. 2005. "Interrupting Positions: Critical Thresholds and Queer Pro/Positions." In L. Brown and S. Strega (eds.), *Research as Resistance: Critical, Indigenous, & Anti-Oppressive Approaches*. Toronto: Canadian Scholar's Press.

Hernandez-Avila, C.A., Bruce J. Rounsaville and Henry R. Kranzler. 2004. "Opioid-, Cannabis-, and Alcohol-Dependent Women Show More Rapid Progression to substance Abuse Treatment." *Drug and Alcohol Dependence* 74, 265–72.

Hiebert-Murphy, D., and L. Woytkiw. 2000. "A Model for Working with Women Dealing with Child Sexual Abuse and Addictions. *Journal of Substance Abuse Treatment* 18: 387–94.

Highcrest, Alexandra. 1995. "Exotic Dancers Lose Regardless of Who Lays Down the Law." *The Eye* October 19.

Hill Collins, Patricia. 2004. *Black Sexual Politics: African Americans, Gender, and the New Racism.* New York: Routledge.

Hine Darlene Clark, and Kate Wittenstein. 1981."Female Slave Resistance: The Economics of Sex." In Filomina Chioma Steady (ed.), *The Black Woman Cross-Culturally*. Cambridge, MA: Schenkman.

Hochschild, Arlie. 1983. *The Managed Heart: The Commercialization of Human Feeling*. UCP, Berkeley: CA.

Hollander, J., and R. Einwohner. 2004. "Conceptualizing Resistance." *Sociological Forum* 19 (4).

Hontz, J. 1998. "25 Years Later: The impact of Roe v. Wade." *Human Rights: Journal of the Section of Individual Rights and Responsibilities* 25: 8–11.

Hood, E.F. 1978. "Black Women, White Women: Separate Paths to Liberation." *Black Scholar* 9(7): 45–56.

hooks, bell. 1981. *Ain't I a Woman? Black Women and Feminism*. South End Press.

_____. 1984. *Feminist Theory: From Margin to Centre*. Boston: South End Press.

_____. 1994. *Outlaw Culture: Resisting Representations*. New York: Routledge.

Howard, Cori. 1992. "Raging Against the Night." *Vancouver Sun*, October 10.

Howard, Keith. 1989. "Those Comic Raging Grannies." *The United Church Observer* 53, 3.

Human Rights Watch. 2004. "Justice at Risk: War Crimes Trials in Croatia, Bosnia and Herzegovina, and Serbia and Montenegro." *Human Rights Watch* 16, 7/D (October).

Humphries, D. 1999. *Crack Mothers: Pregnancy, Drugs, and the Media.* Columbus, OH: Ohio State University Press.

Hunter, Gorde. 1988. "One Man's Opinion." *Times-Colonist* Victoria, August 25.

Hunter, Janet E. 1984. "Sano Manabu." *Concise Dictionary of Modern Japanese History.* Berkeley: University of California Press.

Hydén, M. 1995. "Verbal Aggression as a Prehistory of Woman Battering." *Journal of Family Violence* 10: 55–71.

Immigration and Refugee Board of Canada. 1993. "Guidelines on Women Refugee Claimants Fearing Gender-Related Persecution." Available at <http://www.irb-cisr. gc.ca/en/references/policy/guidelines/women_e.htm> accessed October 2008.

ICC (International Criminal Court) Women's News. 2000. "Annex — Summary of Judgement of Tokyo Tribunal 2000." *International Criminal Court Women's News.* May. Available at <http://www.iccwomen.org> accessed October 16, 2000.

_____. February 2001a. *International Criminal Court Women's News.* Available at <http://www.iccwomen.org> accessed June 25, 2005.

_____. February 2001b. "Tokyo Tribunal 2000 and Public Hearing." *International Criminal Court Women's News.* Available at <http://www.iccwomen.org> accessed June 22, 2005.

Incite! Available at <http://www.incite-national.org/about/index> accessed April 21, 2006.

Iyer, N. 1993. "Categorical Denials: Equality Rights and the Shaping of Social Identity." *Queen's Law Journal* 19.

Jacobs, Harriet. 2000. *Incidents in the Life of a Slave Girl.* A Norton Critical Edition. Nellie Y. McKayand Frances Smith Foster, editors. New York: Norton.

Jacobs, Jane. 2004. *Dark Age Ahead.* Vintage Press.

Jacobs, Ruth Harriet. 1997. *Be An Outrageous Older Woman.* New York: Perennial.

Jalušić, Vlasta. 1994. "Die Funktionalisierung von Vergewaltigungen im Vorkriegs-Jugoslawien." In Uremovif, Olga (ed.), *Frauen zwischen Grenzen. Rassismus und Nationalismus in der feministischen Diskussion.* Frankfurt, New York: Campus Verlag.

James, Carl E. 2003. *Seeing Ourselves: Exploring Race, Ethnicity and Culture.* Third edition. Toronto: Thompson Educational Publishing.

Jang, K.L., L., W.J. Livesley and Philip A. Vernon. 1997. "Gender-Specific Etiological Differences in Alcohol and Drug Problems: A Behavioral Genetic Approach." *Addiction* 92(10): 1265–76.

Janoff, Douglas. 2005. *Pink Blood: Homophobic Violence in Canada.* Toronto: University of Toronto Press.

Jeffrey, Leslie Ann, and Gayle MacDonald. 2006. *Sex Workers in the Maritimes Talk Back.* Vancouver: University of British Columbia Press.

Jhappan, Radha. 1996. "Post-Modern Race and Gender Essentialism or a Post-Mortem of Scholarship." *Studies in Political Economy* 51.

_____. 1998. "The Equality Pit or the Rehabilitation of Justice." *Canadian Journal of Women and the Law* 10 (1).

_____. 2002. *Women's Legal Strategies in Canada.* Toronto: University of Toronto Press.

Johnson, Merri. 1987. "CABE and Strippers: A Delicate Union." In Laurie Bell (ed.), *Good*

Girls/Bad Girls: Sex Trade Workers and Feminists Face to Face. Toronto: Women's Press.

Johnson, Rebecca. 2002. *Taxing Choices: The Intersection of Class, Gender, Parenthood and the Law*. Vancouver: UBC Press.

Joseph, G., and J. Lewis. 1981. *Common Differences: Conflicts in Black and White Feminist Perspectives*. New York: Anchor Press.

Kamen, Paul. December 1993. "Erasing Rape: Media Hype an Attack on Sexual-Assault Research." FAIR: Fairness and Accuracy in Reporting. Available at <http://www. fair.org/index.php?page=1218> accessed October 2008.

Kanuha, Valli. 1996. "Domestic Violence, Racism and the Battered Women's Movement in the United States." In Jeffrey L. Edleson and Zvi C. Eisikovits (eds.), *Future Interventions with Battered Women and Their Families: Visions for Policy, Practice, and Research*. Thousand Oaks: Sage Publications.

_____. 1998. "Stigma, Identity, and Passing: How Lesbians and Gay Men of Color (sic) Construct and Manage Stigmatized Identity in Social Interaction." Ann Arbor: UMI.

Kaplan, S.J. 1979. "Literary Criticism." *Signs* 4(3): 514–27.

Kaplan, T. 1990. "Community and Resistance in Women's Political Cultures." *Dialectical Anthropology* 15.

Kapur, Ratna. 2002. "The Tragedy of Victimization Rhetoric: Resurrecting the 'Native' Subject in International/Post-Colonial Feminist Legal Politics." *Harvard Human Rights Journal* 15: 1–48.

Karumanchery-Luik, Nisha, and Helen Ramirez. 2003. "Teaching for Legitimacy: Or, Teaching from the Margins." In D. Keahey and D. Schnitzer (eds.), *The Madwoman in the Academy: 43 Women Boldly take on the Ivory Tower*. Calgary, AB: University of Calgary Press.

Kauffman, L.A. 1990. "The Anti-Politics of Identity." *Socialist Review* 20(1).

Kawash, Samira. 1999. "Fugitive Properties." In Martha Woodmansee and Mark Osteen (eds.), *The New Economic Criticism: Studies at the Intersection of Literature and Economics*. London: Routledge.

Keahey, Deborah. 2003. "Nine Steps Toward a Twelve-Step Program for Recovering Academics." In D. Keahey and D. Schnitzer (eds.), *The Madwoman in the Academy: 43 Women Boldly take on the Ivory Tower*. Calgary, AB: University of Calgary Press.

Keahey, Deborah, and Deborah Schnitzer (eds.). 2003a. *The Madwoman in the Academy: 43 Women Boldly take on the Ivory Tower*. Calgary, AB: University of Calgary Press.

_____. 2003b. "Introduction: Professional Girth." In D. Keahey and D. Schnitzer (eds.), *The Madwoman in the Academy: 43 Women Boldly take on the Ivory Tower*. Calgary, AB: University of Calgary Press.

Keane, H. 2002. *What's Wrong with Addiction*. Washington Square, NY: New York University Press.

Kelly, Jennifer, and Aruna Srivastava. 2003. "Dancing on the Lines: Mothering, Daughtering, Masking, and Mentoring in the Academy." In D. Keahey and D. Schnitzer (eds.), *The Madwoman in the Academy: 43 Women Boldly take on the Ivory Tower*. Calgary, AB: University of Calgary Press.

Kelly, L. 1988. *Surviving Sexual Violence*. Minneapolis: University of Minnesota Press.

Kesić, Vesna. 2000. *Gender and Ethnic Identities in Transition*. Zagreb: Unpublished Paper.

Ketchner, Elizabeth S. 1999. "Ageism's Impact and Effect on Society: Not Just a Concern for the Old." *Journal of Gerontological Social Work* 32, 4.

Kikuchi, Jin'ichi. 1934. *Shisō hanzai no sho mondai*. Tokyo: Nihon hanzai gakkai kankō.

Kitzinger, Celia, and Rachel Perkins. 1993. *Changing Our Minds, Lesbian Feminism and*

Psychology. New York: New York University Press.

Klein, N. 2001. *No Logo: Taking Aim at the Band Bullies.* U.K.: Harper Collins.

_____. 2007. *The Shock Doctrine: The Rise of Disaster-Capitalism.* Toronto: Alfred A. Knopf Canada

Koonz, Claudia. 1991. *Mothers in Fatherland.* Freiburg: Kore.

Koprince, Susan. 2000. "Childless Women in the Plays of William Inge." *Midwest Quarterly* 3, 251–64.

Korac, Maja. 2004. "War, Flight, and Exile: Gendered Violence among Refugee Women from Post-Yugoslav States." In W. Giles (ed.), *Sites of Violence: Gender and Conflict Zones.* Berkeley, Los Angeles, London: University of California Press.

Korehito, Kurahara. "Kurahara Korehito." In *Nihon shakai undō jinmei jiten.*

Koss, Mary. 1988. "Hidden Rape: Sexual Aggression and Victimization in a National Sample of Students in Higher Education," In A. Wolbert Burgess, (ed.), *Rape and Sexual Assault* Vol. 2. New York: Garland Publishing.

_____. 2000. *Blame, Shame, and Community: Justice Responses to Violence Against Women.* Minnesota: Minnesota Center Against Violence and Abuse. Available at <http://www.mincava.umn.edu/documents/koss/koss.html> accessed October 2008.

Koss, M., T. Dinero, and C. Seibel. 1988. "Stranger and Acquaintance Rape." *Psychology of Women Quarterly* 12 (12).

Koss, Mary P., and Mary R. Harvey. 1991. *The Rape Victim. Clinical and Community Interventions.* Second edition. Newbury Park, CA: Sage Publications.

Koss, M., and C. Oros. 1982. "Sexual Experiences Survey: A Research Instrument Investigating Sexual Aggression and Victimization." *Journal of Consulting and Clinical Psychology* 50 (3).

Kraut, R.E., and R.E. Johnston. 1979. "Social and Emotional Messages of Smiling: An Ethological Approach." *Journal of Personality and Social Psychology* 9: 1539–53.

Krawczk, Bob. June 1991. "Remembering the RTPC." *Gay Archivist* 9. Available at <http://www.clga.ca/Material/Records/docs/remrtpc.htm> accessed October 2008.

Krestan, J.-A. 2000. Addiction, Power, and Powerlessness. In J.-A. Krestan (ed.), *Bridges to Recovery: Addiction, Family Therapy, and Multicultural Treatment.* New York: Free Press.

LaFrance, M., H. Brownell, and E. Hahn. 1997. "Interpersonal Verbs, Gender, and Implicit Causality." *Social Psychology Quarterly* 60: 138–52.

Lahey, K. A. 1991. "Reasonable Women and the Law." In M.A. Fineman and N.S. Thomadsen (eds.), *At the Boundaries of Law: Feminism and Legal Theory.* New York and London: Routledge.

LaMastro, Valerie. 2001. "Childless by Choice? Attributions and Attitudes Concerning Family Size." *Social Behavior and Personality* 29: 231–44.

Lamb, S. 1991. "Acts Without Agents: An Analysis of Linguistic Avoidance in Journal Articles on Men who Batter Women." *American Journal of Orthopsychiatry* 61: 250–57.

Lamb, S., and S. Keon. 1995. "Blaming the Perpetrator: Language that Distorts Reality in Newspaper Articles on Men Battering Women." *Psychology of Women Quarterly* 19: 209–20.

Land, Peggy. 2001. "Moments of Faith at the Wall." *Peace & Environment News* 16 (May/June).

Larana, E., H. Johnston, J.R. Gusfield (eds.). 1994. *New Social Movements: From Ideology to Identity.* Temple University Press.

Laster, Kathy, and Edna Erez. 2000. "The Oprah Dilemma: The Use and Abuse of Victims." In Duncan Chappell and Paul Wilson (eds.), *Crime and the Criminal Justice*

References

System in Australia: 2000 and Beyond. Sydney: Allen & Unwin.

Lattin, Don. 2001. "In Oakland, Moon Stresses Family; Speech of Unification Church Criticizes Childless Women." *San Francisco Chronicle* March 13.

LeMoncheck, L. 1997. *Loose Women, Lecherous Men: A Feminist Philosophy of Sex.* Oxford University Press.

Lerner, Harriet G. 1993. *The Dance of Deception, Pretending and Truth-Telling in Women's Lives.* New York: Harper Collins Publishers.

Letherby, Gayle, and Catherine Williams. 1999. "Non-Motherhood: Ambivalent Autobiographies." *Feminist Studies* 25: 719–29.

Leto, Marisa. 2002. "Whose Best Interest? International Child Abduction under the Hague Convention." *Chicago Journal of International Law* 3, 1.

Levy, Eileen F. 1995. "Feminist Social Work Practice with Lesbian and Gay Clients." In N. Van Den Bergh (ed.), *Feminist Practice in the 21st Century.* Washington: NASW Press.

Lewis, J. 2000. "Controlling Lap Dancing: Law, Morality, and Sex Work." In R. Weitzer (ed.), *Sex for Sale, Prostitution, Pornography, and the Sex Industry.* New York: Routledge.

Lewis, J., and E. Maticka-Tyndale. 2003. "Peer Research in the Sex Trade." *Research Bulletin: Centers of Excellence for Women's Health* 4, 1.

Lewis, Stephen. 2005. *Race Against Time: Searching for Hope in AIDS Ravaged Africa.* Toronto: Anansi Press.

Lightly, Marion. 1989. "Raging Grannies: Singing the Subs Away." *Briarpatch: Saskatchewan's Independent News Magazine* 18, 1 (February).

Lillehoj, C.J., L. Trudeau, R. Spoth, and K.A. Wickrama. 2004. "Internalizing, Social Competence, and Substance Initiation: Influence of Gender Moderation and a Preventative Intervention." *Substance Use and Misuse* 39(6): 963–91.

Lisle, Laurie. 1999. *Without Child: Challenging the Stigma of Childlessness.* New York: Routledge.

Loftus, Ronald P. (ed.). 2004. "Resisting Authority: Fukunaga Misao's *Recollections of a Female Communist (Aru onna kyōsanshugisha no kaisō).*" In *Telling Lives: Women's Self-Writing in Modern Japan.* Honolulu: University of Hawaii Press.

Long, Jane. 2001. "'A Certain Kind of Modern Feminism': Memory, Feminist Futures and 'Generational Cleavage' in Historical Perspective." *Outskirts: Feminisms Along the Edge* 8. Available at <http://www.chloe.uwa.edu.au/outskirts/archive/volume8/long> accessed October 2008.

Lorde, Audre. 1984. *Sister Outsider: Essays and Speeches.* Berkeley, CA: Crossing Press.

Loseke, Donileen R. 1992. *The Battered Woman and Shelters: The Social Construction of wife Abuse.* Albany: State University of New York Press.

Louwe, Ava. 2002. March 23. Personal communication. Ottawa, Ontario.

Luther, Rashmi, Elizabeth Whitmore and Bernice Moreau (eds.). 2001. *Seen But Not Heard: Aboriginal Women and Women of Colour in the Academy.* Ottawa, ON: Canadian Research Institute for the Advancement of Women.

MacDonald, Gayle, Rachel Osborne, and Charles Smith (eds.). 2005. *Feminism, Law, Inclusion: Intersectionality in Action.* Toronto: Sumach Press.

Mackie, Vera. 1997. *Creating Socialist Women in Japan: Gender, Labour and Activism, 1900–1937.* Cambridge: Cambridge University Press.

MacKinnon, Catharine A. 2005. *Women's Lives: Men's Laws.* Boston: Harvard University Press.

_____. 2008. *Are Women Human? And Other International Dialogues.* Cambridge, MA: Harvard University Press.

Maher, F. and M.K.T. Tetreault. 1998. "'They Got the Paradigm and Painted It White':

Whiteness and Pedagogies of Positionalities." In J.L. Kincheloe, S.R. Steinberg, N.M. Rodriguez and a R.E. Chennault (eds.), *White Reign: Deploying Whiteness in America*. New York: St. Martin's Griffin.

Maher, L. 1997. *Sexed Work: Gender, Race and Resistance in a Brooklyn Drug Market*. New York: Oxford University Press.

Mahoney, Martha. 1991. "Legal Images of Battered Women: Redefining the issue of Separation." *Michigan Law Review* 90.

Major, Brenda, Caroline Richards, M. Lynne Cooper, Catherine Cozzarelli, and Josephine Zubek. 1998. "Personal Resilience, Cognitive Appraisals, and Coping: An Integrative Model of Adjustment to Abortion." *Journal of Personality and Social Psychology* 74: 735–52.

Makau, Lynn. 2005. *Milk Matters: Contemporary Representations of Breast-giving, Property and the Self.* Diss. University of Texas at Austin.

Makin-Byrd, Kerry. 2002. "The Doctor and the Woman: Comparing British and American Abortion Law." *Off Our Backs* March-April: 37–41.

Makise, Kikue. 1976. *Kikigaki hitamuki no onnatachi: Musan undō no kage ni*. Tokyo: Asahi shimbunsha.

Mallick, H. 2006. "Pay attention, feminists." *CBC News Online*. Analysis and Views. October 6. Available at <http://www.cbc.ca/news/viewpoint/vp_mallick/20061006.html> accessed June 4, 2008.

Mandel, Laurie, and Charol Shakeshaft. 2000. "Heterosexism in Middle Schools." In N. Lesko (ed.), *Masculinities at School*. Thousand Oaks, CA: Sage.

Maradorossian, Carine M. 2002. "Toward a New Feminist Theory of Rape." *Signs* 27: 743–75.

Marchese, Darci. 2006. "'Raging Grannies' Protest Armed Forces Recruitment." WTOP Radio 103.5 FM. Washington, D.C. 15 February. Available at <http://www.wtop-pnews.com/index.php?nid=25&sid=700078> accessed October 2008.

Marcoux, Lois. 1998. May 18. Personal communication. Victoria, B.C.

Marcus, J. Spring 1982. "Storming the Toolshed." *Feminist Theory* 7(3): 622–40.

Mardiros, Shelley. 2000. "Raging Gracefully." *Alberta Views* 3, 1 (January/February).

Marler, P., and C. Evans. 1997. "Animal Sounds and Human Faces: Do They Have Anything in Common?" In J.A. Russell and J.M. Fernandez-Dols (eds.), *The Psychology of Facial Expression*. Cambridge, UK: Cambridge University Press.

Marolla, J.A., and D.H. Scully. 1979. "Rape and Psychiatric Vocabularies of Motive." In E.S. Gomberg and V. Franks (eds.), *Gender and Disordered Behavior: Sex Differences in Psychopathology*. New York: Brunner/Mazel.

Martin, Del, and P. Lyon. 1976. *Battered Wives*. San Francisco: Glide Publications.

Mason, Mary Ann. 1994. *From Father's Property to Children's Rights: A History of Child Custody.* New York: Columbia University Press.

Masten, Ann S. 2001. "Ordinary Magic: Resilience Processes in Development." *American Psychologist* 56: 227–38.

Mathen, C. 2004. "Transgendered Persons and Feminist Strategy." *Canadian Journal of Women and the Law* 16(2): 291–316.

Matsuda, M.J., C.R. Lawrence III, R. Delgado, and K. Williams Crenshaw (eds.). 1995. *Words that Wound: Critical Race Theory, Assaultive Speech and the First Amendment*. Boulder, San Francisco, Oxford: Westview Press.

Maynard, S. 1991. "When Queer Is not Enough: Identity in Queer Nation." *Fuse Magazine* 5 (1/2).

McAdam, Doug. 1994. "Culture and Social Movements." In E. Larana, H. Johnston,

References

and J.R. Gusfield (eds.), *New Social Movements: From Ideology to Identity*. Philadelphia: Temple University Press.

McCaffrey, Dawn. 1998. "Victim Feminism/Victim Activism." *Sociological Spectrum* 18, 3: 263–84.

McCulloch, Sandra. 1991. "Victoria's Raging Grannies Lead the Battle Against War." *Times-Colonist Victoria*. Dec. 1. Sunday Supplement, p. 18.

McIntyre, S. 2000. "Studied Ignorance and Privileged Innocence: Keeping Equity Academic." *Canadian Journal of Women and the Law: Revue femmes et droit* 12,1.

McLaren, Arlene T. 1982. "The Myth of Dependency." *Resources for Feminist Research/ Documentation pour la Recherche Féministe* 11, 2.

McLaren, Jean. 2002. May 10. Personal communication. Gabriola Island, B.C.

McLeer, Anne. 1998. "Saving the Victim: Recuperating the Language of the Victim and Reassessing Global Feminism." *Hypatia* 13, 1: 41–55.

McNeece, C.A., and D. DiNitto. 1998. *Chemical Dependency: A Systems Approach*. Needham Heights, MA: Allyn & Bacon.

Mesić, Stipe. 2004. *The Demise of Yugoslavia: A Political Memoir*. Budapest: Central European University Press.

Miers, David R. 1983. "Compensation and Conceptions of Victims of Crime." *Victimology* 18, 1–2: 204–12.

Miller, Michelle. 2008. *Branding Miss G: Third Wave Feminists and the Media*. Toronto: Sumach Press.

Minkler, Meredith. 1996. "Critical Perspectives on Ageing: New Challenges for Gerontology." *Ageing and Society* 16, 4 (July).

Misao, Fukunaga. 2004. "Resisting Authority: Recollections of a Female Communist (Aru onna kyōsanshugisha no kaisō)." In Ronald P. Loftus (ed.), *Telling Lives: Women's Self-Writing in Modern Japan*. Honolulu: University of Hawaii Press.

Mock, Michele. 1996. "Spitting Out the Seed: Ownership of Mother, Child, Breasts, Milk, and Voice in Toni Morrison's Beloved." *College Literature* 3: 117–26.

Mohanty, Chandra Talpade. 1994. "On Race and Voice: Challenges for Liberal Education in the 1990s." In H.A. Giroux and P. McLaren (eds.), *Between Borders: Pedagogy and the Politics of Cultural Studies*. New York: Routledge.

Montemurro, B. 2001. "Strippers and Screamers: The Emergence of Social Control in a Non-Institutional Setting." *Journal of Contemporary Ethnography* 30, 3.

Monture-Angus, Patricia. 1999. *Standing Against Canadian Law: Naming Omissions of Race, Culture and Gender*. Halifax, NS: Fernwood Press.

_____. 2001. "In the Way of Peace: Confronting 'Whiteness' in the University." In R. Luther, E. Whitmore and B. Moreau (eds.), *Seen But Not Heard: Aboriginal Women and Women of Colour in the Academy*. Ottawa, ON: Canadian Research Institute for the Advancement of Women.

Mooers, C., and A. Sears. 1997. *Organizing Dissent: Contemporary Social Movements in Theory*. Toronto: Garamond Press.

Moraga, Cherrie L., and Gloria E. Anzaldúa (eds.). 2003. *This Bridge Called My Back – Writings by Radical Women of Color*. Third edition. Third Woman Press.

Morgan, M., and D. O' Neill. 2001. "Pragmatic Post-Structuralism (II): An Outcomes Evaluation of a Stopping Violence Programme." *Journal of Community & Applied Social Psychology* 11: 277–89.

Morrell, Carolyn. 1993. "Intentionally Childless Women: Another View of Women's Development." *Affilia: Journal of Women and Social Work* 8: 300–17.

Morris, R. 2000. "Living In/Between." In A. Gonzalez, M. Houston and V. Chen (eds.),

Our Voices: Essays in Culture, Ethnicity, and Communication. Los Angeles, CA: Roxbury.

Morrison, Toni. 1987. *Beloved.* New York: Knopf.

Moses, D.J., N. Huntington, and B. D'Ambrosia. 2004. *Developing Integrated Services for Women with Co-Occurring Disorders and Trauma Histories: Lessons Learned from the SAMHSA Women and Alcohol, Drug Abuse and Mental Health Disorders who have Histories of Violence Study.* Delmar, NY: Policy Research Associates, Inc.

Mueller, Karla, and Janice Yoder. 1999. "Stigmatization of Non-Normative Family Size Status." *Sex Roles* 41: 901–19.

Mulia, N. 2000. "Questioning Sex: Drug-Using Women and Heterosexual Relations." *Journal of Drug Issues* 30(4): 741–66.

———. 2003. "Conflicts and Trade-Offs Due to Alcohol and Drugs: Clients' Accounts of Leaving Welfare." *Social Service Review* 77(4): 499–522.

Mullaly, Robert. 1993. *Structural Social Work – Ideology, Theory, and Practice.* Toronto: McClelland and Stewart.

———. 2002. *Challenging Oppression, A Critical Social Work Approach.* Ontario: Oxford University Press.

Munro, Eva. 2002. March 13. Personal communication. Halifax, Nova Scotia.

Murakami, Nobuhiko. 1978. *Nihon no fujin mondai.* Tokyo: Iwanami Shinsho.

Myron, N., and C. Bunch (eds.). 1975. *Lesbianism and the Women's Movement.* Baltimore, MD: Diana Press.

Nakamoto, Takako. 1950. *Ai wa rogoku o koete.* Tokyo: Satsuki shobō.

———. 1963. "The Only One." In Jay Gluck (ed.), *Ukiyo: Stories of 'The Floating World' of Postwar Japan.* New York: Grosset and Dunlap.

———. 1973. *Wagasei wa kuno ni yakarete: waga wakaki no ikigai.* Tokyo: Shiraishi shoten.

———. 1987. "The Female Bell-Cricket." In Yukiko Tanaka (ed.), *To Live and to Write: Selections by Japanese Women Writers, 1913–1938.* Seattle, WA: Seal Press.

———. 1999a. *Aiwarogoku o koete: denki Nakamoto Takako* Tokyo: Ōzorasha; reprint of Nakamoto Takako. 1950. *Ai wa rogoku o koete.* Tokyo: Satsuki shobō.

———. 1999b. "Takako Nakamoto." In Jojo Kikaku (ed.), *Onnatachi no nijū-seiki hyakunin shimaitachi yo.* Tokyo: Shūeisha.

NAWL (National Association of Women and the Law). 2003. "Transgender and Women's Substantive Equality, Discussion Paper." Available at <http://www.nawl.ca/lob-trans-dp.htm> accessed March 10, 2006.

Neary, Ian. 1989. *Political Protest and Social Control in Pre-war Japan: The Origins of Buraku Liberation.* Manchester: Manchester University Press.

Nett, Emily. 1982. "Introduction." *Resources for Feminist Research/Documentation pour la Recherche Feministe* 11, 2.

Noonan, S. 2002. "Of Death, Desire, and Knowledge: Law and Social Control of Witches in Renaissance Europe." In G. MacDonald (ed.), *Social Context and Social Location in the Sociology of Law.* Toronto: Broadview Press.

Norman, Alma. 2001. October 22. Personal communication. Ottawa, Ontario

———. 2002, March 23. Personal communication. Ottawa, Ontario.

O'Heron, Connie A., and Jacob L. Orlofsky. 1990. "Stereotypic and Nonstereotypic Sex Role Trait and Behavior Orientations, Gender Identity, and Psychological Adjustment." *Journal of Personality and Social Psychology* 58: 134–43.

O' Neill, D., and M. Morgan. 2001. "Pragmatic Post-Structuralism: (I): Participant Observation and Discourse in Evaluating Violence Intervention." *Journal of Community & Applied Social Psychology* 11: 263–75.

O'Reilly, Andrea. 2004. *Toni Morrison and Motherhood: A Politics of the Heart.* Albany: State

University of New York Press.

Ochiai, Emiko. 1999. "Modern Japan through the Eyes of an Old Midwife: From an Oral Life History to Social History." In Wakita Haruko, Anne Bouchy and Ueno Chizuko (eds.), *Gender and Japanese History: Religion and Customs/The Body and Sexuality* Vol. 1. Osaka: Osaka University Press.

Office of the Prosecutor. 2004. Press release: Address by Carla del Ponte, Prosecutor of the International Criminal Tribunal for the former Yugoslavia, to the United Nations Security Council. CDP/P.I.S/917-e. Available at <http://www.un.org/icty/pressreal/2004/p917-e.html>. Accessed June 20, 2008.

Ōmiya, Nobumitsu. 1999. "Kaisetsu." In *Aiwarogoku o koete: denki Nakamoto Takako*. Tokyo: Ōzorasha.

Omolade, Barbara. 1985. "Black Women and Feminism." In Hester Eisenstein and Alice Jardine (eds.), *The Future of Difference*. New Brunswick, N.J.: Rutgers University Press.

Orr, Catherine M. 1997. "Charting the Currents of the Third Wave." *Hypatia* 12(3): 29–45.

Ostlund, A., F. Spak, and V. Sundh. 2004. "Personality Traits in Relation to Alcohol Dependence and Abuse and Psychiatric Comorbidity Among Women: A Population-Based Study." *Substance Use and Misuse* 39(4): 1301–18.

Page, Cristina. 2006. *How the Pro-Choice Movement Saved America: Freedom, Politics, and the War on Sex*. New York: Basic Books.

Park, Kristin. 2002. "Stigma Management Among the Voluntarily Childless." *Sociological Perspectives* 45: 21–45.

Parkins, W. 2000. "Protesting Like a Girl: Embodiment, Dissent and Feminist Agency." *Feminist Theory* 1 (1).

Patton, Michael Quinn. 2002. *Qualitative Research and Evaluation Methods*. Third edition. London: Sage.

Payne, Julien, and Marilyn Payne. 2006. *Canadian Family Law (In A Nutshell)* Canada: Irwin Law.

Payne, Kathryn. 2002. "Whores and Bitches Who Sleep with Women." In C.B. Rose and A. Camilleri (eds.), *Brazen Femme, Queering Femininity*. Vancouver: Arsenal Pulp Press.

Penelope, J. 1990. *Speaking Freely*. New York: Pergamon.

Pieri, Laura. 2002. "The Therapuetic Community as Treatment in Substance Use Disorders." Available at <http://www.alcoholmedicalscholars.org/tc-out.htm> accessed November 15, 2003.

Pierson, Ruth Roach. 1999. "Nations: Gendered, Racialized, Crossed With Empire." In Ida Blom (ed.), *Gendered Nations. Nationalisms and Gender Order in the Long Nineteenth Century*. Oxford, New York: Berg.

Ponting, J. Rick. 1998. "Racism and Stereotyping of First Nations." In V. Satzewich (ed.), *Racism & Social Inequality in Canada: Concepts, Controversies & Strategies of Resistance*. Toronto: Thompson Educational Publishing.

Prescott, C.A. 2002. "Sex Differences in the Genetic Risk for Alcoholism." *Alcohol Health and Research World* 26(4): 264–73.

Price, K. 2000. "Stripping Women: Workers' Control in Strip Clubs." *Unusual Occupations* 11.

Prittie, Jennifer. 1999. "Exotic Dancers Fight for Rights: Conditions 'Filthy.'" *National Post* September 11.

Profitt, Norma Jean. 2000. *Women Survivors, Psychological Trauma, and the Politics of Resistance*.

New York, London, Oxford: Haworth Press.

Ptacek, James. 2005. "Guest Editor's Introduction." *Violence Against Women* 11.

Quinby, Lee. 1999. "Virile Reality: From Armageddon to Viagra." *Signs* 24.

Raby, R. 2005. "What is Resistance?" *Journal of Youth Studies* 8 (2).

Raging Granny "Carry On" Songbook. 2000. Collected by South West Ontario Grannies.

Ramos, H. 2008. "Aboriginal Protest." In S. Staggenborg (ed.), *Social Movements.* Don Mills, ON: Oxford University Press.

Rasmussen, S. 2000. *Addiction Treatment.* Thousand Oaks, CA: Sage.

Ray, Ruth E. 1999. "Researching to Transgress: The Need for Critical Feminism in Gerontology." In Diane J. Garner (ed.), *Fundamentals of Feminist Gerontology.* New York: Haworth Press.

Razack, Sherene. 1994. "What Is to Be Gained by Looking White People in the Eye? Culture, Race, and Gender in Cases of Sexual Violence." *Signs* 19, 4 (Summer).

_____. 1998. *Looking White People in the Eye: Gender, Race, and Culture in Courtrooms and Classrooms.* Toronto: University of Toronto Press.

_____. 2001. "Racialized Immigrant Women as Native Informants in the Academy." In R. Luther, E. Whitmore and B. Moreau (eds.), *Seen But Not Heard: Aboriginal Women and Women of Colour in the Academy.* Ottawa ON: Canadian Research Institute for the Advancement of Women.

Rees, M. 2004. *Our Final Hour: A Scientist's Warning: How Terror, Error, and Environmental Disaster Threaten Humankind's Future in This Century — On Earth and Beyond.* New York: Basic Books.

Regnier, Robert. 1995. "Warrior as Pedagogue, Pedagogue as Warrior: Reflections on Aboriginal Anti-Racist Pedagogy." In R. Ng, P. Staton, and J. Scane (eds.), *Anti-Racism, Feminism, and Critical Approaches to Education.* Toronto: OISE Press.

Reid, R. 2001. "The Exposure Show!" Available at <groups.msn.com/ExoticDancersAlliance/Exposureshow.msnw> accessed February 15, 2006.

Reynolds, V. 2001. "Wearing Threads of Belonging: The Cultural Witnessing Group." *Journal of Child and Youth Care* 15: 89–106.

Rice, James J., and Michael J. Prince. 2003. *Changing Politics of Canadian Social Policy.* Toronto: University of Toronto Press.

Rich, Adrienne. 1980. "Compulsory Heterosexuality and Lesbian Existence." *Signs: Journal of Women in Culture and Society* 5(4): 631–90.

_____. 1983. "Compulsory Heterosexuality and Lesbian Existence." In A. Snitow, C. Stansell, and S. Thompson (eds.), *Powers of Desire: The Politics of Sexuality.* New York: Monthly Review Press.

_____. 1993. *What Is Found There: Notebooks on Poetry and Politics.* New York: W.W. Norton.

Richie, Beth. 1996. *Compelled to Crime: The Gender Entrapment of Battered Black Women.* New York: Routledge.

_____. 2000. "A Black Feminist Reflection on the Antiviolence Movement." *Signs* 25.

Riessman, Catherine Kohler. 2000. "Stigma and Everyday Resistance Practices: Childless Women in South India." *Gender and Society* 14: 111–36.

Riordon, Ellen. 2001. "Commodified Agents and Empowered Girls: Consuming and Producing Feminism." *Journal of Communication Inquiry* 25: 279–97.

Ritcey, Sheila. 1982. "Substituting an Interactionist for a Normative Model in Gerontological Research." *Resources for Feminist Research/Documentation pour la Recherche Féministe* 11, 2.

Ritter, Kathleen Y., and Anthony I. Terndrup. 2002. *Handbook of Affirmative Psychotherapy with Lesbians and Gay Men.* New York: Guilford Press.

Roberts, D.E. 1991. "Punishing Drug Addicts Who Have Babies: Women of Color, Equality, and the Right to Privacy." *Harvard Law Review* 104(7): 1419.

Roesch, Jen. 2004. "Turning Back the Clock? Women, Work and Family Today." *International Socialist Review* 38: 10–16.

Roiphe, Katie. 1993. *The Morning After: Sex, Fear, and Feminism.* London: Hamish Hamilton.

Ronai, Rambo C. 1999. "The Next Night: Sous Rature: Wrestling with Derrida's Mimesis." *Qualitative Inquiry* 5,1.

Roscoe, Will. 1998. *Changing Ones, Third and Fourth Genders in Native North America.* New York: St. Martin's Griffin.

Rose, Stephen, and Heidi Hartmann. 2004. *Still a Man's Labour Market: The Long-Term Gender Gap in Earnings.* Washington, DC: Institute for Women's Policy Research.

Rosenthal, Evelyn R. 1990. "Women and Varieties of Ageism." *Journal of Women and Aging* 2, 1.

Ross, L. 1998. *Inventing the Savage.* Austin, TX: University of Texas Press.

Rubin, J.W. 1995. "Defining Resistance: Contested Interpretations of Everyday Acts." *Studies in Law, Politics and Society* 15.

Saleebey, Dennis. 2002. "Introduction: Power in the People." In D. Saleebey (ed.), *The Strengths Perspective in Social Work Practice.* Third edition. Boston: Allyn and Bacon.

SAMHSA. 2002. *Benefits of Residential Substance Abuse Treatment for Pregnant and Parenting Women.* Rockville, MD: DHHS-SAMHSA.

Sanchez, L. 1997. "Boundaries of Legitimacy: Sex, Violence, Citizenship in a Local Sexual Economy." *Law & Social Inquiry* 22.

Sangster, J. 1997. "Telling Our Stories: Feminist Debates and the Use of Oral History." In V. Strong-Boag and A. Fellman (eds.), *Rethinking Canada: The Promise of Women's History.* Toronto: Oxford University Press.

Schapiro, Barbara. 1991. "The Bonds of Love and the Boundaries of Self in Toni Morrison's Beloved." *Contemporary Literature* 32 (2): 194–209.

Schechter, Susan. 1982. *Women and Male Violence: The Visions and Struggles of the Battered Women's Movement.* Boston: South End Press.

Scheff, Thomas J. (ed.). 1975. *Labeling Madness.* New Jersey: Prentice-Hall.

Scheidt, R.J., D.R. Humpherys, and J.B. Yorgason. 1999. "Successful Aging: What's Not To Like." *Journal of Applied Gerontology: The Official Journal of the Southern Gerontological Society* 18, 3.

Schneider, Elizabeth. 2000. *Battered Women and Feminist Lawmaking.* New Haven: Yale University Press.

Schnitzer, Deborah. 2003. "Tenure Tracks." In D. Keahey and D. Schnitzer (eds.), *The Madwoman in the Academy: 43 Women Boldly take on the Ivory Tower.* Calgary, AB: University of Calgary Press.

Scott, J.C. 1990. *Domination and the Arts of Resistance: Hidden Transcripts.* New Haven, CT: Yale University Press.

Scott, James A. 1985. *Weapons of the Weak: Everyday Forms of Peasant Resistance.* Westford: Yale University Press.

Segal, B. 2001. "Responding to Victimized Alaska Native Women in Treatment for Substance Abuse." *Substance Use and Misuse* 36(6-7): 845–65.

Seifred, Barbara Calvert. 2002. March 28. Personal communication. Montreal, Quebec.

Senanayake, Pramilla, and Karen Newman. 2002. "The Politics of Abortion in the

Modern Age." *Conscience* 23, 12.

Shaw-MacKinnon, M. 2003. "Portrait." In D. Keahey and D. Schnitzer (eds.), *The Madwoman in the Academy: 43 Women Boldly take on the Ivory Tower.* Calgary, AB: University of Calgary Press.

Shiota, Shobe. 1979. "Korehito Kurahara" In S. Shiota (ed). *Nihon shakai undō jinmei jiten.* Tokyo: Aoki shoten.

_____. 1979a. "Tanaka Kiyoharu," In Shiota Shobe (ed.), *Nihon shakai undō jinmei jiten.* Tokyo: Aoki shoten.

_____. 1979b. "Itō Chiyoko," In Shobe Shiota (ed.), *Nihon shakai undō jinmei jiten.* Tokyo: Aoki shoten: 107–8.

Shunsuke, Tsurumi. 1991. *Tenkōkenkyū.* Tokyo: Chikuma Shobō.

Siegel, D.L. 1997. "The Legacy of the Personal: Generating Theory in Feminism's Third Wave." *Hypatia* 12 (3).

Silver, Angela. 2002. March 27. Personal communication. Montreal, Quebec.

Slavin, Linda. 2001. "Should Have Gone to the Fence." [Letter to the editor]. *Peterborough Examiner* April 24.

Smart, Carol. 2002. *Feminism and the Power of Law.* London & New York: Routledge.

_____. 1995. *Law, Crime and Sexuality: Essays In Feminism: Essays On Feminism.* UK: Sage.

Smart, C., and J. Brophy. 1985. "Locating Law: A Discussion of the Place of Law in Feminist Politics." In J. Brophy and C. Smart (eds.), *Women In Law: Explorations in Law, Family and Sexuality.* London, Boston, Melbourne, and Henley: Routledge & Kegan Paul.

Smith, Barbara. 1979. "Racism and Women's Studies." *Frontiers: A Journal of Women's Studies* 5(1): 48–49.

Smith, D. 2002. "Institutional Ethnography." In T. May (ed.), *Qualitative Research in Action.* London: Sage.

Smith, D. Chad, and Lisa Seymour. 2001. *Identifying Allies, A Safe Space Project.* Winnipeg: University of Manitoba.

Smith, K. 2004. *Environmental Hazards: Assessing Risk and Reducing Disaster.* Fourth edition. New York: Routledge.

Smith, Sidonie, and Julia Watson. 2001. *Reading Autobiography: A Guide for Interpreting Life Narratives.* Minneapolis: University of Minnesota Press.

Snug, Hannah. 2000. "Peel & Play Professor of Strip Mary Taylor Empowers Women by Showing Them how it's Done." *Varsity* October 10.

Sohrabji, F. 2002. "Neurodegeneration in Women." *Alcohol Health and Research World* 26(4): 316–18.

Sommers, Christina Hoff. 1994. *Who Stole Feminism? How Women Have Betrayed Women.* New York: Simon and Shuster.

Spelman, Elizabeth. 1988. *Inessential Woman. Problems of Exclusion in Feminist Thought.* Boston: Beacon Press.

Spivak, G.C. 1988. *In Other Worlds: Essays in Cultural Politics.* New York: Routledge.

_____. 2008. *Other Asias.* MA, USA; Oxford, UK; Victoria, Australia: Blackwell.

Spivak, Gayatri Chakravorty, and Sarah Harasym. 1990. *The Post-Colonial Critic: Interviews, Strategies, Dialogues.* New York; London: Routledge.

Staggenborg, S. 2008. *Social Movements.* Don Mills, ON: Oxford University Press.

Stannard, D.E. 1992. *American Holocaust: The Conquest of the New World.* New York: Oxford University Press.

Stark, Evan. 2004. "Insults, Injury, and Injustice: Rethinking State Intervention in Domestic Violence Cases." *Violence Against Women* 10.

References

Statistics Canada (Robin Fitzgerald). 1999. *Family Violence in Canada: A Statistical Profile 1999*. 85-224-XIE. Available at http://www.statcan.ca/english/freepub/85-224-XIE/0009985-224-XIE.pdf accessed October 2008.

Status of Women Canada. 2004. "Fact Sheets on Violence Against Women for the National Day of Remembrance." Available at <http://www.swc-cfc.gc.ca/dates/dec6/index_e.html> accessed November 12, 2008.

Steinhoff, Patricia G. 1991. *Tenkō Ideology and Societal Integration in Prewar Japan*. New York: Garland Publishing.

Stern, D. 2000. "The Return of the Subject? Power, Reflexivity and Agency." *Philosophy & Social Criticism* 26 (5).

Stiglmayer, Alexandra. 1993. *Massenvergewaltigung*. Freiburg: Kore.

Strauss, A.L. 1987. *Qualitative Analysis for Social Scientists*. Cambridge, UK: Cambridge University Press.

Stringer, Rebecca. 2000. "'A Nietzschean Breed': Feminism, Victimology, Ressentiment." In Alan D. Schrift (ed.), *Why Nietzsche Still? Reflections on Drama, Culture and Politics*. Berkeley: University of California Press.

_____. 2001. "Blaming Me, Blaming You: Victim Identity in Recent Feminism." *Outskirts: Feminism Along the Edge* 8. University of Australia. Available at <http://www.chloe.uwa.edu.au/outskirts/archive/volume8/stringer> accessed October 2008.

_____. 2006. "Is New Zealand a Post-Feminist Paradise?" In Michelle Thompson-Fawcett and Claire Freeman (eds.), *Living Together: Towards Inclusive Communities*. Dunedin: Otago University Press.

Sudermann, M., and Jaffe, P. 1999. *A Handbook for Health and Social Service Providers and Educators on Children Exposed to Woman Abuse/Family Violence*. Family Violence Prevention Unit, Health Canada. Available at <http://www.phac-aspc.gc.ca/ncfv-cnivf/familyviolence/html/femexpose_e.html> accessed October 2008.

Sulliman, C. 2003. "(M)othering in the Academy." In D. Keahey and D. Schnitzer (eds.), *The Madwoman in the Academy: 43 Women Boldly take on the Ivory Tower*. Calgary AB: University of Calgary Press.

Sykes, Gresham M., and D. Matza. 1957. "Techniques of Neutralization: Theory of Delinquency." *American Sociological Review* 22: 664–70.

Tanaka, Yukiko (ed.). 1987. *To Live and To Write: Selections by Japanese Women Writers 1913–1938*. Seattle: Seal Press.

Tarrow, S. 1998. *Power in Movement: Social Movements and Contentious Politics*. Second edition. Cambridge: Cambridge University Press.

Tatlock, Melissa, and Linda Coates. 2003. "Disguising Violence: Violence in Children's Films." Manuscript in progress. St. Thomas University.

Thesenvitz, J. 2002. "Exotic Dancers: Not so Hard-to-Reach After All." *The Update* Health Communication Unit at The Centre For Health Promotion University of Toronto (THCU). Available at <http://www.thcu.ca/infoandresources/newsletters/sprng2002%20final.pdf> accessed November 14, 2008.

Thompson, Allan. 1998. "Are Raging Grannies a Public Enemy?" *Toronto Star* October 11.

Tilly, Charles. 1995. *Popular Contention in Great Britain, 1758–1834*. Cambridge, MA: Harvard University Press.

Times Colonist. 1990. "Raging Grannies Ready for War, Head for Recruitment Centre Today." Victoria. November 2.

Timpson, Anis. 2001. *Driven Apart: Employment Equality and Child Care in Canadian Public Policy*. Vancouver: UBC Press.

Tipton, Elise. 1990. *The Japanese Police State: The Tokkōin Interwar Japan*. Honolulu: University of Hawaii.

Todd, J.L., and Judith Worell. 2000. "Resilience in Low-Income, Employed, African American Women." *Psychology of Women Quarterly* 24: 119–28.

Todd, N. 2002a. "An Eye for an I: Response-based Work with Perpetrators of Abuse." Unpublished manuscript.

Todd, Nick. 2002b. "An Introduction to Response-based Counseling with Victims of Interpersonal Violence." Calgary, AB: Calgary Women's Emergency Shelter.

Todd, Nick, and Allan Wade. 2003. "Coming to Terms with Violence and Resistance: From a Language of Effects to a Language of Responses." In Tom Strong and Dave Pare (eds.), *Furthering Talk: Advances in the Discursive Therapies*. New York: Kluwer Academic Plenum.

Tokyo Tribunal 2000 and Public Hearing. February 2001. *Newsletter: ICC Women*. Available at <http://www.iccwomen.org> accessed June 22, 2005.

Tracey, Lindalee. 1997. *Growing up Naked: My Years in the Bump and Grind*. Vancouver: Douglas and McIntyre.

Trans Programming at the 519. 2006. *The Toronto Trans and Two-Spirit Primer: An Introduction to Lower-income, Sex-working and Street-involved Transgendered, Transsexual & Two-Spirit Service Users in Toronto*. Toronto: 519 and United Way.

Trew, Tony. 1979. "Theory and Ideology at Work." In R. Fowler, G. Kress, and T. Trew (eds.), *Language and Control*. London: Routledge and Kegan Paul.

Trimble, Linda, and Jane Arscott. 2003. *Still Counting: Women in Politics Across Canada*. Ontario: Broadview Press.

Tsurumi, Kazuko. 1970. "Six Types of Change in Personality: Case Studies of Ideological Conversion in the 1930s." In *Social Change and the Individual: Japan Before and After Defeat in World War II*. Princeton: Princeton University Press.

Tsurumi, Shunsuke. 1991. *Tenkō kenkyū*. Tokyo: Chikuma Shobō.

Turiel, E. 2003. "Resistance and Subversion in Everyday Life." *Journal of Moral Education* 32(2): 115–30.

UNICEF (United Nations Children's Fund). 2000. "Domestic Violence Against Women and Girls." *Innocenti Digest* 6 (June). Available at <http://www.unicef-icdc.org/publications/pdf/digest6e.pdf> accessed October 2008.

United States Department of Justice. 1995. "Violence Against Women: Estimates from the Redesigned Survey August 1995." Special Report, NCJ-154348.

van Dijk, J. 1999. "Criminal Victimization and Victim Empowerment in an International Perspective." In J. van Dijk, R. van Kaam, and J. Wemmers (eds.), *Caring for Crime Victims: Selected Proceedings of the 9th International Symposium on Victimology*. NY: Criminal Justice Press.

Van Leeuwen, Raymond C. 2003. "Is it all Right for a Married Couple to Choose to Remain Childless?" *Today's Christian Woman* 25, 24.

Vickers, J.M. 1982. "Memoirs of an Ontological Exile: The Methodological Rebellions of Feminist Research." In G. Finn and A. Miles (eds.), *Feminism in Canada: From Pressure to Politics*. Montreal: Black Rose Books.

Vickroy, Laurie. 1993. "The Force Outside/The Force Inside: Mother-Love and Regenerative Spaces in Sula and Beloved." *Obsidian II: Black Literature in Review* 8 (2): 28–45.

Volksstimme. 1998. Vol. 3. Magdeburg Publication and Printing House GmbH. Magdeburg: Germany. Available at <http://www.volksstimme.de/> accessed December 2, 2008.

Vosko, Leah. 2000. *Temporary Work: The Gendered Rise of a Precarious Employment Relationship.* Toronto: University of Toronto Press.

Wade, A. 1995a. "The Language of Colonialism." Unpublished manuscript. Victoria, BC: University of Victoria.

_____. 1995b. "Resistance Knowledges: Therapy with Aboriginal Persons Who Have Experienced Violence." In P.H. Stephenson, S.J. Elliott, L.T. Foster and J.A. Harris (eds.), *Persistent Spirit: Towards Understanding Aboriginal Health in British Columbia.* Victoria, BC: Department of Geography: University of Victoria.

_____. 1997. Small Acts of Living: Everyday Resistance to Violence and Other Forms of Oppression. *Contemporary Family Therapy* 19(1): 23–39.

_____. 2000. "Resistance to Interpersonal Violence: Implications for the Practice of Therapy." *Psychology.* Victoria, BC: University of Victoria.

Walker, Gillian. 1990. *Family Violence and the Women's Movement: The Conceptual Politics of Struggle.* Toronto: University of Toronto Press.

Walker, Lenore. 1984. *The Battered Woman Syndrome* New York: Springer Publishing Co.

Walker, Moira. 1998. May 17. Personal communication. Victoria, B.C.

Walter, Natasha. 1998. *The New Feminism.* London: Little, Brown and Company.

Walters, K., Jane Simoni, and Teresa Evans-Campbell. 2002. "Substance Use Among American Indians and Alaska Natives: Incorporating Culture in an 'Indigenist' Stress-Coping Model." *Public Health Reports* 117(Supplement 1).

Ware, V. 1992. *Beyond the Pale: White Women, Racism and History.* London: Verso.

Weagle, Robert. 1999. Human Resource Issues in the Exotic Dance Industry. Unpublished M.A, Queen's University. Kingston.

Weaver, Jill, Nick Todd, Cindy Ogden, and Laura Craik. 2005. *Resistance to Violence and Abuse in Intimate Relationships: A Response Based Perspective.* Calgary: Calgary Women's Emergency Shelter.

Weiner, M. 2000. "International Child Abduction and the Escape from Domestic Violence." *Fordham Law Review* 69, 2: 593-706. Available at <http://law.fordham.edu/ihtml/page3.ihtml?imac=1137&pubID=500&articleid=529> accessed November 12, 2008.

West, Candace, and Don H. Zimmerman. 1987. "Doing Gender." *Gender and Society* 1: 12551.

West, Krista, and Linda Coates. 2004. "Respresentation and Responsibility: An Analysis of Sexual Assault Trial Judgments." Saint Thomas University, Fredericton, NB

Westlund, Andrea C. 1999. "Pre-modern and Modern Power: Foucault and the Case of Domestic Violence." *Signs* 24.

White, L.E. 1991. "Subordination, Rhetorical Survival Skills, and Sunday Shoes: Notes on the Hearing of Mrs. G." In M.A. Fineman and N.S. Thomadsen (eds.), *At the Boundaries of Law: Feminism and Legal Theory.* New York and London: Routledge.

Wilkinson, S. 1992. "Old Woman, 'Bearer of Keys to Unknown Doorways'." *Canadian Woman Studies* 12, 2.

Williams, L. Susan. 2002. "Trying on Gender, Gender Regimes, and the Process of Becoming Women." *Gender and Society* 16: 29–52.

Williams, P.J. 1991. "On Being the Object of Property." In M. A. Fineman and N. S. Thomadsen (eds.), *At the Boundaries of Law: Feminism and Legal Theory.* New York and London: Routledge.

Wolf, Naomi. 1993. *Fire With Fire: The New Female Power and How it will Change the 21st Century.* London: Chatto & Windus.

WIGJ (Women's Initiatives for Gender Justice). 2005. "Publications on the ICC and a Dossier of Judicial Candidates." Available at <http://www.iccwomen.org/>. Accessed November 12, 2008.

Women's Caucus for Gender Justice. 2005. "Strengthening Advocacy in Women's Human Rights and International Justice." In International Criminal Court Women's News. Available at <http://www.iccwomen.org/archive/aboutcaucus.htm> accessed June 22 2005.

Wood, E. 2000. "Working in the Fantasy Factory: The Attention Hypothesis and the Enacting of Masculine Power." *Journal of Contemporary Ethnography* 29, 1.

Woodland, Karyn. 1998. "The Raging Grannies: Tackling Serious Issues with Satire." *Focus on Women* 11, 1 (October).

Wurman, Sharon. 2001. July 7. Personal communication.

Yeatman, Anna. 1997. "Feminism and Power." In Mary Lyndon Shanley and Uma Narayan (eds.), *Reconstructing Political Theory: Feminist Perspectives*. Cambridge: Polity Press.

Young, I.M. 1994. "Punishment, Treatment, Empowerment: Three Approaches to Policy for Pregnant Addicts." *Feminist Studies* 20(1): 33–58.

Yuval-Davis, Nira. 1997. *Gender & Nation*. London: Sage.

Zemsky, B. 1991. "Coming Out Against All Odds: Resistance in the Life of a Young Lesbian." In C. Gilligan, A.G. Rogers and D.L. Tolman (eds.), *Reframing Resistance: Women, Girls, and Psychotherapy*. New York: Haworth Press.

Zita, Jacquelyne N. 1998. *Body Talk, Philosophical Reflections on Sex and Gender*. New York: Columbia University Press.

Legal Cases Cited

563080 Alberta Ltd. (c.o.b. Body Shoppe) v. Calgary (City) [1997] A.J. No. 269.

AEAC (Adult Entertainment Association of Canada) v. Ottawa (City) [2005] O.J. No. 3626.

Affidavit of Theo Koumoudouros cited in *OAEBA v. Toronto* (1997), 118 C.C.C. (3d) 481.

Affidavit sworn September 10, 1995, Ms. Johne (intervener licensed under Bylaw No. 20-85).

Algonquin Tavern and Canadian Labour Congress, Chartered Local Union No. 1689, [1981] 3 Can. L.R.B.R. 337 (Labour Board).

Belton v. Belton [1998], M.J. No. 562. (Man. Q.B.)

CABE (Canadian Association of Burlesque Entertainers) v. Algonquin Tavern [1981] O.L.R.B. Rep. 1057.

Calahoo v. Calahoo [2000], A.J. No. 815 (Alta. Q.B.)

Canadian Charter of Rights and Freedoms. Schedule B. Constitution Act, 1982 (79).

Canadian Criminal Code, R.S.C. 1985, c. C-46.

Children's Law Reform Act R.S.O. [1990] C. 12

Divorce Act R.S.C. [1985] (2nd Supp.), c. 3

Finizio v. Scoppio-Finizio [1999], 46 O.R. (3d) 226 (Ont. C.A.)

Geneva Convention Relating to the Status of Refugees 1951 Concluded 28 July 1951

Hague Convention of 25 October 1980 on the Civil Aspects of International Child Abduction, concluded by the Fourteenth Session of the Hague Conference on Private International Law on 25 October 1980 and entered into force *1 December 1983* Can. T.S. 1983, No. 35, 19 I.L.M. 1501

Immigration and Refugee Board "*Guidelines on Women Refugee Claimants Fearing Gender-Related Persecution*." March 1993

Jabbaz v. Mouammar [2003], O.J. No. 1616 (Ont. C.A.)

References

Medhurst v. Markle [1995], 26 OR (3d) 178 at p. 182, 17 RFL (4th) 428.

OAEBA v. Toronto (1997), 118 C.C.C. (3d) 481, aff'd. (1995), 101 C.C.C. (3d) 491.

OAEBA (Ontario Adult Entertainment Bar Association) v. Metropolitan Toronto (Municipality) (1997), 118 C.C.C. (3d) 481, aff'd. (1996), 27 O.R. (3d) 643.

Pollastro v. Pollastro [1999], 45 R.F.L. (4th) 404 (Ont. C.A.)

R. v. Butler [1992] 1 S.C.R. 452 (S.C.C.).

R. v. Caringi [2002] O.J. No. 2367 (Ct. J.).

R. v. Hawkins [1993] 86 C.C.C. (3d) 246 (C.A.).

R. v. Johnson [1975] 2 S.C.R. 160 (S.C.C.).

R. v. Mara and East [1997] 2 S.C.R. 630 (S.C.C.); aff' D (1996), 88 O.A.C. 358 (C.A.).

R. v. Pelletier [1999] 3 S.C.R. 863 (S.C.C), over'd [1998] J.Q. no 4316 (C.A).

R. v. Shalmark Hotels and Municipality of Toronto (1981) 32 O.R. (2d) 129 (Ct. J.)

R. v. Tremblay [1993] 2 S.C.R. 932 (S.C.C.).

Re Koumoudouros and Toronto (1985), 52 O.R. (2d) 443 (C.A.), ov'ed (1984) 45 O.R. (2d) 426 (Div. Ct.).

Roberts v. Roberts [2000] N.S.J. No. 218 (Fam. Ct.)

Sharlmark Hotels v. Municipality of Toronto [1981], 32 O.R. (2d) 12.

Starko v. Starko [1990], 74 Alta. L.R. (2d) 168 (Alta. Q.B.).

The Body Shoppe v. Calgary [1997] A.J. No. 269.

Sauvé v. Canada (Ministry of National Revenue: M.N.R) [1994] T.C.J. No. 1093 (Tax Ct).

Contributors

Suzanne Bouclin is a feminist lawyer working in the areas of equality rights and minority language rights. Her research areas include feminist theories around sex work, law and representation, and marginal labour organizing. She is currently pursuing graduate studies at the University of Manitoba.

Rebecca Bromwich, lawyer, practises predominantly in the areas of family, immigration and youth justice. Rebecca is committed to equality, particularly gender equality and has been involved with feminist work throughout her career. She also teaches at the University of Western Ontario and Fanshawe College. Rebecca completed her LL.B. and LL.M. at Queen's university. Rebecca has published several academic papers and book chapters dealing with subjects relating to international law, youth justice and family law.

Linda Coates, PhD, is an associate professor in the Dept. of Psychology, Okanagan College. She has published and presented widely on the issue of language and violence and how it affects social policy and practice. Linda has a particular interest in the representation of violence and has undertaken extensive analyses to identify problematic practices within the legal system, media and helping professions. Linda has conducted numerous studies demonstrating how language can be used to conceal violence, mitigate perpetrators' responsibility, blame victims and conceal victim resistance.

Ellen Faulkner is an assistant professor in the Department of Sociology at Brock University. For the past few years she has been studying hate crimes committed against gay, lesbian, bisexual and transgender/transsexual persons in Canada. In 2006 she was awarded a SSHRC grant to research and understand what impedes or supports hate crime reporting, documentation and case processing. She has most recently published in the *Journal of Hate Studies* and *Canadian Woman Studies/les cahiers de la femme*.

Doris Goedl is a research fellow at the Institute for Social Research and Development, Salzburg, and a part-time lecturer at the University of Salzburg. In the fall of 2004 she held the Harriman Institute Visiting Fellowship at Columbia University. She coordinated the Austrian Research Fund's two-year study "Political Transformation Processes in Former Yugoslavia," which encompassed Slovenia, Croatia and Bosnia-Herzegovina. Currently she holds the U.S. Institute for Peace (USIP) research grant. Her areas of specialization are the role of gender in nation-building, trauma in the political context and transitional justice and peace.

Gayle MacDonald is a professor of sociology at St. Thomas University. Her areas of interest include sex work, socio-legal studies, social control and deviance. Her most recent books include *Sex Workers of the Maritimes Talk Back* (with Leslie Jeffrey, UBC Press, 2006); *Feminism, Law, Inclusion: Intersectionality in Action* (ed. with Rachel Osborne and Charles Smith, Sumach Press, 2005); *Social Context and Social Location in the Sociology of Law* (ed., Broadview Press, 2002). She has appeared before the Parliamentary subcommittee on prostitution laws and as an expert witness to the Ontario Superior Court on a challenge to Canada's prostitution laws.

Lynn Makau is an assistant professor of English and African and African American Studies at Michigan State University. She is currently at work on a book manuscript exploring contemporary literary representations of intimate transgressions in nineteenth-century American domestic spheres.

Janice Matsumura is an assistant professor of Japanese history at Simon Fraser University. She is currently conducting research on the psychiatric profession in Japan and has most recently published in *Modern Asian Studies* and the *Bulletin for the History of Medicine*.

Debra Mollen is an assistant professor in the Department of Psychology and Philosophy at Texas Woman's University in Denton, Texas. She earned her doctoral degree in counselling psychology with a minor in gender studies at Indiana University. Her research interests and scholarly works centre on feminist concerns, childfree women, multicultural training and education and reproductive freedom.

Lisa Passante (BSW, PBDE) is a social worker and master's student in Winnipeg. Since her own coming out in 1995, Lisa has been an active member of Winnipeg's queer community as a volunteer, educator and activist, while also working in a variety of social work settings. Lisa believes strongly in our individual, allied and collective agency to agitate for and manifest the social change we want to see. Lisa offers gratitude to her partner Jackie Kuryk for being an outstanding source of love, fire and support.

Norma Jean Profitt, a feminist social worker, has worked for over twenty years in women's issues, particularly woman abuse and violence against women, in Canada and Costa Rica. After joining academia in 1996, she continues to participate in women's organizations and feminist activism.

Penny Ridley conducted part of the research for her chapter for her undergraduate honours thesis in psychology at the University of Victoria under the supervision of Linda Coates. Penny is interested in psychotherapy and critiques of theory and practice.

Karen Rosenberg is a doctoral candidate in women's studies at the University of Washington. Her research focuses on legal responses to domestic violence and alternatives to criminalization in domestic violence cases in the United States and Canada.

Carole Roy is the author of *The Raging Grannies: Wild Hats, Cheeky Songs, and Witty Actions for a Better World* and is presently making a film about the Raging Grannies. She currently teaches courses in Canadian studies/women's studies at Trent University while completing a postdoctoral fellowship with the multidisciplinary research team Hidden Costs of Care/Invisible Contributions of Older Adults/Adults with Disabilities. She holds an MA in women's studies and a PhD in adult education. She has been involved in movements for social justice.

Rebecca Stringer lectures in gender studies at the University of Otago, New Zealand. She received her PhD in political science at the Australian National University. Her doctoral research, now under review as a book manuscript, uses Nietzsche's concept of *ressentiment* to examine the politics of the "victim feminism" debate. Her recent work includes research and publications on New Zealand's *Prostitution Reform Act 2003*, the socio-economic status of women in New Zealand, legislative responses to violence against pregnant women and (with Heather Brook) harm minimization versus prohibition in the government of drugs.

Jean Toner joined the faculty at Central Michigan University in August 2005, following the award of her doctorate in social work from Arizona State University. Jean's new career in social work education follows over twenty years of social work practice in a variety of settings, primarily clinical. The intersection of gender, race and class as it interacts with substance abusing behaviours has long been a core professional and personal interest. The dynamics of oppression and challenge and resistance to oppression enacted by women have been overlooked in clinical and recovery literature, leaving an incomplete understanding of women's critical social analysis and personal and collective resilience. Jean addresses and hopes to redress this oversight. She spends part of the year in Arizona, when not teaching in Michigan.